INTERNATIONAL BUSINESS OF WINE:
A World of Producers, Buyers & Cellars

INTERNATIONAL BUSINESS OF WINE:
A World of Producers, Buyers & Cellars

David E. Smith
Darryl J. Mitry
Per V. Jenster
Lars V. Jenster

Nordic International Management Institute Press

INTERNATIONAL BUSINESS OF WINE:
A World of Producers, Buyers & Cellars

© Smith, Mitry, Jenster, Jenster 2013

Authors

David E. Smith, D.B.A.
Dr. Smith is a professor at National University, San Diego, California, and visiting professor at Copenhagen Business School in Denmark. In addition to his teaching and research, he is an editorial board member for the *International Journal of Consumer Studies* and the *Journal of Business and Behavioral Sciences.*

Darryl J. Mitry, Ph.D.
Dr. Mitry teaches for the Graduate School of Norwich University, Northfield Vermont, and is a research fellow of several institutes and member of the Consulting Group Economics Council. His primary research studies are in the field of international trade, strategy and finance.

Per V. Jenster, Ph.D.
Dr. Jenster is chairman and Professor at the Nordic International Management Institute, Chengdu China, and Professor of Nyenrode University, Holland. In addition to his responsibilities for teaching and research, he is also the Managing Director of the Jenster Winery in Mendoza, Argentina.

Lars V. Jenster, MS, MBA
Mr. Jenster , wine master, Jenster Winery in Mendoza, Argentina. He holds an MSc in chemical engineering from the Technical University of Denmark, the Diplome Nationale D'Oenologie from the Ecole Normale Supérieure Agronomique dé Montpellier and a Master of Business Administration from the Rotterdam School of Management.

The authors wish to thank the following individuals for their excellent assistance in developing this book.

Denise Ross - manuscript editorial assistance and support services. (More than Just Words) mtjwords@pacbell.net

Xue Meng - diligence in data review and research assistance. Nordic International Management Institute

REVIEW comments –

The global perspective of this book creates continuing opportunities to visualize the entire wine industry actions and reaction, and it helps me in the process of advising our clients.

**Phillippe Croce-Spinelli, Vignobles Croce-Spinelli,
Consultant to the French wine industry,
Les Arcs, Provence, France**

A brilliant book that has provided real inspiration and it has guided us in the process of defining our strategy and positioning our company.

**Francisco Robles,
Production Manager, Clos de la Tierra Sana,
Mendoza, Argentina**

This is important research, a thoughtful review and analysis of economic and cultural trends impacting the world's wine markets. The book provides significant insight on the many wine countries, regions and markets around the world.

**Dr. Bob Skalnick,
President, Integrated Marketing Resources,
Irvine, California, USA**

This book is invaluable and the authors' analysis of global patterns extremely informative and quite useful. As a winemaker, I enjoyed reading the detailed historical narratives and learning how the global issues affect all wineries in the largest and smallest wineries.

**Gary Zucca, Ph.D.
Zucca Mountain Vineyards, Stocton, California, USA**

Many industry professionals and people interested in wine would very much enjoy reading this timely and well-researched book.

**Ole Esmark,
Chairman, Compenhagen Wine Club, Denmark**

TABLE OF CONTENTS

Introduction

INTERNATIONAL BUSINESS OF WINE: A WORLD OF PRODUCERS, BUYERS & CELLARS

The information presented in this book represents thousands of hours of research and the authors' analytical interpretations. If a reader independently attempted to obtain this information from consultants or various reports, he would be required to spend tens of thousands of dollars, pounds or euros. This is the latest elaboration of an earlier book first published in 2008 (entitled "The Business of Wine: a Global Perspective"), which was the first book to illuminate the many different regions, companies and wine producing countries around the world. Although the organization and historical accounts of the wine business as presented in the earlier book remain, there is also much that has changed.

Immediately following the publication of the 2008 book, the world experienced the greatest economic turmoil in over 60 years, often referred to as a financial crisis and the "Great Recession." The consequence of this disruption has upset many factors and trajectories for international businesses most everywhere. Added to these changes, technology has continued its remarkable advance and introduced further alterations, refinements and adjustments in the business of wine.

This volume, completed and published at the end of 2013, updates the extensive information, tracks the changes, and also looks forward by investigating the most influential trends as we examine the implications for the future of the international business of wine. New tables and graphs replace older versions. The tables and graphical illustrations of data contain basic source citations where applicable, but the use of footnotes within the book has been eliminated in order to improve readability.

Many books have been written about the pleasure of consuming good wine, and the subtle distinctions to be enjoyed between wines from different countries, vineyards and vintages. However, that is not the primary objective of this book. As the title implies, the authors focus more on wine as an international *business* rather than simply a pleasurable pastime. Most everything in the world that involves human activity is some form of a business; and when money and wine come together, it is no different.

In this book, the authors offer a unique and very detailed view of the worldwide wine industry and the commercial, political and global forces interacting with the production, marketing, distribution and consumption of wine. The intensive research and historical narratives provide a framework for the extensive data illustrated in tables and graphs. Furthermore, thoughtful analysis of the data is used to reveal the forces that have shaped the industry while uncovering the important trends for the future.

The first chapter, *Market Overview*, offers a summary of the global business of wine and provides a contextual understanding of the many fundamental components. Chapter 2, *The Vineyards of the World*, presents a detailed statistical breakdown of the world's wine-producing areas, the major differences in methods used in production and aspects that give certain types of vineyards a competitive edge. The third chapter, *Consumer Behavior*, describes and analyzes some of the major changes behind consumption trends, new market parameters, and where growth or decline are evident. In Chapter 4, *Product Categories*, the authors briefly describe the different product types, in order to better identify the various sectors of the wine trade and their relative importance to the global market.

Chapters 5, 6 and 7 examine *Production, Development of the Distribution System*, and *Marketing of Wine* in greater detail. These three chapters focus on each of the specifics of all the essential stages of production, distribution and marketing of wine around the world. Here the authors examine the various methods, and particularly how new methods have been improving products and simultaneously intensifying competition. Chapter 8, *Wine Companies and How They Compete*, illustrates a number of specific examples; instances of strategic competition and how contemporary actors within the industry are channeling their energies. Chapter 9, *Legislation and Political Issues*, describes the background of EU law on the wine trade and illuminates the curiously complex political and legislative developments operating to structure the industry in a developing global market. Finally, Chapter 10, *The Future Outlook*, examines some of the trends and predictions concerning the future of the industry and summarizes the findings. For example, a rather new wine market has arisen, as well as an increasingly resourceful competitor, China. The latest information and implications of this country are investigated.

The history of the wine business is deeply rooted in the European economy, but the industry has spread across the world and experienced radical changes on a multitude of levels. Like many contemporary industries, the wine business now operates within a truly global context. Consumer demand has been decreasing in many areas of traditionally high consumption, while demand is increasing in areas of traditionally lower consumption, such as the UK. Moreover, the nature of demand is in itself dynamic as underlying variables are changing, such as increased customer sophistication, product legislation, and the public's increasing awareness of health issues. All of these factors have been leading toward the consumers' increasing demand for quality over quantity.

Such trends pose little or no threat to the upper echelons of European wine (the Chateau and Domaine produced *premiers crus);* nevertheless, they affect the standard *vin ordinaire* segments of the market, which have faced increasing pressure to improve product and marketing. The EU has consistently overproduced, forcing smaller concerns in the lower two categories to either struggle to upgrade (itself a costly and strictly regulated process), or to become part of a larger organization with sophisticated distribution and marketing strategies. However, the traditional wine producers not only face competition from within the EU, but from the growth in global competitors. The wineries of the "New World" threaten to continue expanding their market share. Australia and the US, for example are each dominated by a handful of extremely efficient monolithic producers that have made considerable inroads into areas such as the coveted UK Market. With stylish promotion, prominent branding and consistency of varietal-identified wines, the New World producers have earned the loyalty of a significant section of mid-range consumers.

Wine, unlike other generic commodities, is a product of literally infinite variety. Elements such as the type and quality of grapes used, soil, climate, weather, plus the huge number of individual styles and refinements available to the wine-maker for fermentation and aging processes all conspire to contribute multifaceted characteristics for the finished product. The growth in global production, the enormous leaps made in the field of distribution and current consumer trends have all contributed to the need for new strategies on the part of producers and marketers of wine. The very diversity of wine as a product and the huge number of small producers means that any trader has a small captive market where consumer choice becomes of paramount importance. The small producer with wine to sell has an especially hard task to differentiate his product and to convince the public that he is offering the best choice.

This book examines the way that the worldwide production base is divided: who exports wine, who imports it, which segments of the public buy wine and what they prefer. The book surveys the innovations in production, distribution, and retailing. Particular attention is given to the area of marketing, which appears to be the single most important factor in the battle for winning larger numbers of customers. Wine is produced by millions of distinct growers worldwide and consumed by many more millions of people. In between vineyard and the glass are tens of thousands of individual business-es. *The International Business of Wine* unravels and details the complexi-ties of the global industry, identifies some of the major companies in today's wine business and explores how companies are responding to changes and influencing the changing demands of the market.

Chapter 1

MARKET OVERVIEW

There are few products in the world that are as varied and popular as wine. Every year, hundreds of millions of people consume it. Wine is important to us as individuals when we enjoy a pleasant meal or in the company with good friends, and it has healthful properties. The businesses associated with wine are the daily work for millions of people, and wine is an important product for many communities, and even a primary industry in some national economies. Wine is a major commodity of international trade. With such significant status, much has been written about wine. However, the previous publications are most often concerned only with the oenological properties of the beverage, while this book takes a different point of view as we focus on the business of wine—its production, marketing, distribution and consumption, or, as economists say, the supply and demand for wine.

Readers will find that this book is filled with statistics, the most detailed being presented in tables and graphs. The reader will encounter numerous variations on this voluminous data. Such distinctions are necessary because different periods of time reflect not only historical anomalies, but also certain trends that are the foundation for the wine industry's future. The authors have selected data according to these important and controlling fundamental factors of production, consumption, and trade. Sometimes the data illustrated is historical, other times it reports the latest data at the time of publication. The information contained in the book represents thousands of hours of research. For a reader to obtain independently this information elsewhere, it would likely cost many tens of thousands of dollars. The perspective of each chapter in this book changes according to the specific factors being analyzed and progresses from the general overview to the most specific. This chapter focuses on a market overview. The reader can easily pick and choose what level of data they wish to examine. For example, the reader may wish to read simply the text accompanying the numerous figures or the reader could choose to concentrate on the graphs and tables alone.

For the sake of clarity, it will be useful to establish exactly what we are talking about when we use the term wine. The definition insisted upon by the European Union (EU), the regulator of the most important sector of the wine industry, is that "Wine is the product obtained exclusively from the total or partial alcoholic fermentation of fresh grapes, whether or not crushed, or of grape must" (Annexure One to Regulation, EU No. 822/87).

Thus, those products regarded by traditionalists as frivolous oddities, such as "apple wine" and other derivatives of fermented fruit juice fail to qualify for the title. Even the use of actual grape juice as a base, as in the case of much so-called "made wine" produced in the UK, is insufficient to earn the recognition of the EU requirement. Wine, therefore, can be seriously produced only where there is access to fresh grapes or grape juice—that is to say principally in countries supporting significant areas of vineyard.

As of 2012, it was estimated that the total world area devoted to the vine stood at 7.6 million hectares, of which Europe as a whole represented about 60% of area under cultivation. The global wine business has witnessed major changes in recent years. Some of these changes are structural, others only new fashions, and some changes are cyclical in nature. However, one of the most significant influences over the past decade has been leveraged credit (loans on problematic collateral) from the global banking system. This has propelled many nations into huge public and private debt burdens resulting in serious economic challenges to most all types of markets and national economies. Recently, new market entrants have increased their wine exports not only to traditional European markets but to other importing regions as well. In contrast, the European producers have experienced declining market shares.

The world vine-growing area rose consistently between the years 1950 and 1980, but thereafter the total area of cultivation started declining. This decline was primarily caused by EU policies encouraging vine grubbing, as well as the extensive wine grubbing carried out in the former USSR. The vine-growing area has fluctuated considerably over the past sixty years. There are many factors involved that often cause forecasts to be off the mark. For example, in 2005 the overall vine-growing area was expected to have reached 8.4 million hectares by 2007, but the actual reported figure fell short of expectation at 7.8. Furthermore, forecasters did not expect the figure would continue to decline and shrink below 7.6 million hectare. The fluctuations have primarily been due to the:

- Changes in governmental regulations, particularly the supranational EU policies.
- New entrants into the industry and new technologies.
- Growth of Chinese vineyards, notably since 1998, which also is expected to continue (note that China's grape production of 487 million hectares in 2005 already exceeded that of Australia, Chile and South Africa combined).

Table 1:1 shows the changes in the worldwide vineyard area. The area peaked around 1980 and then started declining. This trend reversed in 1997-1998, and the areas under vines increased from 1998-2005, and then reversed again in 2006 through 2012.

PERIOD	AREA UNDER VINES (million hectare)
1951-1955	8.845
1971-1975	9.961
1976-1980	10.213
1981-1985	9.823
1986-1990	8.842
1991-1995	8.126
1996	7.744
1997	7.690
1998	7.674
1999	7.732
2000	7.855
2001	7.893
2004	7.919
2005	7.930
2006	7.797
2007	7.757
2008	7.720
2009	7.702
2010	7.672
2011	7.592
2012	7.500

Table 1:1 Developments in Worldwide Area of Vines
Sources: Adapted from OIV Bulletin 2013, and World Reports, and authors' research and interpretations.

We see that again in 2012, there was a decline in area under vine, bringing total vine area down to 7.5 million hectares. While the shrinkage was largely on the European continent, in other regions there were increases in area under vine: the Americas, Australia and Asia. Historically, the Asian sector of the vine-growing world, although significant in world grape-production, had relatively little impact on the wine industry because much of the Asian grape production results in making non-fermented drinks and grape product. In fact, the Asian grape production from Turkey, Iran, Syria, Afghanistan, and Iraq involve cultural traditions and religious prohibition toward the consumption of alcohol. However, the production and consumption of wine in China

7

has increased substantially, and China can be expected to continue to grow in both consumption and production.

Of the total annual worldwide production of grapes, approximately 75% is used for the production of wine. The major production comes from Europe with 4212 thousand hectares and the Asian 1253 thousand hectares in current vineyards. The major sectors are: the Americas with a total area of 1009 thousand hectares (notably in California, Argentina, Chile and Brazil), Africa with 378 thousand hectares (in South Africa, Egypt, Algeria, Morocco, Tunisia, Libya), and the vineyards of Australia and New Zealand, which cover some 206 thousand hectares in all.

Table 1:2 and Figure 1:1 shows how world wine-production is divided among the continents and regions. Of an annual total of approximately 264 Mhl (million hectoliter; where one hectoliter = 100 liters) of wine, Western Europe is still the largest producer and consumer. It is also worth noting that reductions in actual vine area tend to be offset by better methods of production and technology with the net result that the volume of European production has, until very recently, remained fairly stable. EU policy brought about a decline in European production. However, the decline was offset by increased production in Asia, Australia and Africa.

Mhl	Africa	America	Asia	Europe	Oceania	World Total
Production	10.56	50.16	14.52	174.24	13.20	264
Consumption	7.07	53.68	19.27	158.60	6.58	244

Table 1:2 Division of World Wine Production among Continents and Regions

Consumption has, in fact, over a number of years been constantly chasing production; and we see that in America and Asia consumption are greater than their domestic production, presenting significant import/export markets for wine. In per capita terms, France appeared to level off through 2005, but it modestly reduced per-capita consumption through 2010. Likewise, Italy had continued its downward consumption trend. On the other hand, per capita consumption had increased significantly in Denmark and other northern European states. A detailed analysis of this phenomenon is contained in Chapter 10. Other countries with high consumption rates are Croatia, Portugal and Switzerland. Increases in wine consumption are largely due to consumers in United States (US), the United Kingdom (UK) and most recently in China. For example, by 2005, China became the world's fastest-growing wine market, but as of 2013, the European market, as a whole, still dominates the wine industry by a wide margin.

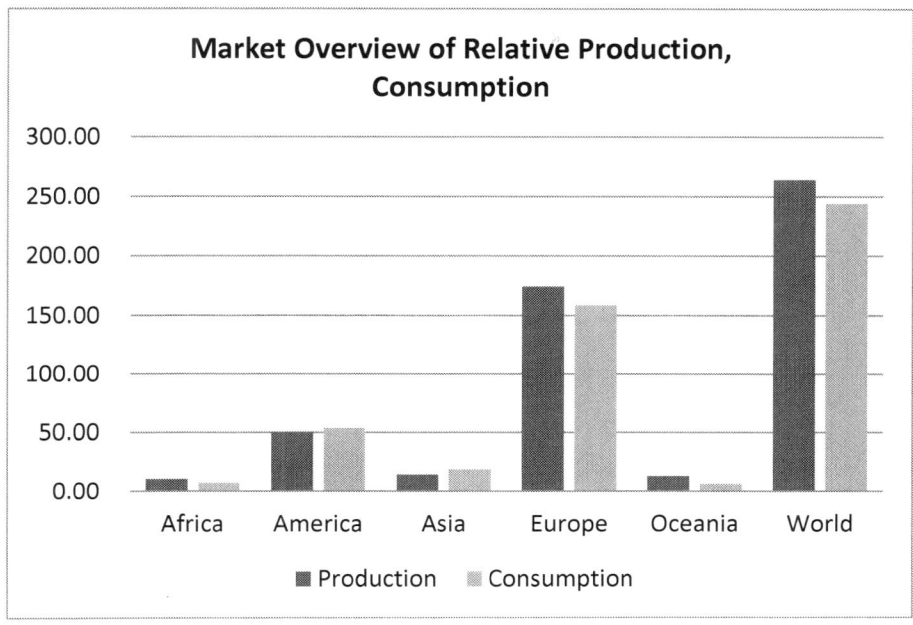

Figure 1:1 Market Overview of Production, Consumption in Mhl
Source: http://www.bkwine.com/features/more/world-wine-statistics-and and OIV, 2013.

Worldwide wine consumption in the first decade of the 21st Century increased 4.56%. In overall terms, as a sub-sector of the drinks market, the wine business continues to hold its own against the ubiquitous soft-drink and the relatively high-volume beer market.

The comparative sizes of the world's major markets can be analyzed by various measures. For example, total liters per year or per-capita consumption or in terms of a monetary unit such as the dollar. All of these measures have their defects and that is why it is necessary to examine each measure in order to better understand the patterns over time. The measures vary from year to year, but show the trending pattern of each market, when viewed over longer periods of time. For example, Table 1:3 depicts changes from 2007-2010, and it shows some countries' markets were generally increasing, while others were in a downturn in terms of wine consumed per capita. The UK is the fourth largest, when viewed from the perspectives of total volume consumed and also in terms of monetary value of wine consumption.

As of 2013, the worldwide wine consumption trend is shown in Figure 1:2. The growth in consumption turned down after 2007 due primarily to the global disruptions caused by the advent of the 2008 financial crisis. Modest growth resumed and is evidenced in 2010 and 2011.

Country changes in importation of wine from 1970 through 2010, are shown in Table 1:3

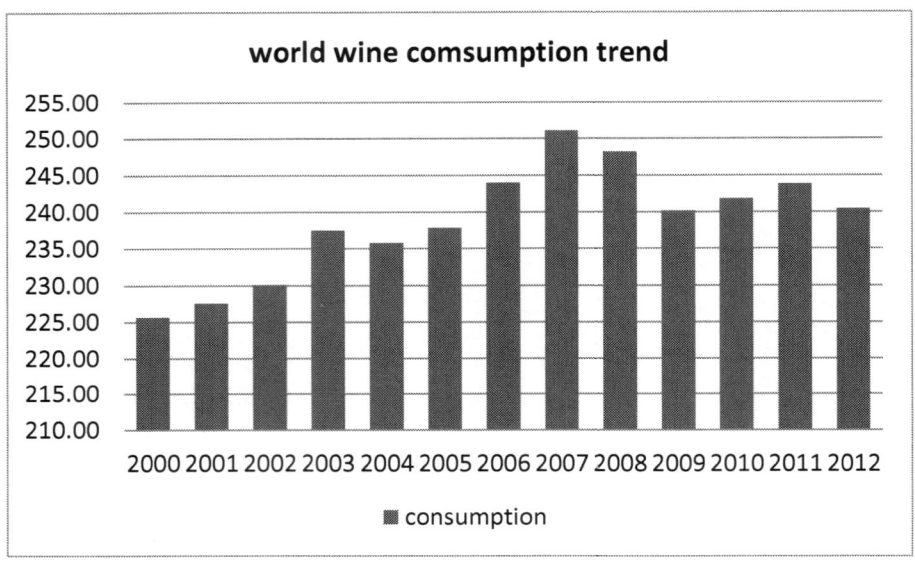

Figure 1:2 World Wine Consumption Trend
Source: OIV, 2013.

It is particularly worthy to note how the UK, for all intents and purposes relatively a non-producer of wine, nevertheless became the fifth largest consumer of wines in 2010 (in terms of a monetary measure or total volume). This explains why the UK (with substantial and rising consumer demand and no indigenous product to fall back on) is so coveted a market by not only the traditional and established exporters of wine, but also by the "new world" competitors (the Americas, Australia, New Zealand).

Tables 1:3 and 1:4 show the import-export patterns for the five major markets over the past three decades in terms of hector-liters of wine.

Beginning in the early seventies, the volume of wine imported to and among the countries of Europe increased steadily by between 1% and 5% per year, until in 1989 when it accounted for 23% of total European consumption. The upward trend continued in the 1990s as well, and by 2002 the volume of wine imported to and among the countries accounted for 27.4% of the total European consumption. As can be seen from the above tables, the largest importer in 2003 was Germany with 11.9 Mhl. However, the largest volume growth since the seventies occurred in the buoyant UK market, which was the number two European importer of wine with 11.34 Mhl in 2003 and 12.5 Mhl by 2010.

Import	71-75	76-80	81-85	86-90	91-95	96-00	2001	2003	2010
France	7,494	7,655	NA	4,786	5,965	5,168	5,111	4,696	4.500
Germany	7,126	8,395	9,705	10,550	9,776	10,796	11,268	11,906	14.200
Italy	455	2012f	276	538	456	563	680	1,447	1.700
UK	2,954	15.000	5,117	6,089	6,587	8,369	9,943	11,340	12.500
US	1,779	4.300	4,865	2,986	2,509	4,096	4,688	6,082	9.300

Table 1:3 Wine Imports in Thousand Hecto liters (after 1970)
Source: faostat.fao.org, http://www.bkwine.com/features/more/world-wine-statistics-2010

Export	71-75	76-80	81-85	86-90	91-95	96-00	2001	2003	2010
France	5,936	7,959	10,164	12,868	11,375	15,014	15,517	14,962	14,900
Germany	636	1,448	2,604	2,714	2,689	2,330	2,372	2,702	3,800
Italy	11,786	15,666	17,319	11,865	13,672	14,830	15,371	12.802	20,000
US	40	129	301	611	1,180	2,314	2,844	3,293	4.100

Table 1:4 Wine Exports in Thousand Hecto liters (after 1970)
Source: faostat.fao.org, http://www.bkwine.com/features/more/world-wine-statistics-2010/

The import/export figures for the year of 2012 continue the trends exampled in the above tables. The non-wine-producing countries of Northern Europe account for about 12% of all European wine imports, while wine-producing France in the south is by far the biggest importer of wine. This seemingly strange situation is explained by two interesting facts: first, 90% of France's imports are table wines, the majority being used for mixing into French vin ordinaries (permitted by law to contain a maximum 15% of foreign wine). Second, the surprisingly high figure for French wine imports is more easily comprehended, if one bears in mind that France is the world's largest market for wine.

Much of France's imported wine comes from Italy, traditionally one of the biggest exporters by volume, followed by Spain. Italy's southern position and climate have naturally led to high yields per hectare, but mostly of grapes suitable for nothing more elevated than table wine. Italy's volume export figures have fluctuated considerably, but in 2010 Italy became the largest exporter by volume, exceeding France by a substantial margin.

In general, the three other largest producers and exporters of wine in Europe are France, Italy and Spain. However, countries in Europe such as Portugal and Germany are also proving to be significant competitors. Still other countries in Europe, like Bulgaria and The Republic of Moldova, are also carving a niche for themselves in the import sector. Furthermore, the non-European wine producing countries like South Africa, Argentina, Chile, USA and Australia presents an even greater challenge. These countries have been consistently increasing their ability to penetrate the European markets.

The US market has grown significantly over the past two decades. The consumption has increased remarkably. This reversal of the downward trend in consumption of some wines in the USA and the significant increases in others is due to the increasing consumer interest in premium wine. This trend was further spurred by favorable health reports based on findings that moderate consumption of red wine may reduce the risk of cardiovascular disease and other potentially fatal ailments. A significant factor of influence that encourages selecting wine over other alcoholic beverages.

In conclusion, it should be noted that the annual volume of international wine trade amounts to around 24% of production. Of this total, the greater part consists of short-haul trading. The actual volume of long-distance international trade in wine is much less considerable, although of relatively high value (in monetary terms) being chiefly the preserve of vintage and fine wines. Figure 1:3 illustrates the top ten importing counties 2008-2012, and shows imports growing in most countries during by 2012. Figure 1:4 illustrates the export changes for the top ten exporting countries 2008-2012.

The New World countries accounted for 30% of the wine exports in volume as compared to the five Old World countries that accounted for the remaining 70%. Most of the New World countries exhibited a year-on-year export increase.

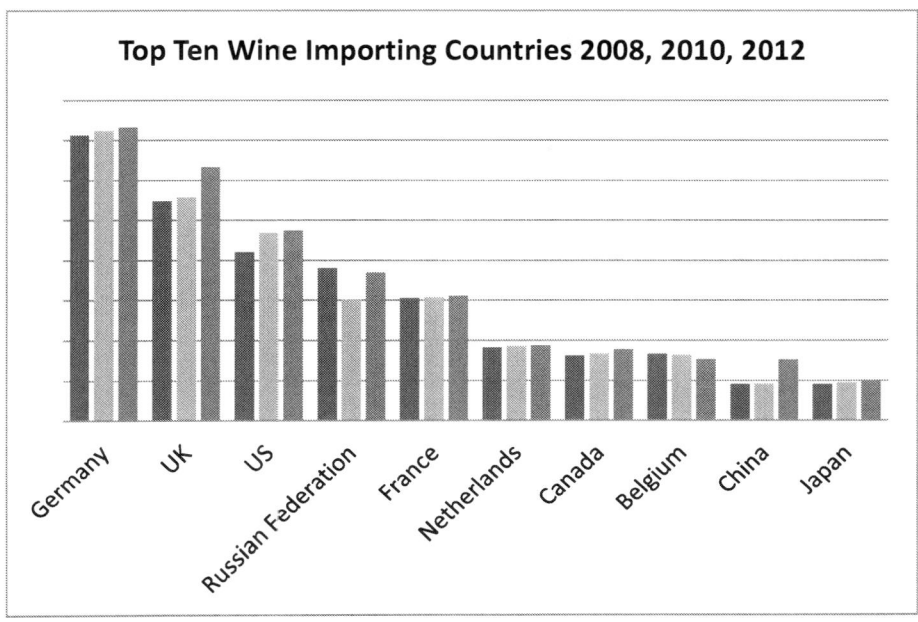

Figure 1:3 Top Ten Wine Importing Countries 2008-2012
Source: http://faostat.fao.org/

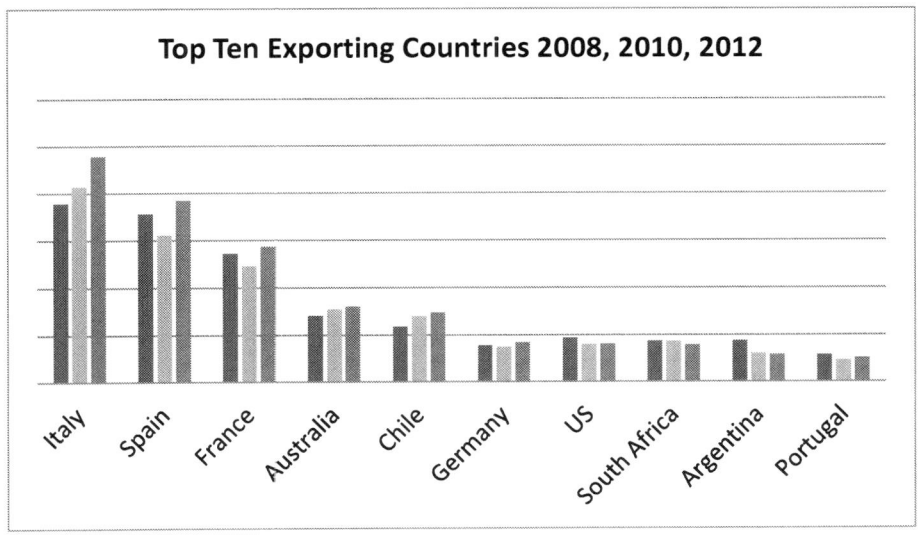

Figure 1:4 Top Ten Exporting Countries 2008-2012
Source: http://faostat.fao.org/

Specific Types of Wine

Wine production in Europe divides into three main categories: still, sparkling and fortified wines. The first category—still wines, which accounts for over 88% of the market, is divided into table wines and fine wines. The fine wines are divided into further segments. Table 1:4 highlights the segments in different countries.

Table 1:5 shows the segments and descriptions for sparkling wines in European countries.

Country	Segments	Description
France	AOC-Appellation d'Origine Contrôlée	An AOC wine comes from a geographically defined and limited area which lays down rules in regard the grape variety, alcohol content, yield, pruning etc.
	VDQS-Vin Démimité de Qualité Supérieure	A VDQS wine is also governed by a set of rules, though not as strict as those in the AOC
Italy	DOC-Denominazione di Origine Controllata	A DOC wine is equivalent to a French AOC wine
	DOCG-Denominazione di Origine Controllata e Garantita	This is like an AOC Wine of France, except that it also guarantees the quality
Spain	DO-Denominación de Origen	A DO wine is equivalent to a French AOC wine
	DOC—Denominación de Origen Calificada	Like an Italian DOCG wine. Only Rioja has DOC
UK	English/Welsh Vineyards Quality Wine	Comparable to a VDQS of France
Portugal	DOC-Denominaçâo de Origem Controlada	Like an Italian DOCG wine.
	VQPRD-Vinho de Qualidade Produzido em Região	Like a French VDQS Wine, but with stricter rules
Germany	Qmp—Qualitätswein mit Prädikat	Equivalent to a French AOC
	QbA-Qualitätswein eines bestimmten Anbaugebietes	Comparable to a VDQS of France

Table 1:5 Wine by Segment in Major European Countries
Source: http://www.internetwineguide.com

The second two categories, fortified wines (vermouths, ports, sherries) and sparkling wines/champagnes (including the German Sekt) represent a relatively small section of the market—although a high-value one. Figures 1:5 and 1:6 highlight the wine market segregated by types of wine.

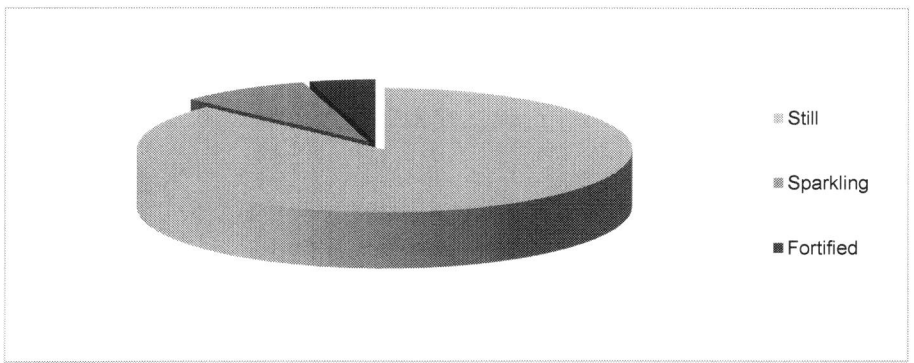

Figure 1:5 Wine by Segment in Major European Countries
Source: Based on Euromonitor Market Report.

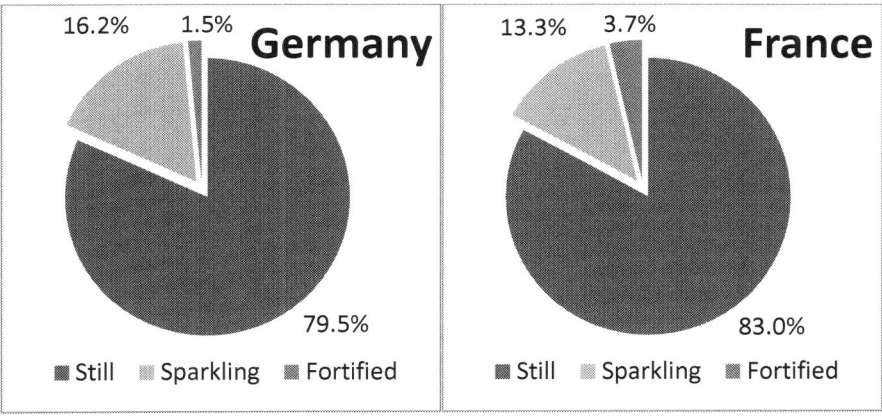

Figure 1:6 Germany and France – Market Share by Type of Wine
Source: Based on Euromonitor International, Country Sector Briefing, France/Germany, 2011.

Wine Coolers are a sparkling mixture of wine, fruit juice, mineral water and flavorings. Coolers initially registered significant growth in the US. Launched in 1982, Coolers swiftly established their place in the market—dramatically increasing in US sales until 1987, when they topped 56 million cases in the year. There followed significant decreases in demand of 10.9%

and 21.4% in the next two years. The Wine Cooler market became relatively insignificant by 2000. The hoped-for burgeoning of demand for Wine Coolers did not materialize as expected by the industry marketers. Nonetheless, the prepared mixed drinks showed steady but limited expansion, and malt-based Flavored Alcohol Beverages arrived on the scene in 2000. These types of sweeter tasting low alcoholic drinks are aimed more at attracting new drinkers into the market and may serve as transitions to more serious alcoholic beverages.

Changes

Highlighting the trends in consumption of everyday "vin de table" (standard wine) and premium wine for Europe is illustrated in Figure 1:7.

As the figure illustrates, the consumption of standard wine has been continuously decreasing and that of premium wines is continuously increasing. As early as 2006, the trend lines crossed, signaling more demand for premium wine over ordinary table wine. While the wine industry can draw some comfort from the fact that these trends can be explained in part by increased consumer sophistication (accompanied by a concomitant willingness to pay for quality), there is a limit to the amount of upgrading that can be achieved within existing mechanisms of production. The inevitable result, unless major restructuring took place, is an increasing quantity of unwanted vin-de table, and eventually a reduction of land used for less valuable vineyards. Therefore, in the second decade of the 21st century, we can better understand why the growers have been dedicating more land to better quality production.

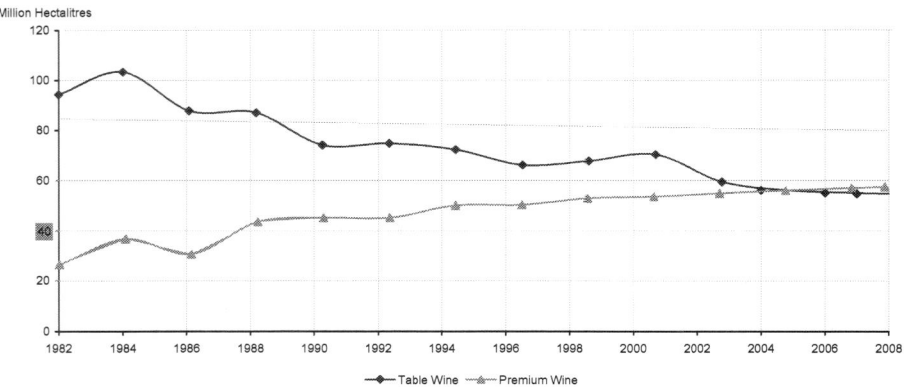

Figure 1:7 Table Wine and Premium Wine Consumption Trends
Source: Based on europa.eu.int/comm/agriculture/markets/

The reasons for this change are many, but can mostly be traced to tradition being eroded and people breaking free from shackles of old habits. Traditionally, wine was the beverage of choice for an accompaniment to fine cuisine and also as an everyday part of European family life; especially in the South. It would have been inconceivable to the average Frenchman of the 1930s, who was happily quaffing some 128 liters a year, that by 2002 his capacity would dwindle to below 53 liters. Who would have thought that the Association Nationale Interprofessionale Des Vins de Table would feel the need to browbeat the Frenchman with advertising slogans like "A meal without wine is like a weekend without telly." It is easy to imagine the Frenchman of the 1930s momentarily prying the cigarette butt from his lips to murmur: "Quel desastre!"

Modern events have overtaken "Mr. Average consumer" and there is a growing tendency amongst young people to elect to substitute one of the many brands of persistently advertised soft drinks on the market for a portion of their drinking behavior. Moreover, there is a growing awareness of the adverse effects on health by over-consumption of alcohol. Spirits and, to some extent, beer have been worse-affected by these changes. But the fact has to be faced that, consumption levels in countries where wine has for centuries been the most popular staple, is now finding a level considerably lower than that of just a few decades ago.

However, that is not to say that everything is doom and gloom for the business of wine. We have already noted that the consumer trend is towards smaller amounts of higher-quality wine, a fact that helps to maintain reasonable buoyancy in the market. In addition, while volume of consumption has been decreasing in the previously high-consuming South, there is a compensatory increase of consumption in the North. At the same time, although producer-consumers have been drinking less of what they produce, there is a gradual and consistent increase in the potential market for their product in the countries of the North. This trend of drinking less of what is produced in the major wine producing countries has continued beyond 2002, but at a slower rate of change. Figure 1:8 shows the consumption trends during the period 1982 into 2011 (where 1982 is taken as base-reference).

A more detailed analysis of these trends is offered in Chapter 10, where we present the per-capita data through 2011 and examine the future implications of the supply and demand for wine by extrapolating the trend line beyond the end of the decade.

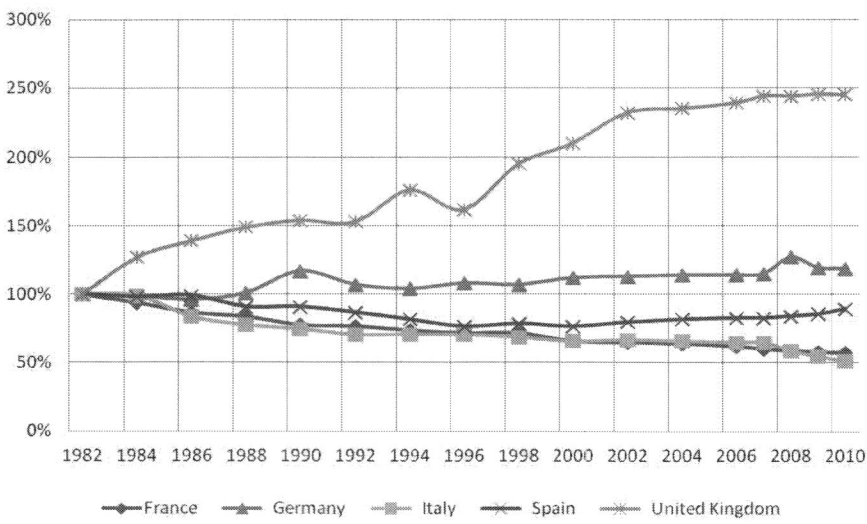

Figure 1:8 National Consumption Trends of France, Germany, Italy, Spain, and the UK

Source: based on data from www.faostat.fao.org (Evalueserve Analysis; World Wine Consumption by Volume & Rank.

Vineyard to Shelf

The industry of wine production and distribution was traditionally highly fragmented, with a very loose network of small producers, many of them selling their product locally or through similarly small-scale merchants. While this has been changing, there are still many small producers. For example, approximately 1.2 million individual agricultural holdings in the EU have less than one hectare of vines. Nevertheless, the owners derive a significant proportion of their income from their efforts in small scale viticulture. These little vineyards account for about 70% of farms with vines and 12% of the total area under vines.

The industry and the individual producer, particularly the very small producer, have benefited from the rise of the Cooperative. There are some 3,000 cooperatives in the EU taking the grapes produced by their membership and vinifying in shared plants. However, if one compares Europe's more traditional methods of production to the US or Australia, where a few and powerful companies dominate and use more mechanized processes, it is easy to see that greater efficiency is to be had by moving towards larger scale operations. This is slowly happening in Europe with a trend towards more concentrated sales through larger retailers, and the future would appear to belong to the large-scale enterprise.

For example, there is a general move away from distribution through the HORECA network (hotels, restaurants and cafes), also referred to as on-trade sales. Previously, much more wine was consumed on such public premises, but the current tendency is for one-stop shopping (often by the woman of the house), which includes the purchase of wine for consumption at home. Wine, well-presented and at reduced prices, is in fact used by many large store chains to entice customers to do their entire weekly shopping at these stores.

This has offered new potential for effective marketing strategies. In former times, unless one made a concentrated study of wine areas, vintages and so forth, choice was primarily dictated by habit or by faith in the word of one's wine merchant. Today, there are only a few people who continue to patronize small specialists in search of rarities. Strenuous efforts have been made by suppliers and distributive-chains selling their own-labels to increase customer awareness of wines. Moreover, by developing the consumers' confidence in selecting the "right wine," the suppliers have gained significant market share. Consistency of quality is a great trump-card wielded by the large-scale supplier and high recognition of brand name. In this, the big wineries of the New World are particularly well placed in the struggle to win consumer loyalty because of their highly technological methods of vinification, and their products based on particular varietals.

The wine business is definitely a large global industry. In the EU, which still produces the majority of the world total, wine growing employs about 5 million people and represents 6% of the gross saleable total of European agriculture. However, the industry is going through a period of profound change. Not only is the emphasis moving away from consumption in the countries of the traditional major producers — necessitating more active export and marketing strategies to neighbor countries — but there is also increasing penetration of the coveted importing markets by more recent producers around the world.

Prices

Looking at regional price behavior, we find that pricing of wine grape juice concentrate, in terms of US dollars per US gallon in the second quarter of 2013, appear to be slightly up from last year, but the trend can be mitigated by changes in the overall year's harvest for each country. As always, a larger crop size pushes prices down, whereas a smaller crop pushes prices up for each country's exports. Therefore, the average price trends for 2013 reflect the behavior of wineries aggregate Demands in response to Supply of harvests.

Red

California	$15.00
Spain	$18.00
Chile	$17.00
Italy	$18.00

White

California	$15.00 to $16.00
Argentina	$10.00 to $11.00

Major Wine Country Overviews

Argentina: By early 2013, volume was showing a 22% increase over the 2012 harvest and this was indicative of a return to an overall average historical harvest.

Australia: There were mixed reports across all regions on the expected size of 2013 crops, with some vineyards reporting slight decreases and others showing average crop yields. The UK remains Australia's number one export destination by volume (e.g. 256 million liters in 2012). The majority of material shipped to the UK is in bulk, reflecting the desire to bottle in the importing country. The US ranks as number two, Canada number three and China is the fourth largest importer of Australian product. The five countries account for 80% of Australian wine exports.

California, USA: Wine volumes sold in the US totaled 360 million cases and exceeded $10.2 billion in revenues for 2012. Strong growth in premium wines (priced $7-$14 per bottle) grew by 6 million cases. The US remains the largest and most lucrative wine market in the world. The US demographics and broad consumer base has been consuming more wine each year. A growing number of traditional sales outlets, Internet and direct-to-consumer websites, as well as the continued removal of archaic distribution laws, have helped sales to increase.

Chile: Grape prices have maintained fairly stable. The expected volume for the 2013 harvest appears to be similar to that of last year, but due to rather volatile weather conditions in December of 2012, diseases such as Botrytis and Mildew affected some areas. The export figures for January 2013 showed an increase by 45% in volume for bulk wine, as compared to January of 2012. Bottled exports also grew slightly (5%), but the forecast was a flat year-end for bottled exports.

France: Compared to the five-year average, overall exports increased by 8% in volume and by 20% in value by year end 2012. In terms of destination, exports within the EU remained stable, but there was a 13% increase in volume exports to third countries.

Germany: The short supply of generic white wines and the over-supply of Riesling during 2012 continued into 2013. The bulk pricing for both categories continued to be approximately the same. Eventually, the usual price difference between generics and Riesling of 0.20 to 0.50 cents is expected to return.

Italy: By the end of the first quarter of 2013, Italian generic wines, continued to be in short supply. Most of the best quality generic red wine had already been sold. The 2013 crop was not yet forecast because of weather conditions such as hail and rainfall was unpredictable.

South Africa: It has been estimated that the 2013 crop will be approximately the same as the previous year (a favorable harvest). The increase in bottling costs and the increase of excise duties for wine has been making it harder for producers to sell wine in the local market. However, there has been a large growth in exports, particularly for bulk wine. The biggest markets for South African bottled wine in 2012 were the UK, Sweden, Germany, Netherlands and the US. The biggest markets for South African bulk wine were: Germany, the UK, Russia, the US and Canada.

Spain: The Spanish market remained subdued in the early part of 2013. The high pricing strategy in Spain, combined with a reduction in allocated volume to historical buyers (especially France and Germany), had led major buyers to favour other country suppliers. As would be expected in a global competitive marketplace, the Spanish cooperatives and negociants began revising their pricing strategies and slightly lowering prices as they attempted to regain lost markets.

Chapter 2

VINEYARDS OF THE WORLD

A scientific researcher and archaeologist, Dr. Patrick E. McGovern, is known as the Indiana Jones of ancient drinks because of his use of molecular tracing of archaeological evidence. He has found evidence of the oldest examples of winemaking (dated to around 5400 BC). His latest results, published in the Proceedings of the National Academy of Sciences (2013), are based on analysis of a stone platforms and pottery jars found at the ancient port of Lattara in southern France. The evidence is consistent with his evaluation that the beginnings of France's vineyards arrived by sea 2,500 years ago from central Italy.

The process of vinification cannot be attributed to a particular individual. It cannot be stated precisely when wine was first produced. In the beginning, wine was simply a natural discovery, many thousands of years ago. The fruit of the vine bears a bloom of natural yeast just waiting for its chance to devour the sugar, as the grape decays and ferments. The grape contains a great amount of sugar, as much as a third of the volume of the grape itself, thus making it one of the sweetest of all fruits. In some past millennia, yeast naturally produced fermentation, and we can assume that early man enjoyed the effects of this natural vinification. At first, prehistoric man probably enjoyed eating the semi-fermented fruit and perhaps later the juice. Somewhere in time, a man or woman decided to control this process of extracting fermented juice to produce a drink with unusual powers. There was probably an immediate overindulgence by someone who first witnessed and enjoyed the exciting effect on man's psyche, at least until the morning after.

From the earliest history of man, we find that the production and consumption of wine takes place as our ancestors began to switch from dependence on hunting to developing an agricultural lifestyle. Accumulations of grape pips serve to convince archaeologists that winemaking was practiced from perhaps as early as 8000 BC in areas such as Turkey, Syria, Lebanon and Jordan. In these earliest times, the grapes used were from wild vines, but at a point somewhere around 5000 BC (pinpointed by means of carbon dating), cultivation of the vine began. The oldest accumulations of cultivated pips, clearly different from the wild variety, have been found in the former Soviet Republic of Georgia. Therefore, wine must be considered the original alcoholic drink, preceding beer that was not commonly in use until 4000 BC. Subsequently, wine was widely used in Babylonian and Egyptian society for perhaps a thousand years or more before entry of other forms of alcoholic beverages.

In the earliest age of winemaking, the emphasis was no doubt on the alcoholic content, rather than on fine points of color or even bouquet. However, the "boon of transcendence," which wine gave to these early peoples, easily explains how it could have established itself as a cornerstone both of mystical rites and conviviality. Equally, notable are its uses as an antiseptic (for thousands of years it was the only one available) and as an aid to digestion. Consequently, wine played a central role in the panoply of things wholesome. The Talmudic dictum that "Where there is no wine there will have to be medicines" is born out even to this day by evidence of the benefits of moderate consumption of wine in the prevention of heart disease.

In ancient times, most wine was drunk as soon as fermentation was completed. In the words of Hugh Johnson, it was "probably somewhere between Beaujolais Nouveau and vinegar." However, with the passage of time, preferences developed for certain "tastes," likely stimulated by trade. After 1000 BC, following the rise of the Grecian and Phoenician maritime states, wine became a highly traded commodity and was distributed throughout the greater Mediterranean. Trade brought market forces into play. People were prepared to pay more to enjoy the qualities of wine from better-situated better-tended vineyards. Eventually, the final luxury was discovered — the storing and aging of wine until it was mature, originally the privilege of the pharaohs. This storing and resulting maturity allowed the "genie in the bottle" to do its highest magic, a truly mysterious amalgam of chemical processes, which is scarcely comprehensible even today, despite all the amazing advances of technology.

The vine, which produces fruit suitable for winemaking is a deciduous shrub of the family Ampelidaceae, genus Euvitis, species Vitis Vinifera. There are others, such as Vitis Labrusca, Vitis Rupestris, Vitis Riparia and Berlandieri, but their chemical make-up is not entirely best; and when grapes are fermented, they have a rather "foxy" flavor. These are the so-called American Vines, which despite their shortcomings, play an absolutely crucial role in the wine industry (more on this later).

The life span of a vine is between 30 and 45 years. In the first year of its life span, roots form. In the second year, some wood is in evidence and a crop of immature berries is yielded. During the next two years, the vine will fruit, but the grapes are not permitted for use in the production of quality wine (at least, not in the EU). At five years old, the vine is producing fully mature grapes, but the plant's full potential in terms of yield is not reached until the ten-year mark. Thereafter, the volume of the yield will decline, although the quality of the fruit tends to go on improving. One of the most significant changes in the quality of the fruit results from the gradual deepening of the roots, which begin to take more and more character from the soil. New vines will produce wine tasting very predominantly of the fruit and nothing else, whereas an old vine's fruit will have much more individuality and, if conditions are right, will have a much better chance of becoming a great vintage.

A vine consists of:

- Roots, which may either spread or push downwards, largely depending upon the nature of the soil
- A solid woody trunk
- Branches (old wood)
- Canes—which are the previous year's growth
- Shoots, which are the new growth and which, if they shoot from the canes, bear the fruit itself. Shoots coming out of the branches will not fruit, but the following year they become canes and produce their own fruiting shoots.

Methods of pruning and of training vines vary enormously. Depending upon the climatic conditions, it may be advantageous to the grower to keep the plants low to the ground, or high in the air. In order to economize on space, it was a custom—particularly in Italy—to train vines across the tops of trees growing in fields supporting another crop at ground level.

Vines will grow and receive sufficient sunshine to ensure a consistent yield and absence of damaging frosts between the latitudes of 30 and 50 degrees—both in the Northern and the Southern Hemispheres; although in the South, the optimal band is 30-40 degrees. Into the Northern band fall a large part of Southern Europe and North Africa, parts of Eastern Europe, and California. In the Southern latitudes, we find Chile, Argentina, South Africa, Southern Australia and New Zealand.

The 21st Century global vineyard surface area has decreased somewhat over the years, and as illustrated previously, it now stands at approximately 7.5 million hectares. The "old world" vineyards are still most important, but the so-called New World has continued growing in percentage and market importance. The percentage distributions of land under vineyards in the five global regions are:

1. Europe   =   57%
2. Asia   =   22%
3. America   =   13%
4. Africa   =   5%
5. Oceania   =   2.7%

The overall vineyard acreage has declined by approximately a half million hectares with the primary shrinkage in the old world wine countries of Spain, France, and Italy. However, some areas do not produce grapes destine for wine production. Therefore, land under vine does not necessarily show the best measure of relative position for the importance of wine production on each continent. This is best illustrated by the actual percentage of wine produced by volume:

1. Europe   =   66%
2. Americas   =   19%
3. Asia   =   5.5%
4. Oceania   =   5%
5. Africa   =   4%

Therefore, it is the continent of Europe that still stands as the most significant, and by all measures dominates the world of wine production.

Europe

There was much expansion in European viticulture during the eighteenth and early nineteenth centuries. The result was that, by the middle of the nineteenth century, the area under vines was already extremely extensive, covering over 5 million hectares (excluding Eastern Europe). However, disaster struck in the form of a tiny burrowing louse called phylloxera. A strain of phylloxera, called vastatrix, originates in the Americas and is a parasite of vines. Phylloxera is essentially an aphid multiplying at a prodigious rate. Phylloxera was first identified in Europe in a greenhouse in the London Borough of Hammersmith in 1863. The life cycle of phylloxera encompasses nineteen separate stages, during which the creature attacks root, cane and leaf of the vine and completely destroys the plant. In its final manifestation (as a small winged insect), phylloxera is capable of flying up to fifty miles downwind, sufficiently far to make its way to mainland Europe.

France first began to feel the effects of phylloxera in that same year, 1863, and by 1870, the insect had been identified in Bordeaux, the Rhone valley and in Portugal. Over the next quarter-century, the pest spread inexorably through the Rhineland, Burgundy, Champagne, Spain's famous Jerez region, Italy, Algeria, and South Africa.

By the end of the nineteenth century, most European vineyards had been uprooted. Phylloxera cannot be eradicated without wholesale destruction of the vines by burning and by sterilization of the soil with carbon disulphide. Therefore, in the early twentieth century, there was a severe wine shortage, due to this one small parasite, which had laid waste to almost the entire European production base.

This is where the American Vines proved to be better. The one great advantage these plants have over Vitis Vinifera is that their roots are resistant to the phylloxera louse and, even when attacked, they can heal themselves by means of scar tissue. The true European vine is incapable of this and, when attacked by phylloxera, in effect "bleeds" to death. The expedient hit upon was to graft European vines onto rootstock of American species. In warmer climates this is done by allowing the American vine to establish itself in situ and then stripping it of leaves and grafting on a scion of the desired variety of vitis vinifera. More generally, grafts are prepared in nurseries by grafting together matched canes of the rootstock and the desired fruiting variety. These are then kept in the hothouse until the cane of the root stock has put down roots and the upper section of the graft has put out shoots. They are then brought outside for maturation, before being replanted in the actual vineyard. In this manner, the march of the pest was halted. The problem, however, has not been totally eradicated and there is currently the threat of another strain, mutant phylloxera "B" that is sharpening its teeth to attack the tougher American roots—a fact which some authorities predict could leave us in exactly the same position more than a century ago. It may take years of insecticide treatments to reverse severe damage. As of 2013, there is still no absolute cure. Even though Europe's vineyards were saved from extinction in the early years of nineteenth century, a large proportion of the devastated areas were never replanted and, by the inter-war period, the Western European total had dwindled to around 4.5 million hectares.

This "downsizing trend" has continued ever since, particularly with the establishment of the EU and its strictures of the CAP. The European Commission has subsidized further reductions and prohibited the planting of new vineyards. The total area under vine cultivation was reduced from 5.04 million hectares to 4.97 million hectares during the period of 1997 to 2001, and Europe accounted for around 63% of total area worldwide. By 2011, Europe accounted for less than 52% of world vine acreage, which may be compared with 69% at the end of the 1980s (O.I V. Statistical Report, 2012, authors' estimates). The only countries of Europe in which the vine is not seriously cultivated are the Netherlands, Poland, Ireland, Sweden, Denmark, Norway and Finland. Table 2:1 lists the area under vineyards in Western Europe.

Country	2011
France	764
Italy	718
Portugal	179
Spain	966
Greece	103
Austria	44
Germany	100
Luxemburg	1.22

Table 2:1 Western European Areas under Vine, in mha, 2011
Source: Eurodata, 2012.

Table 2:2 depicts the wine *production* in Western European countries in 2011. Since the peaks of production were reached during the 1980s, the data show that there has been a reduction of vine and a leveling down of wine production to significantly below the 200 million-liter mark.

Country	Mhl
Italy	46.73
France	45.67
Spain	35.35
Portugal	7.13
Germany	6.98
Romania	3.29
Greece	2.95
Hungary	1.76
Austria	1.71
Bulgaria	1.22

Table2:2 Western European Wine Production in Mhl, 2011

Many European Vineyards Disappear

After the EU directive instituted a subsidized vine-pull scheme in 2008, there were 269,000 hectares of vines "grubbed up" in the member nations. The area now stands at 7.5 million hectares, which represents a decline of 17,000 hectares in 2012 alone. Spain experienced the largest decline (13%). Interestingly, the Chinese used the opportunity for a strategic and very substantial increase in their vineyards.

In 2012, China was the only member of the OIV to have a double digit increase in growth of vineyards, with a 19% increase in 2012 over 2011, for 570,000 hectares of vines under cultivation.

Vine-Growing Areas of the EU

Mediterranean Vineyards
Into this large category fall a large part of the vineyards of Spain, Portugal, the South of France and Greece. The Mediterranean vineyards provide not only a large part of the Community's total eating grape and raisin grape harvests, but also about 70% of wine production.

Within this vast Mediterranean area are two basic categories of wine-growing land. Areas of very high potential yield, the produce of which generally, but by no means exclusively, goes to making vins de table. In the area of middling potential yield, the produce is predominantly used for quality wines. Note the broad correlation between quantity and quality. A grape vine, which yields too much, or is permitted to do so, tends to produce a wine of low grade and low alcoholic content. In France, and similarly in Spain and Italy, this is the major criterion used to determine whether or not a wine deserves a quality denomination.

Atlantic Vineyards
These cover an area of approximately 380,000 hectares in the West and South-West of France and in the North of Portugal and produces mainly quality wines and wine for distillation.

Northern Vineyards
This is not an inconsiderable section, at approximately 250,000 hectares. Much of the area labors under climatic conditions which are at the limit of the grape's tolerance. In the most northerly of these vineyards (Champagne, Alsace, Moselle), only quality white wines are produced. In the slightly more temperate areas (Burgundy, Jura, Savoie), reds and roses, along with white wines, are made.

The Three Major EU Producers: Spain, Italy and France

Spain
Spain is, by quite a long way, the most extensively covered country with vineyard. In fact, it has the biggest single vineyard in the world. It continues to be the country with the largest area under vines in the EU and the world (accounting for more than one third of the total area in the EU, followed by France and Italy with 25% each which represents more than 15% of the

world). Spain has a winemaking tradition that goes back to the Romans. Vines occupy third place in terms of cultivated Spanish area, after cereals and olives.

Wine production, including grape juice, represents 2% of Spain's total agricultural production and 3.3% of the value of crop production. In just five years, between 1995 and 2000, Spain's production rose by 57.6%, the largest increase experienced in the whole Spanish agro-food industry. The sector's percentage share in the overall industry increased from 6% to 8% in the same period. There were 4,055 companies registered in the wine sector in Spain, according to data from the National Statistics Institute, representing a 12.2% increase over 1995. By 2004, 1.04 million hectares were in production (no changes under vine over the previous five years) and a slight decrease by 2009 and 2011. Spain's imports, exports and production 2001-2011 are shown in Table 2:3.

Million liters	2001	2002	2003	2004	2005	2009	2011
Production	3,636.1	2,957.3	3,735.9	4,191.1	3,520.9	3,429.0	3,397.0
Imports	25.2	26.1	28.9	29.0	35.8	61.0	59.0
Exports	1,057.2	1,036.6	1,280.9	1,469.0	1,421.8	1,292.0	2,232.0

Table 2:3 Spain Wine Production, Imports and Export in tons, 2001-2011
Sources: University of Adelaide Press | Global Wine Markets, 1961 to 2009, and GAIN Report, 2/25/2013.

Spain's wine-producing vineyards are spread widely throughout the country, but are to be found in concentration in a number of particular locations—notably La Mancha, a broad plain between 500 and 700 meters above sea level, the continental climate of which supports about 49% of the country's vines. Despite the enormous areas under cultivation, however, Spain's production of wine falls very short of her big EU rivals—partly explained by Spain's substantial output of eating grapes and raisin grapes, but chiefly the result of generally low yields.

In countries with higher fertility, restricting the yield of very fruitful vines can improve the quality of the wine produced. However, unfortunately for the Spanish economy, the converse does not hold true and low yield does not automatically mean the result will be high-quality wine. Of Spain's wine to-tal, around 38% is considered premium wine, and the rest being standard wine.

The Spanish wine industry has been active over the past couple of decades in a move away from predominantly Vine de table (formerly accounting for around 85% of total). Now, instead of concentration on the cheap (largely white) wine, emphasis is being placed on quality reds. The production of quality wines in Spain received a considerable boost from the establishment and maturation of the Institute National des Denominations d'Origine.

Other factors have been even more influential in bringing change to the Spanish vineyards and bodegas. The gradual integration of Spain into the EU, which began in March 1986, was of enormous significance—not only to Spain itself, but also to the wine industry in general. The EU established a very complex network of progressively applied rules and regulations that was partly aimed at ensuring that Spain did not become a "monster producer" upsetting the European balance.

In the vineyards themselves, a handful of forward-thinking individuals have sown the seeds of future developments with ideas such as the introduction of the "noble" grape varieties. Notably in the Penedes region, the blending of wine made from imported grape varieties with those produced from traditionally grown local varieties led to some extremely successful new lines, which are now held to be among the country's best. Another leap forward by the growers of Penedes has been the growth of the very considerable sparkling wine industry, which, as far back as 1982, had already begun turning out over 500,000 hecto liters per year.

The bodegas have likewise been re-equipped to make them more efficient and able to compete in the EU Market, which would have been otherwise impossible. This created a profound effect on the style of wines produced. Spanish whites are changing rapidly, moving away from the ponderously "oak-like style" of their forbearers towards a fresher, fruitier type of wine, which currently is the wine increasingly in demand. These latter changes have been brought about by technological leaps in the bodega already mentioned and by the careful timing of the harvest, at a point when the grapes are still slightly under-ripe.

The changes of method and style have enabled the Spanish to penetrate a wider range of markets, and the increased speed at which these new-style wines can be produced has had a very salutary effect on cash flow.

There are three major categories of Spanish wine:

- Vins de table—these are either drunk as they are or more frequently they are blended. The table wines are generally high in alcohol, between 11 and 15%, and low in acidity.
- Fine wines (Denomination d'Origine)—these are predominantly

reds and roses, the most sought-after of which are produced in the North and the East of the country (Rioja, Tarragona, Navarre; and Valdepenas in La Mancha)

- Specialty wines—most of which qualify for the Denomination d'Origine and include Sherries, Montillas, Malagas and also the sparkling wines known by the generic term of "cava."

Italy

In 1980, there were 1.22 million hectares under cultivation, but by 2001, Italy had reduced vineyards to only about 897,600 hectares of vineyard yielding just over 52 Mhl of wine. The decrease of land devoted to production continued, and in 2003 the vine area stood at 800,000 hectares. Similarly, the wine production had dropped to 44 Mhl of wine and slightly over 25.3% were characterized as "Quality Wine." By 2004, production had reversed and was up over the 2002 level; but again in 2005, it reversed again. Production continued to decrease and by 2012 had dropped considerably. Table 2:4 shows production, for 2001 through 2012.

Million liters	2001	2002	2003	2004	2005	2009	2012
Production	5,229.3	4,460.4	4,415.4	5,084.3	4,794.5	4619	4082

Table 2:4 Italy Wine Production, Imports and Exports: Total Volume
Source: Euromonitor International; OIV, 2012.

After the strong decline reported during the 1980s and the 1990s, Italian vine area appears to be stabilizing at slightly less than about 800,000 hectares, with production down in 2012 by 8% (GAIN Report IT1307, 2013). The Italian wine industry is particularly fragmented over hundreds of thousands of individual holding, most quiet small.

Besides the actual size of holdings, however, there is another, more general kind of fragmentation in evidence. There is no such thing as the *Italian* approach to winemaking. Italy itself is a diverse collection of old fiefdoms and only comparatively recently a unified state. Italian wine making does not have the consistency of approach throughout as is the case in France. The various regions of Italy have clung to their own traditions and, to a great extent, continued to their own practices. While this helps maintain a degree of individuality and character among Italian wines, it has also meant that Italy as a whole has been somewhat held back in recognizing the full potential of her wines as a prestige export asset.

Nevertheless, as elsewhere in the EU, new technology and better equipment is leading to greater efficiency and a production base that is more responsive to the market. Much of the credit for the initial impetus towards modernization came from the cooperatives; more than eight-hundred now exist throughout Italy—predominantly in the South of the country. These cooperatives account for about 40% of Italy's total output of wine and many of them, particularly the larger ones, have made great strides in the modernization of vineyards and wineries. The cooperatives have also been instrumental in consolidating vineyards in order to achieve greater levels of economy in their cultivation and to encourage conversion to the mono-cultural vineyard (where vines constitute the unique crop rather than being one of several). However, 24% of Italian vineyards still use a style known as "promiscuous cultivation."

The innovations practiced by the new generation of oenologists with better technological methods and a willingness to experiment with new grape varietals, such as Cabernet Sauvignon and Chardonnay, unfortunately encountered hurdles when it came to negotiating the strictures of the DOC regulations (in many ways even tighter than those insisted upon in France).The Italian DOC rules dictate the following characteristics of wine:

- Color of a wine
- Where can the wine be legitimately grown
- Which varieties of grape (and in what proportions) may be used
- Minimum (but not maximum) alcoholic content
- Aging procedures

Serving to protect traditional standards of wine production for each specific type, the strictness of the Italian regulations has served to ossify methods of production of DOC wine. This has prevented new strains of wine entering the coveted *quality* category. Consequently, many new wines of a very high standard produced by some prestigious companies are having to be described as Vino de Tavola—the only alternative to DOC. Meanwhile, some less creditable producers fearfully hang on to their DOC by close attention to the rules, knowing that if they were to lose the prestige of the Denomination they would have a great deal of difficulty in selling their wine.

The introduction of the even more prestigious DOCG category could never do anything to alleviate the situation as described above. But it has, by its stringent system of checks throughout the vinification process and analysis of wines, provided a quality demarcation even more rigorous than the DOC. The net result has been generally improving the quality of regional production.

Another innovation which has been of benefit to the Italian wine producer was the introduction in 1992 of an equivalent of the French Vins de Pays category—the *Indicazione da Geogralrca Tipica*—which serves to lend cachet to wines of a certain level of quality from specific regions of the country. There are 121 wines in Italy that are classified as Indicazione Geografica Tipica (Typical Geographic Indication) for a total of 25 million hector-liters each year. The Italians have what has been termed rather catholic tastes in grape varieties, favouring according to region, such as Sangiovese, Nebbiolo, Montepulciano, Pinot Grigio, Chardonnay, Trebbiano, Barbera, Bombino Bianco, Lambrusco, Merlot, Cabernet Sauvignon, Verdicchio and more.

In Italy today, experimentation is holding its own against tradition. As has already been mentioned, the "noble" varieties of French grapes are being groomed in certain areas, while at the same time the two best known Italian varieties of red Sangiovese and white Trebbiano are being used to make changes in the style of wines produced, particularly in the South where those grapes are not native. In the far Northeast, in the Friuli-Venezia-Giulia area, the tendency has been to move into the production of varietal-identified wines, rather than using blends of different grapes. Here, because of less deeply established traditions, the setting up of varietal DOC zones has been possible. This system of often overlapping zones, based on the grape rather than on historical methods, may well prove to be the way forward for other areas also.

One tradition that is swiftly passing into history is the habit in certain areas for growers to profit by the abundant sunshine that grows grapes so full of sugar that they can ferment into wine with an extremely high alcoholic content—sometimes up to 15 or 16 per cent, without the aid of any fortification. The newer vinification equipment available to many growers and a greater sensitivity to the demands of the consumer has led to a general abandonment of this rather heavy-hand approach.

Table 2:5 shows the important areas of wine production in Italy and the relative average production.

Wine	Number of DOC/DOCG
Piedmont	2.30
Lombardy	1.10
Trentino Alto Adige	1.06
Friuli Venezia Giulia	1.00
Veneto	6.84
Emilia Romagna	5.68
Other North	0.10
Total North	18.15
Tuscany	2.31
Umbria	0.77
Marche	1.25
Latium	1.25
Total Center	7.21
Abruzzi	3.80
Campania	1.76
Apulia	5.58
Other South	1.14
Total South	12.29
Sicily	6.20
Sardinia	0.72
Total Islands	6.93
Grand Total	**44.60**

Table 2:5 Number of DOC/DOCG Wines in Italy
Source: GAIN Report IT3029.

Machines in the Vineyard

An example of the introduction to Italy of modern methods is machine harvesting. Begun in the US, these machines were used for a very significant proportion of the harvest in America. Even highly traditional wine-producing countries, such as France, started accepting this method, despite the erosion of the festive spirit of the *vendange*, which it inevitably entails. Mechanical harvesting has certain advantages over hand-picking, the chief of which is that machines can bring in a whole crop at optimum ripeness, whereas the ranks of pickers, with however good a will they worked, usually had to start when a crop was just under-ripe and finish when it was just over-ripe.

Harvesting can be performed in the cool of the night, which has advantages particularly for white wines, and requires only two operators per machine. The machines work by straddling the vines and violently shaking the trunk to make the fruit fall onto a conveyor-belt. Flexible paddles at either side perform a similar function for the more far-flung bunches of grapes. It might be thought that such violence would prove disastrously damaging to the fruit. However, since it is passed directly along the conveyor belt, past a blower which removes leaves and to a crusher, and then to a tank, any damage the fruit sustains is of little or no consequence.

The disadvantages of the mechanical method are that it requires a big cash investment and vineyards have often to be adapted to permit using the machinery—indeed, some vineyards are so steep that current models could never cope. The machines fail to harvest approximately 10% of the fruit, which is clearly a consideration, and there are still flaws in the blowing mechanism for the removal of leaves from the crush.

France

Although not the largest in area of the EU big three, France represents the biggest single market in value terms, due to a high proportion of quality-wine production. From 1995 to 2000, the total of France's vineyard area declined by 2.7%. AOC/VDQS plantings rose by 5.2%, while vineyard area under other wines was reduced by 9.9 %. For the past ten years the average wine production in France was about 54 million hl. The split of this production was about three quarters red and one quarter white. The domestic market was 4.8 Mhl. There were around 110,000 wine growers, most who are small growers and place their grapes in cooperatives. The average size is about 8 hectares. Only one grower out of five produces his own wine. A decade ago, there were more than 200,000 vine growers.

In 2006, total wine sales declined by almost 3% in volume terms, to 2.5 billion liters, and fell by 1% in value terms, to €24 billion. But in 2011, it was up at €25.2 billion, and nearly the same volume at 2.47 billion liters. Facing a structural decline of wine consumption and the decreasing number of consumers in France, French wine industry players have adopted new marketing methods and endeavored to develop new product.

By 2012, the major export markets for France, in terms of volume, were Germany, The UK, Belgium, Netherlands and China. The US ranks sixth in volume terms, but second in value terms. Despite being such an ingrained element of French culture, vine growing in France, as is true of everywhere, is by no means a comfortable way of making a living. Indeed, 28% of vine-holdings in France are of less than one hectare and a mere 4.5% occupy an area greater than 30 hectares. Due to pressures of the market and EU strategies in response to those pressures, an ongoing program of restructuring has been followed. Small growers are pooling their resources into cooperatives. And there is a movement towards replanting on existing vineyards with an eye to upgrading to "noble" grape varieties and to improving access for mechanical harvesting. New methods of crop spraying are reducing losses and raising quality of the fruit, which naturally passes through to the quality of the wine.

Of the 61 Mhl produced in France during 1989, around one third were premium wines. More recently, the premium wines have contributed about 50% of the total production. During the early nineties, a system of grants by both the French Government and the EU were making it possible for even individual small-holders and minor cooperatives to modernize their wineries (e.g. acquiring new presses, installing temperature-control equipment for the fermentation process and moving over to stainless steel vats).

Main areas of production by administrative region were the following:

- Languedoc-Roussillon (appellations include Corbières and Côtes du Roussillon, but the region also includes part of the southern Côtes du Rhône)
- Aquitaine (mainly Bordeaux, but also Bergerac)
- Provence-Côte d'Azur (Côtes de Provence, Côtes du Ventoux and part of southern Rhône, including Châteauneuf-du-Pape);
- Rhône-Alpes (Beaujolais, Northern Rhône, Savoie)
- Pays de Loire (Muscadet, Anjou)
- Centre (Touraine, Sancerre)
- Midi-Pyrenées (Cahors, Gaillac, Madiran and Côtes du Frontonnais)
- Champagne
- Bourgogne
- Alsace
- Corse

The areas of Bordeaux, Cotes-du-RhBne, Loire, Champagne, Alsace supply wines of world of renown, besides wine for the elaboration of Cognac, Armagnac and other spirits. Even before the EC grubbing policy began to take full effect, vineyard area in France was in retreat. Between 1979 and 1985, the drop in wine production was particularly marked:

- Midi-Pyrenees—a drop of 26% between 1979 and 1985 and the marginalization of vines in the overall agricultural picture for the region. The drop in total wine cultivation area continued from 41,033 hectares in 1990 to 38,429 in 2002.
- Corsica—a drop of 30%, mainly as a result of distribution- and marketing problems of the final product—in particular the wines of

eastern Corsica. The drop in total wine cultivation area continued from 9,715 hectares in 1990 to 7,287 in 2002.

- Cognac region—a drop of 15%, mostly from the areas on the periphery whose white wines were fetching prices greatly inferior to those produced in the central "Grande Champagne" and "Petite Champagne" areas.

The actual number of growers has been decreasing. The catastrophic frosts of April 1991 destroyed up to 70% of certain French vineyards and drastically reduced that year's wine-production by some 30% immediately. The repercussions of this disaster were bound to be felt for several years to come. Despite the reduction in production-base and other legislative ploys of the EU, over-production was stimulated in part by improved methods of cultivation, and pest and disease control. Over production continued to pose a problem. More recently the EU policy of yield-limitation has been more effective in bringing production more in line with consumer demands.

Germany

In 2003, Germany had a total of 104,000 hectares of land under vine cultivation. Due to climate and geography, German wine production varies significantly in quality and quantity from year to year, despite the rather strict maximum harvest regulations based on the EU wine regime that continues to influence the fluctuations in annual production. In 2004, Germany produced approximately 10.5 Mhl of wine, up 27% from 2003. There was 1% volume and current value decline over 2005 to €9.7 billion. Still rosé wine sold well in 2006, with 1% total volume growth over the previous year. Its popularity continued to increase with German wine drinkers, as people are now better informed about this type of wine and no longer believe it to be a mixture of still red wine and still white wine. More companies launched new still rosé wines, innovating with bottles and packaging in general. Key and growing export destinations include the UK, the US and the Netherlands. In the past few years, German producers proved successful in emphasizing the high quality of German wine.

In 2012, German wine exports were 1.3 million hectoliters, with a value of €321 million. As the German Wine Institute announced, the average price of wines from the German growing regions exported in 2012 increased year over year. Exports to Norway, Canada, Japan and Sweden have shown an increase in both value and volume (value increases of 4% to 10% and approximately similar increases in quantity). In recent years, the Norwegians have been increasing their purchases of German wines. One third of the wine bottles Norwegians purchase comes from Germany.

The production area in Germany is divided into 13 different growing regions. These regions include Rheinhessen, Pflaz, Baden, Württemberg, Mosel-Saar-Ruwer, Franken, Nahe, Rheingau, Saale-Unstrut, Mittelrhein, Ahr, Hessische Bergstrasse and Sachsen. The names of these regions are used for region of origin labeling. The commercial production of wine outside of these designated regions is not permitted.

Based on the rules of the EU wine regime, the German wine law allows regional authorities to stipulate which grape varieties can be produced in the production regions. Table 2:6 indicates the relative the area under vine cultivation in each of these areas.

Region	Area (Hectare)
Rheinhessen	26,444
Pflaz	23,461
Baden	15,906
Württemberg	11,511
Mosel-Saar-Ruwer	9.034
Franken	6,063
Nahe	4,155
Rheingau	3,125
Saale-Unstrut	685
Mittelrhein	461
Ahr	558
Hessische Bergstrasse	439
Sachsen	462

Table 2:6 Main Area Under Vine Cultivation (Hectares) Germany, 2008
Source: www.deutscheweine.de, Deutscher Wein Statistik.

Germany is predominantly a white wine region with 68.5% white wine areas. However, due to consumer preferences, vintners are gradually switching over to produce more and more red wines. In 1991, only 20% of the grapes were of red varieties compared to 32.5% in 2003. Now, about 50% of the replantings are currently in red wine varieties. Based on area, Germany is the sixth largest wine grape producing country in the world and ranked seventh in terms of wine production, recently surpassed by Australia.

As early as 2001, the German wine industry invested significantly in quality. The introduction of two new classification terms (Classic and Selection) forced the industry to take steps to simplify its labeling and become much more consumer-driven. The development of branded wines in the mid-price sector, with an emphasis on dry wines, led to these wines becoming more available in major retailers. The introduction of more modern packaging also helped to raise the profile of German wines, as part of a marketing initiative incentive open to all producers.

Portugal

In 2011, Portugal produced 7.34 MH liters of wine. Domestic consumption, due to the deep economic crisis gripping the country, continued to negatively affect domestic demand for wine in Portugal. This has resulted in consumers increasingly shifting from on-trade to off-trade, as well as migrating from more expensive brands to cheaper ones. As the fate of the euro and the EU political landscape remains in flux during 2013, the Portuguese economy struggles with high unemployment, debt burdens and lack of growth. Therefore, wine may be expected to see total volume sales growth of less than 1% over the foreseeable future.

The vineyards of Portugal cover an area of around a quarter million hectares. Average production is about 60% red wine and 40% white wines. Table 2:7 shows the main areas of production and the most important grape varieties grown in each region. Compared to other European producers, Portugal is relatively one of the most stable of the wine-producing countries of Europe in terms of methods. Wine-growing in Portugal is on a large scale, but concentrated in small-holdings. The vineyards are chiefly in the North and the Central regions of the country and support a work-force of a little less than a quarter of a million, in addition to the landowners themselves. Approximately 80% of the producers have less than one hectare of land, and only 1% have more than 10 hectares of land devoted to wine production.

As might be expected from the generally small nature of the growers, cooperatives play an important role in the life of the Portuguese vineyards. There are some 120 coops across the country, which account for a total of 40% of production. While the export market (chiefly of port and roses) is managed by the British and by big companies like Sogrape—producers of Mateus Rose—and JM da Fonseca (who are permitted to draw on grapes from undemarcated regions anywhere in the country), the cooperatives still tend to make the old-style, highly alcoholic wines preferred by the domestic market. The new styles, less heady wines popular elsewhere, do not stand much of a chance when co-operatives still pay growers according to alcohol potential of their grapes. About 55% of production qualifies as premium wine, coming from eight major regions, the principal of which is the Douro area, whose world-wide fame is assured thanks to its being the home of Port.

Port production is a centuries-old tradition in Portugal and has an important role in fortified wine and vermouth production in the country. Climate change is expected to have important impacts on global temperature and precipitation patterns. There are expectations that this may significantly reshape viticulture zoning in Europe and be favorable to the Port wine producers. Today, port is exported to over 100 countries. The European countries account for 92% of total volume and 83% of value. The North American market contributes approximately 7% and 12% respectively. Wine has provided supermarket chains with much higher margins than those they achieve in other food products and therefore plays an important role. The buying power exerted by the supermarket chains affects the distributor relations of the Port producers. Total Port production in 2010 was in the region of 6.7 million cases, a reduction of 10% since the highpoint year of 2007. The major export market for Port is France, which accounts for around 29% of total exports. This business of Port remains primarily focused on the export trade. The most significant trend in recent times has been the rise in share taken by premium Port, which indicates the emphasis placed on securing value returns as volumes stagnate or decline. Premium Port accounts for almost 40% of revenue.

Area of Production	Important Grape Varieties Grown
Estremadura	Fernão Pires, Arinto, Joao de Santarem, Bastardo, Alfrochiero Preto
Douro	Malvasia Fina, Gouveio, Viosinho, Touriga Nacional, Touriga Francesa
Minho	Alvarinho, Loureiro, Trajadura, Brancelho, Perdal, Vinhão
Ribatejo	Arinto, Fernão Pires, Esgana Cao, Periquita, Cabernet Sauvignon, Merlot
Alentejo	Antão Vaz, Arinto, Diagalves, Fernão Pires, Alfrochiero Preto, Aragonez
Terras do Sado	Moscatel de Setúbal, Arinto, Chardonnay, Aragonez, Cabernet Sauvignon
Beiras	Arinto, Bical, Cercial, Baga, Bastardo, Camarate
Bairrada	Bical, Maria Gomes, Rabo de Ovelha, Baga, Castellão Francês, Tinta Pinheira
Dão	Encruzado, Assario Braco, Barcelo, Alfrocheiro Preto, Bastardo, Jaen

Table 2:7 Main Areas of Production and the Most Important Grape Varieties, Portugal
Source:http://www.harperswine.com/winereports/portugal.cfm

Many of the zones in the DOC region are very small and somewhat obscure. For example, three small zones around Lisbon produce no more than 720,000 bottles between them. The Portuguese DOC system is widely held to be out of date. Currently, many of the largest selling wines in the home market are either branded or are good wines produced in regions such as Ribatejo and Estremadura (the largest producer of table wine), which are still not demarcated. The demarcation system itself is more or less identical to the French one and was one of the first to be established in 1908. In Portugal, a wine is either standard or it is premium.

Greece

The vineyards of Greece cover a total area of approximately 113,000 hectares. Over the last two decades, there has been a considerable decline in the area under vine cultivation in Greece. The area under vine cultivation declined from 192,000 hectares in 1980 to approximately 113,000 hectares in 2010. Production shows a significant decline each year from 2008 to 2011, going from 3,869 in 2008 to 2,750 in 2011 ('000 hectoliters), with a modest increase reported in 2012.

Most of Greece's exports currently go to Germany and France, and exports to the UK remain relatively small. This isn't helped by the fact that Greece is probably the only wine producing country of the western hemisphere that is spending next to nothing on the generic promotion of its wines. The changes experienced in all sections of the Mediterranean vineyard areas are reflected in Greece.

Main areas of vine cultivation include Peloponnese, Macedonia, Cephalonia, Attica, Rhodes and Crete. Major wine producers in Greece include Harlaftis and Hatzidakis.

The Peloponnese and Cretan regions in the South represents the entire Greek production of raisins, but also table wine, dessert wines (such as Samos and Muscat), plus some quality wines (such as Nemea and Mantinia). Macedonia, Thrace and Thessaly in the North produce a number of quality wines including Naoussa, Amynteon and Port-Caras. Central Greece and the Ionian Isles produce mainly white resinated wine from the Savatiano grape. This traditional style of wine, generally known as Retsina, is achieved by the addition of a small amount of pine resin during the fermentation process.

The rest of quality Greek wine divides between reds, whites, naturally sweet and dessert wines. But Greece was slow to respond to the idea of quality denominations and has had them in place for only the past couple of decades—more as a result of EU than of domestic demand.

Elsewhere in Europe

Russia

The first Russian wine guide-book was published in 2012. The book describes 55 wines from 13 wineries. The leading Russian sommeliers who contributed to the wine book hope that the emergence of truly outstanding Russian wines would not be too many years away. Before 1985, domestic wines produced from locally grown grapes dominated the Russian wine market. However, during an "anti-alcohol campaign" in the mid-1980s, most local wineries were destroyed. As a result, domestic wine production fell by 80%. By 2011, Russian wine production was recovering and production was up to 640 million liters. Perhaps as much as four-fifths of wines sold in Russia are of rather poor quality semi-sweet varieties, and often involve the use of imported concentrates. The reason for the preference of sweet varieties dates back to Soviet times, when Russians' taste for semi-sweet and sparkling wines was formed. Many Russians today continue to dislike dry wines, considering them too sour. The preference has been attributed to Soviet dictator Joseph Stalin, an ethnic Georgian, who promoted this tradition of sweet wines.

The Russian consumers are continuing to switch from vodka to "softer" alcoholic beverages, and wine consumption has been on the rise. This trend is expected to continue, particularly among younger, more affluent Russians. The general labor-class in Russia still has the idea that vodka is the "manly" drink. Russia is a land of extremes. It has one of largest extremes in incomes and, therefore, one of the largest discrepancies in wine consumption.

Wine in Russia was only the drink of the aristocracy before the 1917 revolution. However, this changed under Stalin, who believed that wine had to be affordable for every Soviet citizen. Scientists were recruited to resolve the problem, and they managed to produce frost-resistant, high-yielding varieties of grape. As might be expected, the quality suffered and wines made from these grapes were barely palatable, due to their high acidity. The remedy chosen was to add grape sugar and often ethyl alcohol to the wines (this practice is reported to still be widely used in the Russian wine industry). Nevertheless, there are now serious attempts to produce quality wines in Russia.

Makers of quality Russian wines have been pushing for minimum retail prices for wines in Russia (e.g., at least $4 per bottle) because they just cannot compete in the economy segment of box wines of low quality. Some of the winemakers have asked the government to ban the cheap wines altogether, because they believe that existence of very poor quality wines discredit the entire winemaking industry. Nevertheless, such a ban appears unlikely.

Ever since 2006, Russia has seen the emergence of good quality wineries, which have started to adopt European techniques and standards. The Abrau-Durso winery in the foothills near the Black Sea port of Novorossiisk is considered to be the flagship of Russia's new wine industry. Quality-orientated companies include Chateau le Grand Vostok, Lefkadiya, Vedernikov and a handful of others.

In 2003, the average per capita consumption of wine was 4 liters, but by the beginning of 2012, consumption was reported to have increased to 7.14 liters per capita. Therefore, the per capita consumption of wine in Russia has increased significantly. However, this may be compared to per capita wine consumption in Europe of three times as much.

Traditions of wine consumption in Russia are very specific:

- 40% of wine is purchased for a national or family holiday.
- 25% purchased for meeting with friends.
- 15% when eating out.

Red wine accounts for the largest share of wine consumption for all price categories in Russia. The quantity of Russian wine imports had increased steadily during the period 2000 to 2005, and exports show a slight decrease in 2004, depending on statistical sources, and then increased considerably by 2011. Likewise, with the new vineyards, by as early as 2011, wine production had increased by more than double the output of 2001, as shown in Table 2:8.

Million liters	2001	2009	2011
Production	282.6	509	640
Imports	165.7	302	-
Exports	0.1	3	-

Table 2:8 Wine Production, Imports and Exports: Total Volume
Source: Euromonitor International, Country Sector Briefings, Russia.

The other European wine producing countries include Switzerland, Bulgaria, Romania, Yugoslavia and Hungary. All these countries are small producers. The following section provides a brief overview of wine cultivation in these countries, and then considers the other regions of the world.

Bulgaria
In 2012, wine production in Bulgaria was estimated at 1.2 Mhl, which was 2.1% higher than 2011. Bulgarian vineyard area was estimated at 78,468 Ha in 2011. Total Bulgarian viniculture area has been decreasing since 2000. The high number of small vineyards and farms led to substantial problems with investment and marketing. As a result, total vineyard area declined by 51% over the last 10 years. Red varieties (mainly Merlot, Cabernet, and Pamid) account for 62% of total area under vine. Bulgaria is home to some of the finest wines. The development of viticulture in the Bulgarian region was mentioned in early Greek mythology. Legend has it that Dionysius, the mythological "Greek god of wine and agriculture," began the winemaking tradition in Bulgaria by bringing a tiny root of vine to the Thracian valley.

Champagne has become one of the highest growing categories. Bulgarians drank wine mostly at home (80%), and these are largely low-priced wines.

Local wine companies are the sales leaders, as imported wine still commands an insignificant share of the market. The per-capita wine consumption is around 6 liters, which is below that of major wine-producing countries, largely because wine is still thought of as an occasional drink in Bulgaria rather than an everyday indulgence. Therefore, much of the good Bulgarian wine is exported. The wine industry in Bulgaria is quite diverse, with premium wines on one side of the spectrum and extremely cheap wines on the other. An increasing number of Bulgarian producers and some foreign producers are competing for affluent consumers.

Producers and exporters have adopted strong branded approaches to their export markets, and branded wines also became increasingly popular in the domestic market.

Romania

The estimate of growth in 2011 was 9% in constant monetary terms, and such revenue growth has been driven by quality wine and price increases. Romania has an old world winemaking tradition with a history of oenology and viticulture for thousands of years. Despite political and ideological setbacks, Romania is becoming one of the interesting wine producing nations in Europe with a growing reputation for individuality in terms of its indigenous plantings. The diversity of Romania allows expression through its several different regions; some supporting international grape varieties and others are mostly indigenous varietals.

Sales of wine have shown increases in value terms, while the volume has been decreasing since the high volume point reached in 2009. For example, in 2009, volume was 6.7 million hectoliters and in 2012, the estimate of production was only 4.0 Mhl. The vineyard area has been decreasing, falling from 184,400 Ha in 2009 to 175,000 in 2012. According to official data, white varieties account for 85% of production, and red varieties for the remaining. Leading red varieties are Merlot and Cabernet Sauvignon.

Switzerland

Geographically speaking, Switzerland is a tiny country with a population of only 8 million and its land area is one-tenth the size of the wine producing state of California. However, Switzerland has sustained some 16000 ha of vineyards producing around 1.1 Mhl wine (statistical estimate of the 2012 production).

It is perhaps not surprising that the Swiss, surrounded as they are by the major wine-producing countries, of France, Italy and Germany (not to mention Austria), should have their own tradition of winemaking. Swiss wines are so little known abroad and this is largely explained by the fact that domestic demand is sufficiently strong to account for all but a very small amount of the country's yearly output. Up until 2003, Switzerland produced more white wine than red wine. After 2003, the trend was for an increase in red wine production and by 2009, there was more than 11% of red wine over white wine being produced. Official statistics for 2010 showed that wine production accounted for only 4.4% of its total agricultural output. To put this in value perspective, the estimated total of wine grapes and wine was around 700 million Swiss Francs in 2011.

In 2012, the Swiss consumed 276 million liters of wine, which is 6.6 million liters less (2.2% less) than in 2011. The market share of Swiss wine stands at 36.3%, with that of white wine twice as high as that of red. Wine production in 2012 was over 10% below output in 2011, due to less than ideal weather conditions.

Few Swiss winegrowers produce and sell their own wine directly, and *very few indeed* derive their principal income from their vineyards. Due to constant division of inheritances, most Swiss wine-producers operate on a very small scale.

The wine-producing regions of Switzerland—like the country itself—divide three ways: French-speaking Suisse Romande in the West, German/Austrian influenced Eastern Switzerland (the North and East of the country) and the Italian canton of Ticino in the South. It is in the Western cantons of Suisse Romande that the great majority of Switzerland's vines are to be found. The main grape variety grown in Western Switzerland is the white Chasselas, although being what some might consider rather bland is grown more commonly as a table-grape. However, it is the relative neutrality and subtle variety of the Chasselas that lends individuality to the wines of Western Switzerland.

Besides Chasselas, certain red grapes are increasingly cultivated in Western Switzerland—chiefly Pinot Noir (Blauburgunder) and Gamay which are either pressed separately and sold under varietal labels or combined to produce an excellent marriage of the qualities of the two—known as Dole (in Valais) and Salvagnin (in Vaud). The importance of these latter labels has been increasing over the past decade and a half. The name Dole, for example, is under State control and can only be used under strictest regulation as to grape content (at least 51% Pinot Noir) and Oechsle levels (sugar content). Those which do not come quite up to par, can only be marketed as Goron—usually a lighter but often extremely palatable wine.

The fiercely individual streak, so predominant among the Swiss, makes for a rather bewildering labeling system. In most of the Western cantons, varietal labeling is the norm, however, the Chasselas grape is known as Fendant in Valais, and as Perlan in Geneva and Neuchatel. In Vaud, on the other hand, traditional village appellations are used, such as Mont-sur-Rolle, Fechy and Dezaley, to name but a few.

The scale of wine-production tends to be rather small. In Valais, for example, the less than 5,000 ha under vine is shared between almost 20,000 owners. Consequently only about 2% of the Valais growers produce their own wine for direct sale to individuals and friends, while the vast majority work through cooperatives. Some 60% of Valais wines are produced by the Union des Negociants en Vin du Valais, and 30% by the growers' cooperative of Provins Valais. The increasing efficiency of such organizations has led to many and varied improvements in the quality and commercial viability of Swiss wine. The Federation de Caves Genevoises, for example, (known throughout Switzerland as "Vin-Union") has established state-of-the-art plant in Satigny at which the various varietals can be vinified separately and under strict control.

There are seventeen German-speaking cantons, all of which produce wine, if only in very modest quantities. German-speaking Switzerland accounts for two thirds of the country in terms of geographical area, but only for about one sixth of Switzerland's total wine. Wine in Eastern Switzerland is of mainly local importance, most of it being consumed locally. Stringent restrictions on suitability of cultivated land and advances in vinicultural technique have improved the quality of Eastern Swiss Wines and demand is outstripping production. The wine produced in Eastern Switzerland is predominantly red, and made virtually exclusively from Pinot Noir (known as Clevner). The chief white wine grape is the Riesling/Sylvaner cross which is extremely well-known throughout the rest of the world as the Muller-Thurgau. The creator of this phenomenally successful 19th century hybrid was Professor Muller-Thurgau from Switzerland. Ironically, Switzerland is now the only country which fails to honor his memory by attaching his name to the grape. Ticino is Switzerland's most southerly canton and is strongly influenced by neighboring Italy. Ticino's mild climate, good rainfall, infrequent frosts and topography of south-facing slopes combine to produce some very high quality wines. At the beginning the 20th century, the region sustained 7,000 ha of vineyard, much of it grown in the Italian pergola style where the vines are grown on overhead trellises supported by granite pillars. Now, the method of cultivation has almost universally changed and the area under vine has drastically reduced to less than 1,000 ha. There are two principal reasons for this huge reduction: the European infestations of phylloxera and mildew. The arrival of these two scourges destroyed centuries of work within a short period of time. However, soon afterward a phylloxera-resistant root stock was developed and imported from the US.

In the Sottoceneri region, the 1,000 ha of vineyard in the region are now divided among some 10,000 small growers. Given this statistic, one could be forgiven for assuming that production would be purely domestic and perhaps rather primitive. While this may be true for a large part of Ticino, in particular the North, there does exist mainly in the Sottoceneri area, a powerful and efficient system of cooperatives and negociants. Many of these either own or lease estates, which produce fine wines of great interest to the connoisseur.

It is not easy to make many generalizations about the Swiss wine business. There is no comprehensive register of vineyards and their wines, let alone any kind of official classification. Some claim that that there are over 15,000 different labels in the country as a whole, each one as individual as its producer. There is, however, one unifying thread and that is the high standards and the respect for regulations which are so deeply ingrained in the Swiss national character. To carve out even a small place for them in the international market, this tiny nation has always had to go for quality over quantity. This is equally true of the wine business and the rigorous controls of accounting and cellar methods adhered to by Swiss producers, and they are now earning accolades for their product in International competitions. A tourist in Switzerland can be assured to find high-quality domestic wine available for his or her pleasure.

The Vineyards of Egypt and Africa
The chief wine-producing countries here are South Africa, Egypt, Algeria, Morocco, and Tunisia. This section gives a very brief overview of the relatively small domestic wine industry in all these countries.

Egypt
The wine producing sector in Egypt is still small with a rudimentary market and not developed for exporting. In 2012, wine production continued to increase slightly. In fact, production has been a little over 4 Mhl annually since 2006, and stood at 4.5 in 2012. The two primary wines that are under cultivation in Egypt are Pinot Blanc and Cabernet Sauvignon. The Pinot Blanc brands are Grand Marquis Pinot Blanc, Omar Khayyam Pinot Blanc, Gianaclis Cru Des Ptolemees Pinot Blanc, Gianaclis Château Grand Marquis Pinot Blanc, Gianaclis and Obelisk Pinot Blanc. The Cabernet Sauvignon wines are Grand Marquis Cabernet Sauvignon, Omar Khayyam Cabernet Sauvignon, Gianaclis Omar Khayyam Cabernet Sauvignon, Gianaclis Château Grand Marquis Cabernet Sauvignon, Obeslisk Cabernet Sauvignon, and Château Des Reves Cabernet Sauvignon.

Unlike the different quality levels offered in beer and spirits, wines in Egypt are all of the same quality. This is because wine is regarded as a drink for the elite in Egypt and is mainly consumed by the sophisticated Egyptians. Total area currently under vineyards is about 64,000 ha. Total wine production was approximately in the neighborhood of 4,000 hl.

Algeria

Algeria has 81,000 ha in grape production. Interestingly, during pre-independence days, Algeria was supporting some 350,000 hectares of vineyards which was more than the 1991 total for Africa as a whole (326,000 hectares). In Algeria's case, the primary cause for the decline stems from Independence from France, who was formerly the biggest consumer of Algerian wine. After Independence and up until 1970, France continued to support the Algerian vineyards by buying an agreed minimum of their product, but by the time this agreement (The Evian treaty) expired, France was already part of the European Common Market in wine. Besides such basic economic factors, however, the decline in wine production is accounted for by the rise of Islamic fundamentalism and the dictate that no Muslim should drink alcoholic beverages.

The total area under vineyards was further reduced to 60,400 and total wine production in 2011 was approximately 47, 000 hl.

Morocco

The main areas of production include El Jadida, Meknès, Sidi, Slimane, Skhirate, Berkane. The area under vine cultivation was around 10,000 ha. Wine production from the 2011 harvest was 33,000 hl.

Tunisia

Total are under vineyards was approximately 27,000 ha and the total wine production in 2011 was approximately 23,000 hl.

South Africa

In 2012, of the country's estimated total annual harvest of 1095.1 million litres, 79.5% was devoted to the making of wine, 5.7% to wine for brandy, 11.% to distilling of wine and 3.7% to grape juice concentrate and juice. In terms of global wine production in 2011, South Africa ranked number eight in volume of wine produced, and 3.8% of the world's total wine. Exports of natural, non-fortified, packaged wines for the 2012 calendar year reached 160.5 million litres, a decrease of 9.79% on the previous year. Red wine exports accounted for 39% of all natural wines exported.

The Vineyards of South Africa have a 300-year history of considerable experience. There are over 4,000 wine producers working throughout the producing areas alongside 3,500 wine cellar staff and 345,000 farm workers. Since 1994, there has been a significant increase in the area under vine, with the highpoint in 2005, and only slightly less since. In 2010, South Africa had 131,000 ha area under vine cultivation.

The total wine production (excluding wine for distillation) was 9 Mhl. The major vineyard areas in South Africa include Orangeriver, Olifantsriver, Malesbury, Klein Karoo, Paarl, Robertson, Stellenbosch, and Worcester. Figure 2:1 shows reported observations for the growth in area under vine from 1994 to 2010. Table 2:9 illustrates the area under vine cultivation and number of vines in each of these regions.

Figure 2:2 shows the percentage of total area for several of the different varieties (during the period 1996 through 2011) and illustrating the significantly increasing Cabaret and Shiraz varieties.

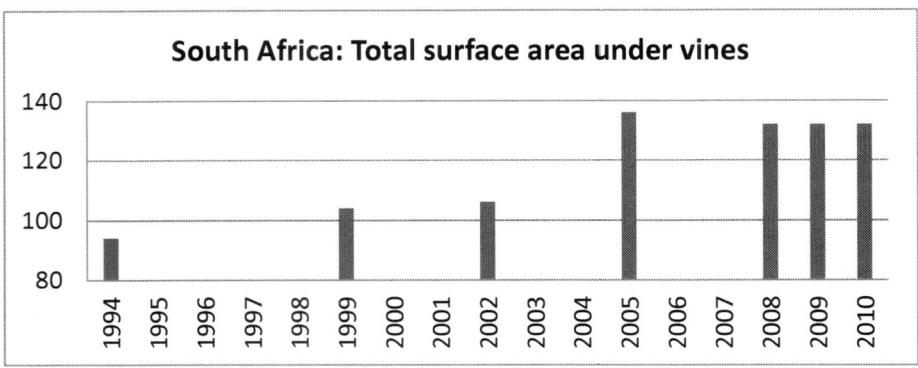

Figure 2:1 South Africa: Total Surface Area Under Vines
Source: GAIN, OIV.

District	2000 (ha)	2010 (ha)
Orange River	5024.50	5077.98
Olifants River	9015.06	9996.76
Malmesbury	13669.59	14224.38
Little Karoor	3167.62	2821.52
Paarl	17248.97	16567.62
Robertson	12227.36	14004.28
Stellenbosch	16112.21	17107.04
Worcester	6805.08	8648.84
Breedekloof	10385.25	12567.78

Table 2:9 Distribution of Wine Grape Vineyards (Red & White) Per District of SA
Source: SAWIS.

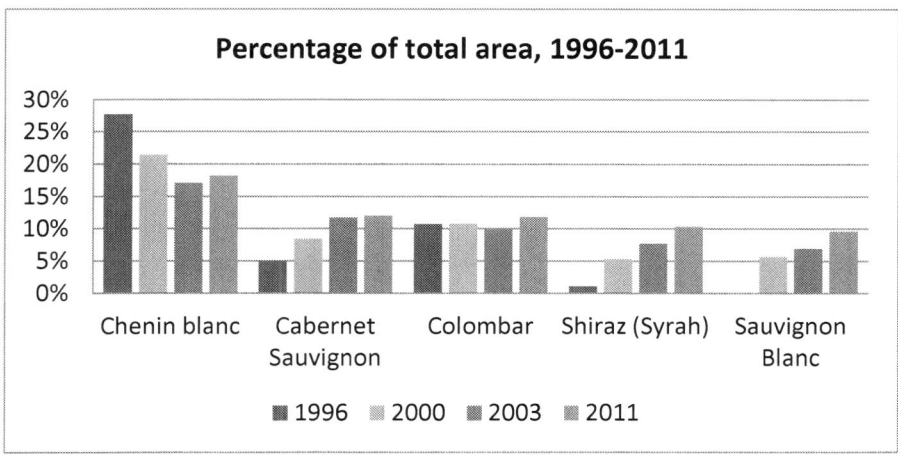

Figure 2:2 Percentage of Total Area for Different Varieties SAWIS

The producers in these areas divide between 66 cooperative cellars and 90+ private wine cellar estates. Besides this, there are over 300 private wine cellars-non-estates and 16 producing wholesalers. The company KWV Ltd. has been a pivotal figure in the South African wine industry. It was initially formed in 1918 as a cooperative. KWV also had an official role for many years in regulating and administering South African wine, in general. In recent years there have been major changes to its organization. The administrative and regulatory functions were transferred to a new organization called the Wine Industry Trust, and the commercial side of the business became KWV International. Then at the beginning of 2003, KWV International spun-off the cooperative side of the business (known as the Wijngaard Cooperative, concentrating solely on the interests of producers), and focused solely on commercial goals (KWV Ltd). The organization's mission is now to take full responsibility as an employer, competitor, partner, buyer and supplier. The company sources wines and grapes from the best viticultural regions in South Africa. KWV is known internationally for brands such as Roodeberg, KWV Wines, Laborie, Golden Kaan, Cathedral Cellar, Café Culture, Wild Africa Cream and their brandies.

South Africa's wine industry operates under a free market system, as buyers and exporters deal directly with the vineyards. Buyers can also now buy on-line. Since 2000, South African wine exporters have been targeting the Asian countries as the new market to explore. South African wine producers have participated in several wine exhibitions in countries such as Japan, Singapore and Hong Kong. Advertising of SA wine is already taking place in Japan.

Wines of South Africa (WOSA), a non-profit organization responsible for the generic promotion of SA wines on international markets, has worked hard to ensure that South African wine gained volume and market share in off-shore market, especially Britain and Holland. Its effort has resulted in excellent penetration in Canada, and 20% growth in other markets. WOSA promotes SA wines in the international markets, with offices in London, Switzerland, Germany, Toronto and New York. IMOYA, a brandy mainly for export, won last year's best brandy of the year in the international market. In California, SA wine is sold under the label Cape Indaba.

South Africa applies a general duty of 25% on wine imports. That duty, combined with the weakness of the Rand and the fact that South Africa is a surplus producer, means that there is only a limited market for imported wines in South Africa.

Vineyards of Australia

Last year, Australia produced 11.3 Mhl. The total bearing area of wine grapes declined significantly between the years 2008 and 2010. According to the ABS, 8164 hectares or 5% of total bearing areas were removed during this period. Previously, the area under vine has been increasing steadily with total production about 14.3 Mhl in 2006 and 2007. Red wine accounted for 58% and white wine accounted for 42%.

In 2011, the cost of production in many regions increased due to a more intensive spraying program to control disease caused by the wet conditions. In the future, the Australian wine industry is expected to continue to face strong competition in both the domestic and export markets, and wine grape prices are expected to remain stable. It is estimated that there are more than 4800 hectares of non-bearing vines that may be expected to come into bearing in later years. In addition, the exceptionally wet season in eastern Australia in 2010 to 2011 boosted irrigation dams, which reduced uncertainty of the availability of water for the near future in most wine producing areas. A greater proportion of wine exports is being shipped in bulk, contributing to downward pressure on wine prices and average wine grape prices. By 2010, Australia was shipping 40% of its total wine exports in bulk (compared with 13% ten years earlier). In terms of value, bulk wine accounted for 14% of total exports, which may be compared with only 4% in the previous decade.

The major wine producing areas in Australia include South Australia, Victoria, New South Wales, Western Australia, Queensland and Tasmania. Table 2:10 depicts the area under vineyards in each of these areas.

Region	Area under vineyards
South Australia	71,543
New South Wales	40,944
Victoria	25,839
Western Australia	11,346
Queensland	785
Tasmania	1,251

Table 2:10 Major Vineyards in Australia (hectares)
Source: Australian Bureau of Statistics Vineyard Estimates, 2010.

A total of about 1,465 wineries buy grapes from approximately 4,000 private winegrowers. Over the past decade, grape production has varied considerably due to the shifts in weather conditions. Over the past three decades, there has been a continual movement towards premium varieties. Whereas in 1992, Chardonnay, Shiraz and Cabernet Sauvignon accounted for about a quarter of production, these three varieties alone now account for the majority of the crop. There has also been a shift from white to red. The projected estimate of wine production for 2013 was 1.7 Mhl. Shiraz is expected to remain the highest-volume wine grape variety produced in Australia in 2013. Chardonnay is expected to be the next largest variety, followed by Cabernet Sauvignon. Collectively, these three varieties account for nearly 60% of total Australian wine grape production. Merlot and Semillon remain the next largest varieties produced in Australia, followed by Sauvignon Blanc.

The industry is made up of predominantly Australian-owned private companies, but a major feature of the Australian wine industry is that of the 2,572 wine-producers, the top 10% make over 90+% of the country's wine, leaving hundreds of producers to fight for the remaining much smaller share of market. This predominance is especially pronounced in the export market.

The Australian Wine and Brandy Corporation regulate the wine industry, which is a statutory authority of the Australian government established under the Australian Wine and Brandy Corporation Act (1980). The AWBC's responsibilities include the following:

- Export regulation compliance
- Promotion of Australian wine (domestically and internationally)
- Maintaining the integrity of Australia's wine labels and wine making practices
- Defining the boundaries of Australia's wine areas
- Addressing international market access issues on behalf of the industry.

Two thirds of the total vineyard area is in the South and mostly still clustering around the chief centers of population. The reasons for this are easily understood; fear of the unknown led the early settlers to remain as close to civilization as possible, moreover, the demand for wine from the mother country (Britain) meant it was sensible to produce it close to the ports from which it was ultimately to be exported. In this, the establishment of the Australian vineyards followed the same pattern as even the most prestigious of Europeans. For example, Bordeaux owes its geographical situation much more to considerations of proximity to markets and transport than to any particular excellence of soil.

However, the producers of Bordeaux were able to compensate for the paucity of nutrients in their land with careful husbandry, and had the enormous advantage of enjoying the optimum climate for cultivation of the Cabernet Sauvignon grape. The growers of Australia were traditionally battling against one *very* major disadvantage: excessive heat, certainly in many of the traditional vineyards near the cities. It has proven to be nearly impossible to produce truly fine wine under such conditions.

In the past three decades, the Australian vineyards have improved their winemaking industry. Pre-1939, Empire wines were crude, but steady sellers on the British market; fortified wines were most popular on the domestic front. In the 1960s, the national staple drink was beer, but it was increasingly in serious competition from the newly developing quality of Australian red wines. Wine producers in the sixties began employing every conceivable device to combat the heat and raise the standard of their wines, both red and white. Today, even the smallest Australian winery boasts expensive stainless steel equipment, hi-tech presses and a comprehensive laboratory.

Practices such as harvesting at night, pressure fermentation and must-chilling have served to minimize the danger of oxidation and resulted in lighter, fresher wines. Likewise, filtration, centrifuging and the addition of chosen yeast strains have all contributed over recent decades to producing extremely "clean" wine, even from grapes which had an inauspicious start to life on the sunbaked plains. However, such emphasis on technology has its detractors who claim that excessive "tinkering" leads to uniformity and robs a wine of its natural identity.

The Australian producer cannot deny the benefits accruing from technology, There is among the new generation of Australian growers a tendency to eschew the excesses of the "old school" and to avoid Australia's leading wine schools, and choose instead to learn their trade in Bordeaux, Dijon or in the Californian schools, such as Davis or Fresno. The idea is gaining currency that great wine begins in the vineyard. Many people are now looking carefully at the relationship between yield and quality.

Australia's first vineyards, as we have seen, were planted without much regard for factors such as terrain and climate. The choice of grape varieties was equally erratic. To begin with, a wide range of varietals was planted. It soon became clear that varietals such as Shiraz and Grenache, though not in the top rank of nobility, were the safest all around bet for reds, since they could be turned into either table or fortified wines. Australia's early selection of Hite grapes consisted chiefly of sherry and brandy grapes like Muscat, Alomino, Pedro Ximenez and Doradillo. These varieties dominated the Australian scene until the boom of the 1960s.

In Australia, there has been a surge in production of red grape varieties, which has led to overproduction and downward pressure on prices. Conversely, the little or no growth in white wine grape area and production led to tight supplies and more favorable prices. As a result, a higher percentage of new plantings consisted of white varieties, particularly Chardonnay. Of note, white varietals plantings outstripped red in 2003, the first time this has occurred since 1995. This type of change in response to market conditions appears characteristic of Australian wine production. The total exports of wine in 2012 earned approximately $1.82 billion (AUD).

New Zealand

In comparison to Australia, the New Zealand wine industry is tiny. However, the New Zealand wine industry is a significant contributor to the New Zealand economy. With annual export earnings of around $1.2 billion in 2011/2012, the New Zealand wine industry is now ranked as New Zealand's eighth most valuable export earner. As in most other wine producing countries, the New Zealand wine industry has experienced the adverse impacts of the "Global Financial Crisis," supply imbalances, wavering high external debt levels, and the increased presence of bulk wine sales, and therefore, wineries have struggled. Nevertheless, a real turnaround has occurred within the industry, and it shows signs of sustainability.

In 2012, the New Zealand grape harvest was intentionally reduced, and consequently wine production was reduced by estimation of 200 million liters, which helped the move toward better average prices, both for grapes and for wine.

North Island accounts for three quarters of total vineyard area, which is concentrated in the Gisborne and Hawke's Bay regions. South Island, once insignificant, is now of very great interest to wine producers. Since 1973, when Montana pioneered plantings at Blenheim, people have become persuaded that the climate (considerably drier than that of North Island) is suitable for the cultivation of vines, and there was a rush to acquire land on which to grow, in particular, Sauvignon Blanc grapes (which form the basis of some of New Zealand's most phenomenally successful wines).

New Zealand's weather benefits greatly from the maritime influence. No vineyard is more than 120km (80 miles) from the sea in either North or South Island. Overall, the climate is cool-temperate and, while this means some areas tend to have a slight deficiency of sunshine, nevertheless the New Zealand climate avoids the extremes found in Australia and enjoys a longer and slower growing season. This in turn means the fruit has longer time to draw more nutrients and, hence, more complexities of flavors from the soil.

It is thus in the area of very fine wines that New Zealand's export future lies, and in little more than a decade this small country has proved capable of producing some thoroughly world-class wines. Technology has always been state-of-the-art in the New Zealand wineries, partly as a spin-off from the country's all-important dairy industry. Also, due to New Zealand's isolation and difficulty in obtaining spares, the grower will often by necessity become servicing-engineer and repair-mechanic, thereby acquiring an intimate knowledge of the machinery he is using and how it functions.

In the 1960s and 1970s, when volume-wine sales were booming and vines seemed a good bet as a cash crop, planting was encouraged on a large scale and taken up by many non-wine-makers. This has had adverse effects on costs and quality, but the trend is now beginning to reverse with the trend for planting, particularly in South Island.

The main areas of grape production include Marlborough, Hawkes Bay, Gisborne, Auckland, Nelson, Wellington, Central Otago, Canterbury/Waipara and Waikato/Bay of Plenty. The most important varieties of grapes grown in these areas include Sauvignon Blanc, Chardonnay, Pino Nor, Merlot, and Cabernet Sauvignon, of which the most important is Sauvignon Blanc. Table 2:11 depicts the important varieties of grapes cultivated in the above-mentioned areas:

Vinyard	Important grape varieties grown
Marlborough	Sauvignon Blanc, Chardonnay, Pinot Noir
Hawkes Bay	Chardonnay, Merlot, Cabernet Sauvignon
Gisborne	Chardonnay
Auckland	Chardonnay, Cabernet Sauvignon, Merlot, Cabernet Franc
Nelson	Chardonnay, Sauvignon, Pinot Noir, Riesling
Wellington	Pinot Noir, Sauvignon Blanc, Chardonnay
Central Otago	Pinot Noir, Chardonnay, Pinot Gris, Riesling
Canterbury/ Waipara	Pinot Noir, Chardonnay, Riesling,
Waikato/Bay of Plenty	Chardonnay, Cabernet Sauvignon, Sauvignon Blanc

Table 2:11 Major Vineyard
Source: http://www.harpers-wine.com

The New Zealand Grape Growers Council and the Wine Institute of New Zealand combined to form "New Zealand Wine Growers," with currently 1,000 wine grower members and 700 winery members. This is the organization that promotes, represents and researches the interests of NZ grape growers and winemakers. There has been a large influx of international ownership, particularly from UK and Australia. There are four large companies, a large base of small companies and a core of medium size wineries that control the process.

China

As of 2013, China's wine industry continued to have the remarkable yearly increases of 15%. Grapes have been grown in China for more than 2000 years, but efforts were negligible until the founding of the People's Republic of China. Then, the area under cultivation of grapes and their production were only about 3,200 hectares and 39,000 tons, respectively. Following rapid economic growth, fruit production, including grape production, increased rapidly in the country, especially since the 1980s. The land area under grapes and their production in 1998 were respectively estimated to be 55.6 and 60.5 times greater than in 1949.

At present, grape production now ranks fifth in fruit production in the People's Republic of China, estimated to be 178,000 hectares. Under the influence of the "red wine rush" in the Asian countries, grape growing again became the focus of people's attention in China from the early nineties. Thus, the area under cultivation of grapes continued to increase again from 1992 to 20,200 hectares by 1998 (about 15% more when compared with that of 1997) and 2,358200 tons, 18.7 times more than in 1979. Most of this production was for table grapes and only about 10% for wine making, and another 10% for raisins. The main areas of expansion are located in the north. The five leading provinces that contributed more than two thirds of the total grape production in the country in 1998 were Xingjiang (32,000 hectares), Hebei (31,500 hectares), Shangdong (20,900 hectares), Liaoning (14,200 hectares), and Henan (11,300 hectares).

At the time of the founding of the People's Republic of China, the estimated annual production of wine was 85 tons per year. Although the wine industry has developed rapidly since that time, wine production only contributes a very small fraction towards the total alcoholic beverage production in the country. Following a rapid growth in wine production, most of the provinces are now engaged in the industry. By 1997, more than 400 wine companies and wineries were established in 26 provinces and municipalities operating directly under the Central Government. Then years later, China had over 500 wine companies operating in 2007. The leading provinces in order of production were Shandong ,Hebei, Tianjing, Beijing, Anhui and Henan.

However, the major areas for growing wine grapes are essentially located in the North of China, such as in the Northeast, including Bohai Bay, Shacheng and Changli (Hebei), Qingxu (Shanxi), Yinchuan (Ningxia), Wuwei (Gansu), Tulufan Basin (Xinjiang), Shihezi (Xinjiang), as well as the ancient course of the Yellow River valley and Yunnan Maitraya.

Among hundreds of grape varieties grown in China, the important wine varieties for white wine are Chardonnay, Italian Riesling, Ugni Blanc, Chenin Blanc, Gewurztraminer, Sauvignon Blanc, Semillon, White Riesling and Rkatsiteli. The main varieties for red wine are Cabernet Sauvignon, Cabernet Franc, Merlot, French Blue, Muscat Hamburg, Pinot Noir, Syrah, Carignan and Saperavi.

China's Planting Material

China is fortunate in not having any phylloxera pest problems. Most of the grape planting material used in the country is therefore propagated by cuttings. In some cold areas, however, vines are grafted on cold-resistant rootstocks, such as Beta (a probable hybrid between *Vitis riparia* and *V. labrusca*) and lines from *Vitis amurensis*.

Although the wine industry has made rapid progress in recent years, the per capita production of wine remains small, as low as about 0.2 L per person. This is far below the average wine consumption in the world (about 7 L per person), thus not satisfying the current consumption requirements of the Chinese people. This deficiency in production has resulted in many new wine companies and wineries in recent years. There were about 240 wine companies and wineries by 1995, after a development phase spanning over a century in China. But an additional 200 wine companies and wineries were founded only during 1996 and 1997. Secondly, the area under cultivation of grapes has increased rapidly all over the country, especially during the last two or three years. This rise in the cultivated area has focused on wine grapes. Lastly, China experienced a sharp increase in wine imports, especially from European countries, with nearly 5,900 tons of wines being imported into China in 1996, which amounted to 7.7 times more than that of 1995. Import of wines continued to increase substantially during the following years.

This development underscores the change in consumption habits of alcoholic beverages in modern China. Chinese have had a tradition of consuming alcoholic beverages, especially drinking of spirits distilled from sorghum and maize. This habit has been changing since the 1970s. Beer production in tonnage was more than 50% of the national alcoholic beverage production by the end of the 1980s. Since the early 1990s, consumption of wines has become a trend of the times. More and more people consume wine instead of spirits, and the demand for wine is expected to continue to increase in the following years. China accounted for 6% of the world wine market in 2006, which can be compared to the US that accounted for 11% of the market. There is no question that Chinese consumers present an enormous upside opportunity for the wine marketers of the world, because the current per-capita consumption amounts to only 1.12 liters in China. There is considerable room for significant increases, when we take into account that France has a per-capita of 54 liters and Italy has a per-capita of 49 liters. The per-capita consumption of China will increase and presents a valuable market for imported wines.

By the late 1970s, wineries numbered more than 100, and the wine output reached 64,000 tons in 1978, up from only 200 tons in 1949. Vineyards and production bases were found in Xinjiang, Gansu's dry areas, the plains around the Bohai Sea, in the former Yellow River bed, the Loess Plateau dry lands, the Huai River region, and in the Changbai Mountains. Table 2:12 shows the production, sales and profits in 2006.

The history of wine is long, and while there have been commercial wineries in China since the end of the 19th Century, production has only evolved into a serious industry in the past two decades (see Figure 2:3).

The current per capita volume of wine consumption in China is only 19.9% of the world's average. According to China Alcoholic Drinks Industry Association, 93.76% annual wine production comes from ten provinces, namely, Shandong, Hebei, Tianjin, Jilin, Xinjiang, Beijing, Henan, Gansu, Ningxia and Yunnan. According to Euromonitor database, grape wine produced in Hebei, Shandong and Tianjin accounted for 70% of the total volume. Southwest (particularly Yunnan) and Northwest China (particularly Xinjiang) have abundant grape supplies, but are undeveloped in terms of wineries and wine brands.

Industries	No. of enterprises above designated size	Output value (bn RMB)	Sales Income (bn RMB)
Alcohol	19.8	54.8	47.4
White Spirit	160.9	279.3	242.2
Beer	59.3	132.0	122.4
Yellow rice wine	12.8	11.7	9.0
Wine	24.8	31.0	28.6
Other	18.7	15.7	12.0

Table 2:12 Key Figures of China's Alcoholic Drinks Industry, 2010
Source: National Bureau of Statistics of China.

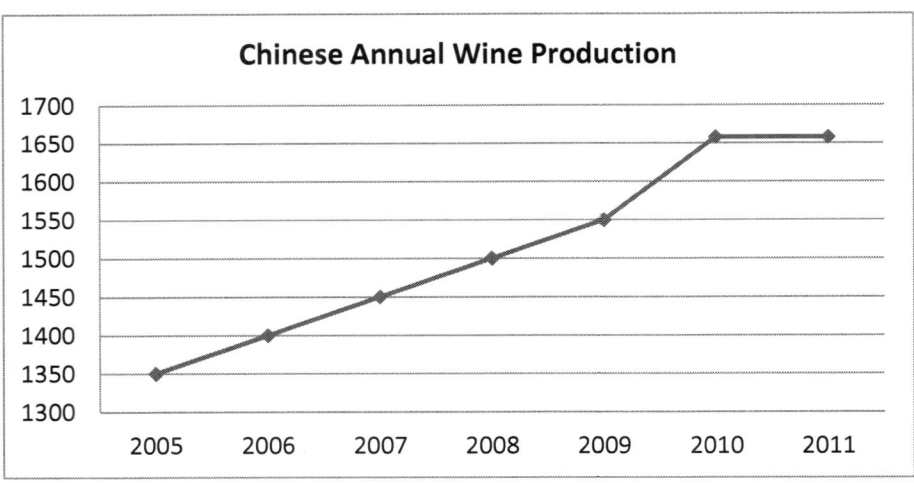

Figure 2:3 Chinese Annual Wine Production, 2007–2011, in thousand tonnes
Source: faostat.fao.org

By 2007, China had over 500 wineries in operation. According to the China Alcoholic Drinks Industry Association, the top ten wineries represented 60% of the total production and the top four domestic wine firms produce approximately 51% of the Chinese wine.

Australia, America and Chile have become France's major competitors in China. As early as 2009, new-world wines show a respectful position in the Chinese market of wine imports (Table 2:13).

Country	Volume (ML)
France	48.1
Australia	43.7
Italy	7.9
Spain	8.4
America	11.5
Chile	55.6
Argentina	3.6

Table 2:13 Importers of Wine in China in 2009
Source: University of Adelaide Press | Global Wine Markets, 1961 to 2009.

The Americas

The United States

In 2010, the US recorded 20.89 Mhl in wine production, a lower production of wine than in 2005 (22.9 Mhl), but close to production levels in 2003. California is the major North American wine producing region, containing approximately 55% of all US vineyards, and approximately 90% of the total wine produced in the US comes from California.

The climate of the region is near-perfect for the cultivation of wine grapes. From early springtime to late autumn, the interaction between the cool sea breezes and the warmer air above causes a bank of fog to develop on the sea, all along the Californian coast. As the inland valleys warm up through the day, a low-pressure-system is created and the cool air and fog is drawn inland from the sea, acting as a natural air-conditioning system. This ensures cool nights and evenings to help maintain acidity-levels in the ripening fruit and, at the same time, moderates the consistent sunshine to a perfect temperate mean.

The "appellation" system employed in California operates on several levels. The largest, naturally, is the name "California" itself. To earn this, all the grapes used in a wine must have come from within the State. Wines bearing this label will often have been blended from grapes coming from various regions in the state. Next come wines from smaller geographical or political subdivisions, such as particular counties. Such wines are required by law to contain at least 75% grapes from that specific area. The approved AVA (American Viticulture Area) is determined according to factors such as natural boundaries, topography, soil, climate and sometimes historical considerations. To earn this designation, a wine's grape content must be 85% from a specific AVA. The smallest of the subdivisions in the Californian system comprises specific named vineyards. Fully 95% of grapes used in such a wine must have come from that vineyard, each of which has to state an officially-recognized appellation for the Estate identification.

The term Estate Bottled may only be used on labels of wine where the bottling winery is located within the appellation named on the label. Therefore, the grapes must be entirely grown within the named appellation on land owned or controlled by the bottling winery. In addition, the fermentation, finishing, aging, and bottling of the wine must be done in one continuous process, with the wine at no time having left the premises prior to bottling.

Technology is of a very high standard in the wineries of California and State law is strict. For example, the process of the addition of sugar during fermentation, which is widespread in Europe, is completely outlawed in California. Despite this, the average alcohol-content of California wines is around 12% to 14%. This is, of course, a result of the benign weather conditions—the length and evenness of the ripening season, which in addition to the high alcoholic yield helps to achieve good balances of residual sugar, acidity and tannin.

Grape Varietals Grown in California

Among the white wine type grapes grown in California, Chardonnay varietals covers the maximum acreage. Out of a total 190,594 acres used for over 25 white wine type grapes, Chardonnay covers more than half the area, i.e., 98,743 acres. It is generally regarded as the grape of greatest potential for fine white-Burgundy type wines. Chardonnay has a tendency to be virus- and pest-prone, but considerable efforts have been made in the research laboratories of California's universities to improve stock.

Next is the French Colombard varietal, which covers about 18% of the total area under cultivation of white wine grapes. A grape of quite high acidity, it long served as the mainstay of many white wine blends and also as a useful element in the sparkling sector. With the rise of temperature-controlled fermentation and increased use of stainless steel, Colombard has, since the 1960s, become a staple varietal wine.

Chenin Blanc is one of the oldest known varieties in the business. It is a reliable and trouble-free vine producing wine of a similar character. The other important varieties among the white wine include Sauvignon Blanc, Muscat of Alexandria, Pinot Gris and Malvasia Bianca.

Of the red grape varieties, the most abundant in California is Cabernet Sauvignon, to which are devoted approximately 26% of the total red wine producing acres. It benefits from climatic conditions similar to those found in the maritime Bordeaux area. This grape could be said to be the basis of California's international renown in that it was the flagship of varietal labeling. Since the seventies, Californian Cabernet Sauvignon has been more than able to hold its head up in international competition. The other major red wine grape is Merlot, which covers nearly 18% of the total red wine cultivation area.

Next is the Zinfandel variety, which covers 17% of the total of red wine grapes planted. Zinfandel was long regarded as a mystery. Nobody knew from whence it came—probably due to an accident in the labeling of cuttings. Modern research, however, has revealed that it is a descendant of the Italian Primitivo, which was not particularly renowned as a wine grape, but the vine's 135 year sojourn in California has transformed Zinfandel into something very special. This is due perhaps in part to the fact that it is a demanding grape to cultivate and the Californian growers have risen to the challenge. Other varietals of the red wine type grown in smaller quantities include Pinot Noir, Syrah and Rubired.

The modern industry is really only about seventy-five years old. In the period after the Second World War, when the Californian vineyard was expanding, the growers enjoyed the enormous advantage of being able to embark on totally new plantation. This was a clear palette on which to begin, unhampered by having to uproot old stock and gradually change. Soon, the American spirit of competition was starting to click in. They wanted to prove to the world that they could produce wine as fine as anyone else's, even that of the famous French wineries. It is not surprising, therefore, that they chose to plant the noble varieties such as Cabernet Sauvignon, Sauvignon Blanc and Chardonnay. However, in their initial haste, they failed to approach the question of specific microclimates for particular vines with as much care as they might have done. The Napa Valley—a typical "clean palette"—planted over the past generation or so, is probably not the perfect climate for Cabernet Sauvignon and Chardonnay. Carneros, just a little closer to the sea and enjoying the cool breeze at its freshest, probably bears closer kinship with the climate of Atlantic and Continental France than does Napa Valley. Nonetheless, in the American Bicentennial tasting in Paris in 1976, Napa Valley Cabernet Sauvignons and Chardonnays came out on top of those of Burgundy and Bordeaux, so the American producers should not be too heavily censured for their early enthusiasm.

The US wine industry is highly fragmented. There are over 3,650 bonded wineries in California that produce a vast number of products, most with only a small market share, and most are not exporting wineries. Many small growers bottle their own wine and others sell to large wineries. The medium size wineries with their own production facilities are primarily aimed at the domestic market. However, the largest companies have been acquiring many of the medium producers and forming international brands with large shares of the export market. This trend of consolidation has continued to expand both winery and vineyard ownership with largely international markets. As evidence of growing consolidation in the US wine market, the top 10 wineries in the US sold nearly 76% of all US wines. E. & J. Gallo is the largest wine producing company in the world, with nearly 4% of the world market, and accounts for 23% of US market. Canandaigua Wine Company, a division of Constellation Brands Inc., is the number two US wine seller by volume. These companies have succeeded in gaining the largest market shares through strategic acquisition by purchasing other wineries.

Argentina

Of all the wine-producing countries of South America, easily the most important is Argentina, with extremely large areas under vine cultivation The excellent weather conditions in Argentina have allowed for the production of more than 50 grape varieties. Among them, Cabernet Sauvignon, Malvec,

Merlot, Bonarda, Syrah and Tempranillo are the most planted in the red range, and Chardonnay, Chenin, Torrontes Riojano, Ugni Blanc, Pedro Gimenez, for white wine. Table wine varieties represent about 29% of the processed grapes. These wines are Criolla Grande, Cereza, Muscatel Rosado, Gibi and Bequignol.

In 2003, Argentina exported approximately 0.625 Mhl of wine; this was approximately 5% of its total wine production. The value of Argentina wine trade in just the two major export markets of the UK and US was estimated at $62 million. Wine production in Argentina has about 1,196 wineries.

Argentina offers a wide range of geographical and climatic variations and hence a broad spectrum of different kinds of wine. In 2005, the market share of still wines divides between 45% whites and 55% reds, while the contribution of still, sparkling and fortified stood at 94%, 1% and 5% respectively.

Wine production in Argentina dates back to the early days of Spanish colonization at which time it was mainly concentrated around the city and Province of Buenos Aires (following the classic pattern of remaining close to the major center of population). The industry really began to grow when more modern techniques were developed, with the arrival of larger numbers immigrants from wine-producing regions and with the advent of the railway, which served to turn viniculture into an important pan-national industry. Between 1887 and 1895, the vineyards of Mendoza increased in area at the rate of 15% per year, as part of an overall Government project to establish agricultural wine-growing communities. Between the years 1907 and 1911, land planted with vines increased even faster, at a rate of 20% per annum. It was during this period that a group of entrepreneurs founded the Argentine Viniculture Association, which still dominates the industry.

The National Institute of Viticulture-Viniculture has jurisdiction throughout the country over all aspects of wine-production. The same act of Government, which brought the Institute into existence, also lays out clear rules with which all traders must comply regarding standards of hygiene, quality and labeling.

The establishment of the National Institute was simultaneous with the start of a planting boom in the 1960s, encouraged by tax concessions on investments. In 1988, as the grape harvest grew by 30%, consumption of ordinary wines declined by 27%, following the same pattern as in most other countries of the world.

The Argentine vineyard takes the form of a large band of territory to the West of the country, varying in altitude from between 500 and 1,500 m above sea level and is dominated by the Andes. The major areas are:

- *The North Andean region* comprising the provinces of La Rioja, Catamarca, Salta and Jujuy. The high-altitude climate of the region produces wines of high quality.
- *The South Andean region* consisting of two principal production centers, the Provinces of Mendoza and San Juan, which now account for about 71% and 24% of total Argentine production respectively. However, one-third of the new wineries are beginning to establish in areas other than Mendoza, due to less expensive land and tax incentives to spread production in other areas of the country. Again, an area of high altitude, over 500 m, with a very favorable set of weather conditions: low humidity, very little rain and plenty of warmth and sunshine during a good long growing season. The region produces a high yield of excellent table wine and a good deal of fine wines of outstanding quality.
- *Patagonia* comprising the provinces of Rio Negro, Neuquen, the South of La Pampa and the Southern tip of Buenos Aires province. This region swoops down from 850 m at Chos-Malal to the Atlantic coastline itself and so contains a wide variety of microclimates, many of which are favorable for cultivation. A broad range of grape varieties can be brought to ripeness here. Although, since the weather is generally colder in this Southern region, early and late frosts can pose problems. Table wines and fine wines are produced in Patagonia, characterized by higher levels of acidity than elsewhere.
- Other areas which cultivate grapes include the central region to the East of La Rioja and San Juan where small amounts of sometimes remarkably fine wine are produced.

Grape Varietals in Argentina

The wide climatic variations already noted permit a similarly wide range of grape varietals. Red Malbec and White Torrontés are the two main grapes produced in Argentina. The climatic condition of Argentina is suited for growing Red Malbec. The grape's deep, rich colors and intense, fruity flavors are largely responsible for making the country well-known to wine consumers. Torrontés white grape is a spicy aromatic variety, which produces some of Argentina's most distinguished white wines. The rest of the vineyard regions have a huge variety of vines grown including many of the classic noble varieties and a good showing of Italian varietals.

In response to the production boom of the 1960s and 1970s, the National Institute established a series of legislative checks, support prices and later production restrictions and quotas for wine-making and distribution. In 1990, most of these restrictions were greatly simplified and the National Institute resumed what many regard as its proper role as monitor of quality rather than quantity. The State in general made its presence in the wine market considerably less intrusive by a program of privatization, permitting certain large companies to revert to the private sector.

However, as of 2013, despite the large potential of Argentinean wine production, the future prospects are seriously threatened by the unfortunate policies of the government. As in the past, the national financial challenges are once again threatening to destroy the exports and prospects of the industry. The foreign exchange difficulties, starting in 2012, has almost entirely halted the export of bottled Argentinean wine and thus the international branding of leading vineyards. In 2013, most of the exports were carried out as bulk wine, but at dramatically smaller volumes. This has caused great pain to the domestic vineyards, which now are struggling for survival.

Chile

The Conquistadores of the 16th century brought Jesuit Priests with them to Chile who required wine for the celebration of Mass. Whether the Spanish brought cuttings with them or found an indigenous variety already there, the haciendas, given to the conquering heroes by their leader Pedro de Valdivia, were soon producing liberal quantities of a grape known as Pais. Throughout the 17th and 18th centuries, production of good wine increased to such a degree that in 1803, orders came from the Mother country (Spain) for the uprooting of vineyards in Chile, because Spanish wine could not compete. Happily, however, Chile fought for and obtained Independence before these orders could be implemented.

In the 1850s, it became the fashion for rich Chileans to do the Grand Tour of Europe. From this, another fashion grew—the emulation of the chateau-owning classes of Bordeaux. People returned to their own country resolved to build themselves beautiful mansions surrounded by noble lush vineyards, and the grapes, like those of Bordeaux and Burgundy. Not only did they import European technology and expertise, but more importantly they imported stock of all the noble varietals.

In 2012, Chile had a total of 117,000 ha of area under vineyards. Out of the total planted area, approximately 76% are red varietals. During the period 1998 to 2004, Chile's annual wine production averaged around 5 Mhl, but Chile reached its highest point with 10.46 Mhl of wine in 2011. Table 2:14 and Figure 2:4 depict the annual wine production in Chile, during the period 1982 to 2012:

Year	Area Planted (Th. Has)	Production (Mill. Liter)	Per Capita Consumption	Export	
				Mill. Liter	Mill. US$
1982	105	603	52	8	11
1990	65	398	25	43	52
1992	62	370	17	74	119
1994	53	411	13	111	143
1996	56	481	16	185	294
1998	75	547	17	251	540
2000	104	679	15	276	585
2002	109	574	15	356	610
2004	112	655	16	474	845
2006	115	845	15	520	965
2008	118	869	16	591	1,384
2009	118	1,009	16	696	1,390
2010	117	915	16	733	1,554
2011	117	1,046	17	667	1,703
2012*	117	1,030	18	700	1,787

Table 2:14 Wine Production, Consumption and Exports of Chile
*Estimate.
Sources: National Agricultural Society (SNA) and Central Bank.

Chile is basically a strip of land never more than 180 km wide, but with a coastline 4,300 km long, bordered on the West by the Pacific Ocean, and to the East by the Andes Mountains. The primary wine vineyards are concentrated in the Central and South Central regions from north of Santiago south to Temuco. Running parallel to the Andes through this region are a second range of lower mountains, the Cordilleras de la Costa. This divides the wine-growing area into two distinct parts—a major central valley between the two ranges of mountains, which receives virtually no rain but which is liberally supplied with melt-water from the Andes, and the area between the Cordilleras and the coast, which receives sufficient enough rain not to require irrigation. The purity of the water, abundance of the sunshine, and the nighttime temperature contribute to make Chile a viticultural paradise.

Chile exports nearly 60% of its wine production, which has the highest exportation to sales ratio of any country. Figure 2:4 depicts the quantity of Chilean wine exports during the period 1998 to 2012.

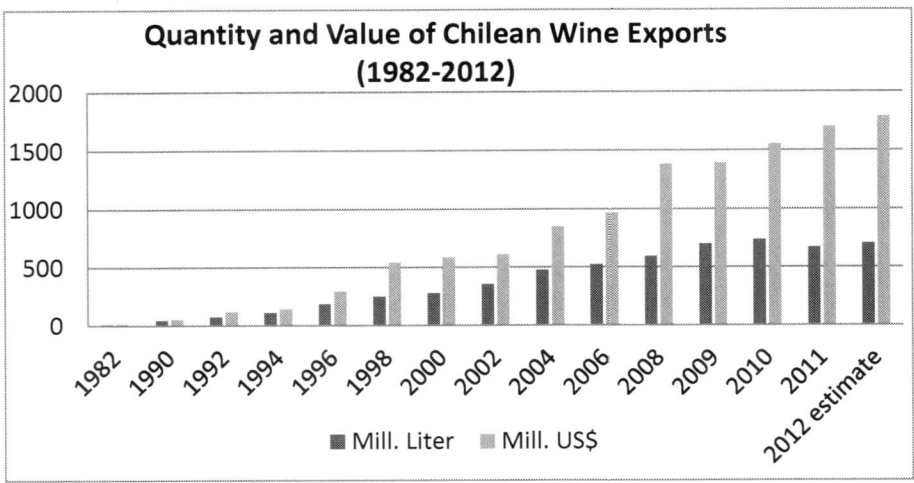

Figure 2:4 Quantity and Value of Chilean Wine Exports (1982-2012)
Source: GAIN.

Before the 1980s, there were a few quality producers in Chile, but their wines were not well known outside of the country. However, in themid-1980s, Chilean wines were "discovered" in Europe and North America. Since then, there has been considerable investment in the vineyards, and also in the wineries. The old-established wineries have entered into partnerships with producers in other countries, and foreign consortia have established new operations.

Chile has an estimated 8,000 producers of wine grapes, but only 250 commercial wineries of which 100 are large exporters. The wine industry has expressed some concerns about the explosive increase in the planted area during the last few years. Total planted area has increased over 70%. Beginning in 2005, the main exports targets of Chile were expansion into the rest of the EU and Asian markets (additional to the existing US and UK markets), and these targets continue into 2013.

Brazil

Consumption in Brazil has been growing and Brazilian consumers are becoming increasingly interested in wines. Indeed, local wineries have more recently been investing in infrastructure to accommodate the market.

With increasing local production of fine wines, as well as more wines entering the country, competition in Brazil is rising. Demand is expected to continue to grow with consumers becoming more knowledgeable about wines. Industry sources expect that tourism will continue to be a key strategy in maintaining growth in domestic wine consumption and in promoting Brazilian wine abroad, and several vineyards are investing heavily in this area. Tourism is a significant development, and the tourists enjoy visiting the local wine facilities. There is now a theme park winery and a hotel vineyard, and five wineries with bed and breakfasts. Industry sources believe that tourism in Brazil offers significant potential, and wine consumption is expected to exhibit even higher growth.

Sparkling wine in particular is expected to benefit as the high quality of Brazil's muscatel grapes are an important part of domestic production. Brazil increased wine production from 2001 to 2006 by a sharp 33%; and between 2007 and 2010, it increased another modest 2.08%; and in 2011, there was another sharp increase in growth bringing production up 39%. Over the past decade, Brazil has been one of the world's fastest growing economies.

The Brazilian economy continues to grow, and it is expected that on-trade consumption will benefit from consumers switching from lesser drinks, such as cider to local sparkling wines. By 2011, Brazil showed high constant value growth in wine sales translating to a monetary value measure of approximately $2 billion.

Chapter 3

CONSUMER BEHAVIOR

Worldwide wine consumption increased over the period 1990 to 2007, and then declined following the economic recession that was experienced in many nations around the globe. After 2010, most areas were again on an upward projection. As of mid-2013, consumption has continued to revive, but appears that it is not quite up to the pre-recession levels and trajectories. However, in regions like Asia, the total consumption of wine has actually increased considerably, particularly in China.

The expert forecasters at the United Nations Food and Agriculture Organization had previously expected worldwide demand to continue rising uninterrupted through the end of the decade, at least in monetary terms (with any decreases in overall volume sales being accompanied by a concomitant rise in sales of premium higher-priced wines). However, the unexpected financial debacle of 2008/2009 proved the estimate to be invalid. In addition to this phenomenon was the substantial numbers of drink options open to consumers, particularly new and widely available non-alcoholic drinks being marketed. Such options include various bottled waters and a growing number of fruit juices and soft drinks. The sheer variety of alternative beverages has also, to some extent, encroached on the wine sector.

Consumers that elect to have an alcoholic drink also find a wider choice open to them. The three traditional categories available are beer, spirits or wine. Spirits and wines fortified with spirits have become less popular, due to a general consumer trend towards drinking less alcohol. Consequently, it is beer and wine that vie for the middle-ground of the overall market. Consumer behavior in the 21st Century has essentially moved in the same direction globally; for example, greater levels of beer-drinking in the formerly wine-drinking south of Europe, and conversely a significant increase in the north of wine-drinking at the expense of beer consumption.

There is also a further sub-category of low-alcohol and alcohol-free beers, wines and wine coolers. There is even alcohol-free beer now available in France. In this way, the alcoholic drinks industries have managed to hold on to segments of the market, as they introduce new products and appeal to consumer changing preferences. An interesting aspect of consumer behavior is the growing market for low-alcohol wines. There has been a rapid growth in sales of low-alcohol wine. Estimates indicated a volume growth rate of 50% in 2011 over 2010. Sales appear to have greatly benefited from consumers' health concerns. The health image of wine is largely because of media reporting that its high antioxidant and polyphenol content is highly desirable.

France: A Major Producer and Consumer of Wine

As a producer, France ranks first in the world with production of 47.5 million hectoliters in 2011. This is 11% lower than the average during 2000 to 2005. Twenty-four percent of French wine production is sold within the EU (primarily to the UK, Germany, Belgium and the Netherlands). Exports outside the EU are primarily to the US, Japan, Canada, and Switzerland. Therefore, understanding the variables that affect consumer patterns in France helps to understand some of the most important aspects of consumer behavior in global wine consumption.

Overall French domestic consumption, both in terms of volume and constant-value, has been decreasing for decades. Based on a study conducted by a French consumer-polling panel, consumption increased in Appellation of Origin wines (AOC), to the detriment of table wines. This consumer behavior, movement away from table wine and toward higher quality wines, is expected to continue in the future. Total bottled wine sales in hyper-supermarkets (without hard discounts) in 2005 dropped 2.7%, compared to 2004. This poll also reported that volumes purchased by the food service sector (traditional restaurants, cafeterias and company restaurants) decreased 3% in volume and 6% in value, during calendar year 2005. Quality wines (VQPRD) comprise the largest share of food service sector purchases. This trend has continued for another 7 years into 2012, albeit it was somewhat constrained due to the financial crisis of 2008/2009 and the subsequent advent of the recession.

Wine is fundamental to the culture and the economy of Southern European countries, but the percentage of the population claiming never to drink wine is consistently and markedly higher in these countries of traditionally high consumption when compared to Northern European countries. In the Northern European countries, consumption tends to be spread more evenly, with a large number of people drinking relatively small amounts on a moderately frequent basis.

A third of the French population is not wine consumers. Of the two-thirds that are consumers of wine, about 37% of the population dilutes their wine with water. Nevertheless, it is interesting that France's per capita consumption of wine is still among the highest in the world.

Regular and Occasional Wine-Drinkers

According to an ONIVINS survey, approximately 23.8% of the total of wine-consumers in France can be classified as frequent drinkers. Frequent drinkers are defined as people who drink wine almost every day. In France, wine is considered principally as an accompaniment to food, and frequent wine drinkers can also be defined as people who drink wine at practically all of their main meals. The percentage of frequent drinkers has decreased significantly over the past couple of decades, from 50.7% in 1980 to 23.8%.

Occasional drinkers are those who drink wine once or twice per week, and they are about 17.5% of the population. The percentage of occasional drinkers (including people who have wine less frequently than once a week) has increased from 30% to 42.6% over the past two and half decades. These occasional drinkers account for only about 20% of the total annual wine consumption. This increasing segment of occasional drinkers tends to reserve wine for special occasions, particularly ones to which guests have been invited. This coincides with the fact that there has been a 35% increase in the frequency of consumption of quality wine. Therefore, hosts are now offering their guests better quality wines instead of non-vintage or table wine.

The fact that the French use wine traditionally with food means that changing eating habits, such as fast-food outlets and canteen lunches, have had a major impact on consumption. About 48% of those who consume wine are drinking it when eating at home. However, only 21.5% of these consumers drink wine with meals consumed outside the home. For example, the midday meal during the working week, often eaten at the workplace, indicates that wine consumption has dropped even further (to below 18%). Contrast this with a traditional French restaurant lunch on a Sunday where there will be more than 50% wine drinkers.

Simultaneously, there has been a reduction in the total number of visits to restaurants and generally in all the on-trade consumption of wine at hotels, restaurants, cafes and bars (HORECA). Therefore, there have been lifestyle changes brought about by changes in workplace and consumer information. These are some of the factors behind the current situation where consumers are in general drinking smaller quantities of wine. In order to better understand consumer behavior, we can also examine such lifestyle factors as income, occupation and gender.

Class, Gender, Income Bracket, and Occupation

Figures from the ONIVINS Survey reveal very clear correlations between social status and wine consumption patterns. A high correlation exists between the level of involvement in the process of wine selection and drinking and the social status of a person. The amount of interest, pleasure and importance attached to wine consumption determine the level of involvement. The influence of income is reflected by the statistic showing that consumers in the least well-off income bracket have a higher percentage (52%) of people with low involvement. Likewise, in the most well-off income bracket, only 22% of households show low involvement. It is principally in the well-off households that the drinking of tap water, which is a major competitor to wine drinking, is seeing a marked upswing. Table 3:1 shows how the socio-economic status of a household relates to the involvement level.

Based on the observed correlation between involvement and consumption frequency, it can be said that "frequent drinkers," to a great extent, are "involved" customers. Over 80% of the frequent drinkers show a high level of interest in wine selection and consumption. Table 3:2 summarizes the relation between frequency of consumption and level of involvement.

Level of Involvement	1 (Least well-off)	2	3	4	5 (Most well-off)	Average (All Status)
1 (Highest)	16	21	21	24	31	22
2	16	18	18	20	29	19
3	16	17	16	21	19	18
4	18	18	20	17	11	17
5 (Lowest)	34	27	26	18	11	23

Table 3:1 Involvement and Socio-economic Status of Households
Source: ONIVINS Surveys.

Frequency of Consumption	1 (Involved)	2	3	4	5 (Uninvolved)
Frequent Drinkers	54	28	13	4	<1
Occasional drinkers	19	26	27	19	8
Non-consumers	2	4	9	25	60

Table 3:2 Frequency of Consumption and Involvement
Source: ONIVINS Surveys.

The following Table 3:3 summarizes the current status among French wine consumers. It shows the degree of correlation between various factors and consumption frequency.

As shown in this table, this study also indicates consumers under 35 years of age purchased both still wines and sparkling wines (88% bought still wines and 48% bought sparkling wine at least once). This age group (23% of total French households) buys less than the seniors.

Consumers from 35 to 49 years old (30% of French households) comprise 25% of wine purchases. They purchase still-white and sparkling wines (except champagne) in larger quantities than any other age group. Nonetheless, the 50-64 years old group is the leading buyer of wine in all categories, with a preference for red wines. The 65+ category, along with the 50-64+ category, represents nearly half of total French households that buy still wines, consisting mostly of table wines. The 50+ consumers are also the major consumers of champagne.

	Group 1	Group 2	Group 3	Group 4	Group 5
Numbers in Groups	556	696	663	619	835
(Base 100 : Total 3339)	16.6%	20.8%	19.8%	18.5%	25%
Consumption freq.	+++	+	-		---
Involvement	+++	+++	-		---
Taste of wine	+++	+++	+	++	---
Thirst-quenching	+				
Good for health	+++	++		+	--
Prefers other drinks	---		+++	++	+++
Wine is cheap	+	--			
Special occasions		++	+++	+++	
No meal without wine	+++		---	---	---
Socio-economic status	--	+++	+++	---	--
Sociability degree		++	++	-	-
Sex	Male	Male	Female	Female	Female
Dominant age group	>45	36-55	<45	>56	<25

Group 1: Daily die-hard drinkers

Group 2: Occasional involved drinkers

Group 3: Occasional uninvolved drinkers

Group 4: Occasional drinkers for tradition

Group 5: Non-consumers

The + and – signs indicate the weight and strength of the variable allocated to each group. The absence of a sign indicates a neutral or median positioning.

Table 3:3 Typology of Wine Consumers in France
Source: ONIVINS-INRA Survey.

The gender factor is significant. The division between male and female consumers in France continues to be marked—with men consistently the more frequent and higher volume wine drinkers. Moreover, women are twice as likely as men to dilute whatever wine they do drink with water. Culturally, in rural areas especially, it has rarely been seen as fitting for women to be wine consumers. With the substantial move from rural areas to cities, and the general emancipation of women, such strictness is no longer operating. However, the fact that women still consistently drink less can be explained, at least in part, in terms of the calorific value of the alcohol-content of wine which causes many calorie conscious females to restrict their intake of wine

The tendency towards urbanization and the increase in the number of sedentary occupations that this implies appears to go against regular wine consumption.

Public Opinion

Traditionally, an outsider's perception of the French tends to cast them as a nation obsessed by wine, and proud of their viniculture heritage. However, recent statistics show that for the bulk of the French population, wine is a matter of indifference. Fully 75% of non-consumers expressed slight or nonexistent level of involvement in wine consumption. These same views are shared by 27% of occasional wine drinkers. On the other hand, as may be expected, 82% of frequent drinkers express a high degree of involvement.

Young people are particularly prevalent among non-consumers. Of those coming from families in which there are no regular consumers of wine, only 10% between the ages of 15 and 25 claim to be regular consumers themselves. The consumption patterns can be explained partly by the growth of the soft-drink segment as well as flavored alcoholic beverages, which target a young clientele. The appeal for these beverages may also have something to with the perennial disdain felt by the young for the habits of their parents.

There is also a marked preference currently for more stimulating mood-enhancers than alcohol (whether in the form of officially-proscribed substances or as sparkling drinks made with such additives as extract of the jungle vine Guarana). It is expected that a large number of young people will remain true to the habits they have acquired in their youth and continue to be part of the non-consumer category.

Wine as a Beverage versus Wine for Pleasure

The general, in France as well as in the rest of Southern Europe, there has been a move away from wine as an everyday beverage to its use as a means to enhance special meals and other occasions. People are simply drinking less wine, but what they do drink is of higher quality with premium prices. Table 3:4 shows consumer preferences for different types of wines between 2003 and 2006. These preferences began to change in the late 1990s. The data shows an increase in per capita consumption of rosé and sparkling wines, which are considered to be of superior quality than the regular still wines. This indicates that there has been a shift towards higher quality wines, and the sales of quality wines continued to increase over each of the following years through 2013. This has been a remarkable trend for 16 years and has not yet shown any tendency to abate.

Wine Category	2003/04	2004/05	2005/06
VQPRD Wines	15,821	17,608	17,536
Table Wines	17,069	15,312	15,730
TOTAL	32,890	32,920	33,266

Table 3:4 French Consumption by Category, 2003 through 2006 (in 1,000 HL)
Source: DGI/DGDDI (General Customs Office).

Table 3:5 shows the change in consumer patterns for different types of wines and depicts an interesting movement of most of the major markets to an increase in consumption of sparkling wines and champagnes. These data support the hypothesis that wine in France is becoming increasingly used for special occasions or celebrations. However, notice that this trend is reversed in Germany, as well as the US.

Country	Still white	Still red	Still rosé	Champagne	Sparkling	Fortified/ Vermouth
Italy	-16.8%	21.7%	-28.9%	4.1%	22.3%	-13.5%
US	7.1%	29.9%	-8.5%	-3.2%	-5.3%	-7.7%
Germany	-5.5%	35.8%	11.4%	-29.0%	-4.2%	-8.0%
UK	15.4%	32.5%	-26.5%	14.0%	11.0%	-10.0%
France	5.3%	-8.7%	11.0%	0.8%	8.4%	-3.3%
Spain	3.6%	-2.8%	-8.9%	38.9%	15.3%	12.6%
Portugal	-0.3%	-5.6%	-5.2%	38.6%	30.4%	-
World	**-2.5%**	**17.1%**	**-6.5%**	**-1.9%**	**7.2%**	**-4.6%**

Table 3:5 Percentage Change in Consumption Patterns
Source: Country Trade reports.

The traditional midday meal is also changing to lighter meals and quicker alternatives, such as a sandwiches accompanied by either beer or soft drinks. Trends in evening meal habits are also moving towards a lighter meal taken at an earlier time. With formal occasions becoming fewer, the aperitif (vermouth or other fortified wine) have become less popular.

White wine is still featured as part of the younger social drinking scene; however, the overall trend is toward drinking smaller quantities with better qualities.

The UK—One of the Most Highly Targeted Markets

The UK can be considered an example of a newer and growing market for wine in Europe. According to Government data, there has been no significant decrease in overall volume of alcohol consumed in Britain, despite the anti-alcohol lobbies.

Per capita consumption for beer and cider continues to be significant, but beer has seen the most dramatic decline, losing £2.2 billion in revenue between 2006 and 2011. This has been attributed largely to the dramatic decline of the UK pub sector. Cider consumption is now about equal to beer consumption. Cider's gains have been attributed to it attracting the younger drinkers. However, cider is a sweet drink and not suitable as a beverage to accompany a meal, whereas many wines are the perfect accompaniment to foods, and wine continues to do well in the UK. Within the EU, the British consume more alcohol than the Netherlands, Greece, Italy, Finland and Poland.

In worldwide terms, the UK ranks in the middle of the top 30 countries for alcohol consumption. Wine is now consumed by almost two thirds of the UK population, and the UK ranked 10th in the world in per capita wine consumption by 2011. The average wine consumer now drinks 32 (75cl) bottles per year. Wine consumption was steadily rising during the previous decade. This was related to increasing personal disposable income in the UK and an influence of lifestyle from continental Europe. The more recent economic turbulence has not appeared to reduce alcoholic consumption in the UK, but there has been a shifting between choices of alcoholic beverages.

Beer may still be wine's greatest rival in the UK, despite beer consumption being in decline. The largest consumer group for wine is affluent consumers, over 35 years of age. The increase in wine sales is driven by this largest consumer group drinking more quality wines, as opposed to younger consumers being attracted to wine. Interestingly, a slightly higher percentage of women drink wine: 68.5% compared to 62% of men.

The French wine imports to the UK, in terms both of volume and market share, have declined slightly. This is probably due to price and quality challenges. For example, Australia's share of the UK market has reached 24%, which is substantially more than only a decade ago. A similar trend has been observed for imports from the US, which accounted for about 17.9% of the total UK wine imports, as recently as 2005. Product knowledge and price awareness have changed the purchasing patterns of many British consumers of quality wine, and many consumers have been willing to taste New World wines. They have discovered clean and fruity wines at reasonable prices. As in France, there is a general tendency among UK consumers to be aware of the quality of what they are buying and to be prepared to pay a little more to obtain better quality. For the UK consumer, the extra cost of upgrading to better quality is dwarfed in relation to the extremely high taxes paid on each bottle.

The role of female consumers in the UK market has been of considerable significance. In the past, the fashion was for women to drink a glass of wine instead of beer because this was considered more genteel. Women have continued to spearhead the purchasing of wine, a fact which has been greatly enhanced by retailing trends so heavily biased towards the supermarkets, where female customers out-number men. Euromonitor data demonstrates that in the UK, young women are consuming more alcohol and are more relaxed about drinking without men in public, than in the past.

Table 3:6 shows the preferences of UK wine consumers. Consumption of white wine is skewed towards women in the 35 to 54 age range, particularly those from more affluent backgrounds. Red/rosé wine is a bias of men in the 45 to 64 age range, again those from more affluent backgrounds. Red/rosé continues to be more expensive than white wines. Presently, the split between red/rosé and white wine is almost even in the UK retail market. This is attributed to the more fruity styles of the New World wines in comparison to the fuller dry reds from traditional European suppliers. Since 2003, New World wine imports have surpassed imports from traditional suppliers. Rosé jumped 34% in 2006, and is seen as a niche market that is growing, an example is the success of White Zinfandel among young female drinkers.

Color of Wine:		White %	Red %
Sex	Male	31.0	49.4
	Female	69.0	50.6
Age Group	18-24	8.5	4.7
	25-34	17.1	14.8
	35-49	34.0	32.2
	50+	40.3	48.3
Social Grade	AB	38.4	45.5
	C1	34.1	32.7
	C2	14.6	13.0
	DE	12.9	8.7

Social Grade Definitions:
AB: Upper Middle/Middle Class i.e. Higher/intermediate managerial professional
C1: Lower Middle Class i.e. Junior managerial professional
C2: Skilled Working Class i.e. Skilled manual worker
DE: Working Class i.e. Unskilled manual worker

Table 3:6 Profile of Wine Drinker by Wine Color
Source: The Drinks Pocket Book.

Taxation

Countries outside the EU, such as the US, must pay import duty (tariffs) on exports, while EU countries are exempt. Duty Receipts on wine have essentially remained at a rather high level. Sales of non-EU wines are at a consumer price disadvantage. Table 3:7 shows the import duties applicable in UK on different types of wines.

Wine Type	Tariff/Import Duty
Sparkling wine	32.0 Euros per hecto liters
Still white wine 12.5% abv	13.1 Euros per hecto liters
Still red wine 14.0% abv	15.4 Euros per hecto liters
Vermouth < 18% abv	10.9 Euros per hecto liters
abv = alcoholic strength by volume	

Table 3:7 Tariffs on Wine Imports into the UK
Source: USDA Foreign Agricultural Service, GAIN Report.

The UK is one of four EU Members to practice punitive levels of taxation on alcohol; the others are Ireland, Sweden and Denmark. The Irish excise duty on wine is similar to that of the UK. The natural boundary of the English Channel makes it less likely that the UK government will meet demands for complete tariff unification. Figure 3:1 compares the excise duties for 21 countries.

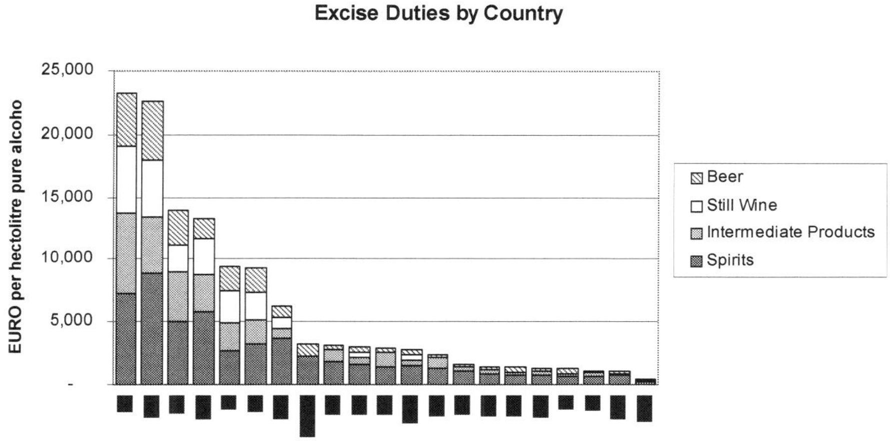

Excise Duties by Country

Figure 3:1 VAT and Excise Duties Data by Country
Source: GAIN.

The Wealthy Wine Connoisseurs

Someone asked, "Is $17,000 too much to pay for a bottle of wine?" One could also ask, "Is $300,000 to much to pay for a bottle of wine?" The answer is, as with anything else, the price of a wine is determined by the consumers' desire and ability to pay with respect to the offer of sellers in a marketplace. In the terminology of the social science of economics: Demand and Supply.

The extremely wealthy wine enthusiast is a type of consumer that has not yet been mentioned. The person is a devotee of the world's most rare examples of wines. He or she is also very rich, with a wealth that can be measured in hundreds of millions or thousands of millions of dollars.

This type of wine consumer could be referred to as a "Connoisseur," and he or she is an extraordinary devotee of fine wine. The wealthy customer also believes that a bottle of wine can be a "store of value," much like an art object created by famous artists. These individuals can often be found frequenting such places as the grand wine auctions of Sotheby's and Christie's. These two auction houses are the world's largest brokers of fine art, jewelry, real estate, and collectibles. Sotheby's and Christie's are longstanding rivals for the status of the world's preeminent auctioneering brokerage. Sotheby's has presence in 40 countries and 90 cities with flagship auctions in the major hubs such as New York, London and Beijing. Buyers can register to bid in person at Sotheby's offices or online. Sotheby's requires that buyers provide government-issued proof of identity and a bank reference. If the buyer is approved, there are four ways he/she can bid: in person at the auction, online in real time, by registered telephone, or using a representative from Sotheby's. When a client has the winning bid, he/she can choose to pay with cash, check, money order or wire transfer.

An example of a winning bid for wine is the purchase made of six-bottles of Hermitage, La Chapelle 1961 Paul Jaboulet Aine for the amount of $102,850. The online auction catalogue described this particular wine as:

> A masterpiece of gigantic proportions. The colour is barely touched by age. A great bouquet of smoky violets and smoked reindeer meat. The extraordinary richness on the palate is astonishing. Sheer, rich coffee. Unparalleled glycerol. Rich leather, black winegums and liquorice. A later bottle had an incredible nose of damp forests and a deep, violet and iron taste. Gloriously sweet and ripe. Drunk recently with Petrus '61 and Latour '61 and, for some, it was the winner! One can understand why.

Another example was the amount paid for a bottle of 1947 Château Cheval Blanc: $304,375. Until recently, no winery had sold recent wines directly to customers at six-figure prices. However, in 2012, the Australian wine producer *Pinfolds* decided to offer twelve bottles of its "limited editions" 2004 Block Cabernet Sauvignon for the price of $168,000 per bottle. You may ask, "Will someone actually buy this wine?" As of the date that the authors of this book were writing the page that you are reading, it was undetermined. However, a Screaming Eagle Cabernet Sauvignon 1992 went for $500,000 in 2012. One can only conclude, as the French say, "pourquoi pas?" The wine producer responds, "à votre santé!"

Chapter 4

PRODUCT CATEGORIES

There are many product categories for wine; however, the primary categories are easily understood. As previously identified, the main classifications are still wines, sparkling wines, and fortified wines. Moreover, each of these three product categories are further refined into sub-classifications. For example, natural still wine in Europe divides as follows: Standard/Table wines (Vin de Table, Vin de Pays or equivalent where applicable), Premium wines (AOC, VDQS or equivalent), Super Premium wines (High-priced Chateau-bottled AOC). Each of these last three is further subdivided into color types of Red, Rosé and White.

Still Wine

Looking at the major world markets for wine, we see the dominance of still wine varies from country to country (see Figure 4:1). Because of the fragmented nature of the wine industry and the enormous variety of individual characteristics between product from specific countries, regions, villages and estates, the need for further classification was recognized. The purpose was to assist the consumer and, simultaneously, protect the producer by instigating legislation to differentiate the quality wine from the every-day varieties. To this end, specific EU regulations have a standard framework covering uniform production rules for all wines produced throughout the Union of member nations. There are over 450 registered designations in France alone, over 300 in Italy, around 28 in Greece, 75 in Germany, 62 in Spain, 8 in Portugal, plus the Luxembourg wine-producing area.

Labeling is guided by similar requirements in the EU member nations:

- Labeling information is divided into "compulsory and optional information." Information not listed as part of either of these two categories may not be displayed on the bottle.
- Labels must contain nominal volume information.
- The amount of alcohol per volume.
- The presents of sulfates, if any.

- Regulations include requirements for how grape varieties and vintage may be mentioned on the label.
- Requirements and procedures for "protected designations" for origin for wine.
- Label indications for degree of dryness to sweetness are regulated in terms of residual sugar content.
- Traditional bottle types may only be used for wines from specific origins

The following graphics in Figure 4:1 illustrate the country differences in percentage, of wines produced as to wine-color and effervescent. These are labeled: 1 = Still Red; White = 2; Rosé = 3; Champaign = 4; Sparkling = 5; and 6 = Fortified.

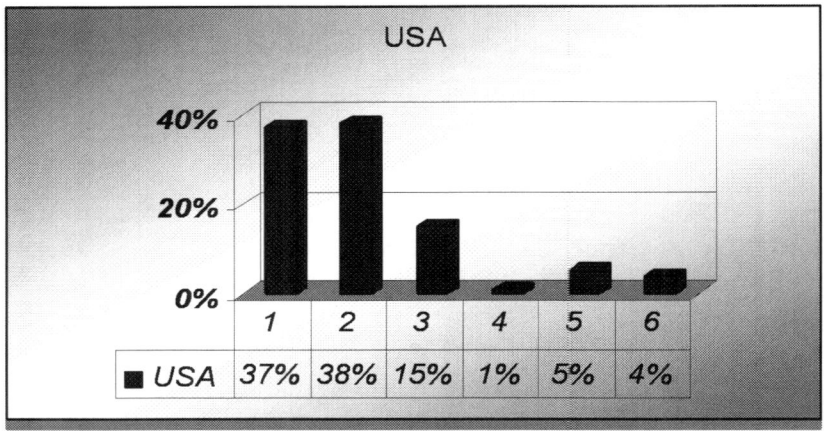

	1	2	3	4	5	6
■ USA	37%	38%	15%	1%	5%	4%

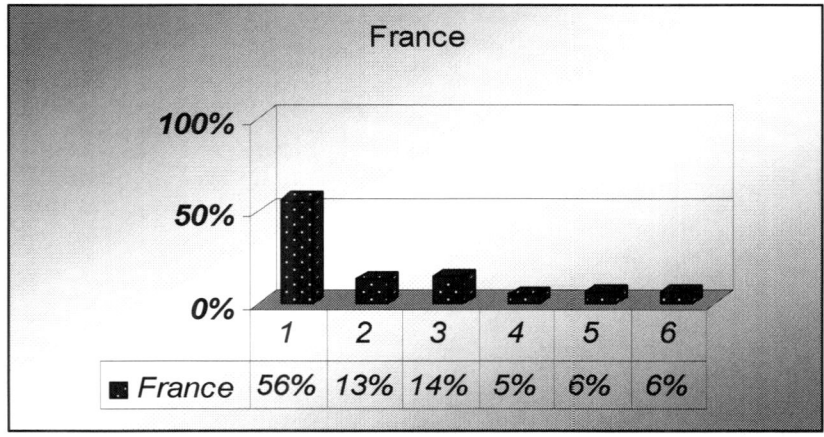

	1	2	3	4	5	6
■ France	56%	13%	14%	5%	6%	6%

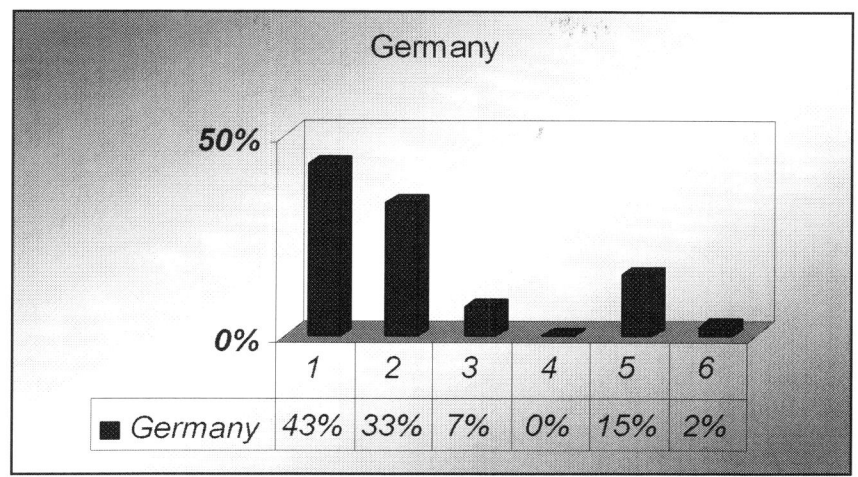

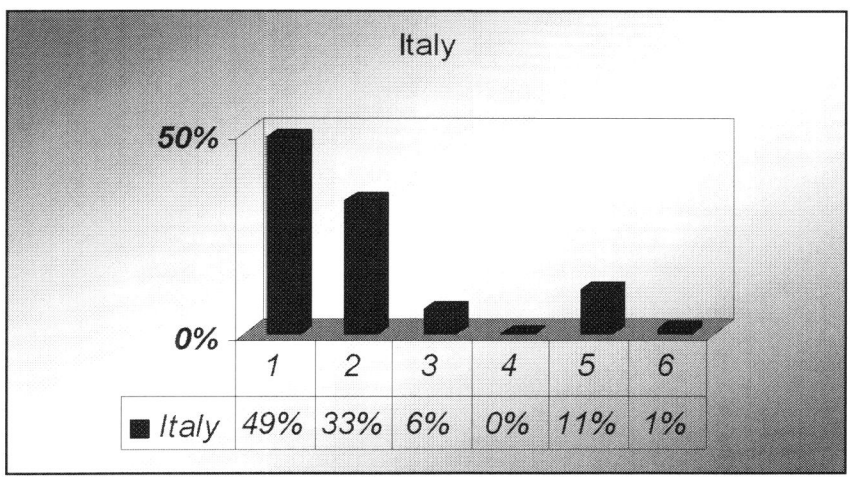

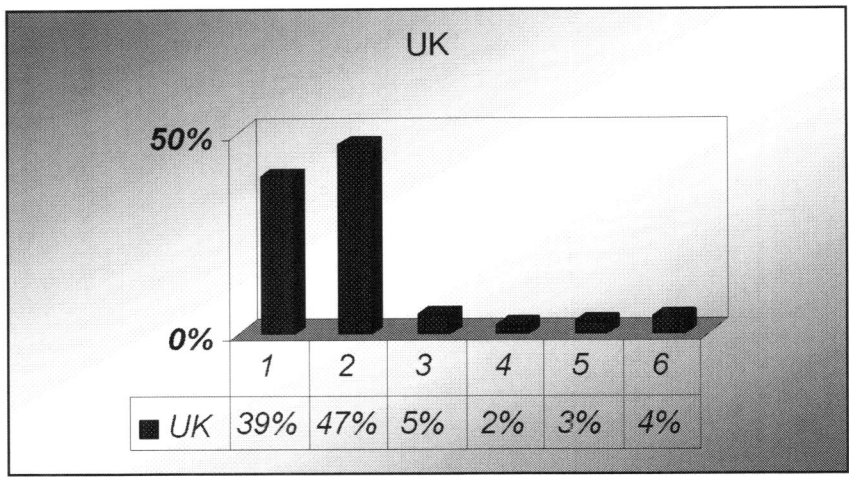

Figure 4:1 Percentage of Primary Categories, Average Total Volume
Source: Based on estimates from Country Sector Briefings.

Note that the EU standards predominate, but many non-EU wine-producing countries compete successfully without any formal appellation system or other quality league. Some countries have their own quality control structures, but lack EU recognition. The bottom line, as with any other product, is that the consumer becomes aware of relative price and quality from personal experience. Consequently, the producers compete for market share by adopting the best practices for making and marketing their products.

France

Demarcation exists in France primarily between VCC (Vin de consommation courante) and AOC (Appellation d'Origine Contrôlée). The first of these two overall categories is further divided between Vin de Table and Vin de Pays. Vin de Table is chiefly blended wine—sometimes containing up to 15% foreign product. Vin de Pays must come from a particular, demarcated region. VDQS wines come next—as a sort of halfway house between Standard and Premium. They must come from legally designated regions and merit recognition as being better than mere vin de table, but not properly qualifying for inclusion in the AOC bracket. VDQS is now being overshadowed by the Vin de Pays category, which serves a similar function, but which is legislatively less complex.

The Appellation d'Origine Conti-616e evolved as a legal mechanism for the protection of certain renowned areas, notably Bordeaux and Burgundy, but had previously been somewhat besmirched by abuses of imitation and adulteration. To this end, the wine-producing lobbies of the major regions have established exclusive rights to the production of AOC wines from certain grape varieties. The AOC system, being originally designed as a means of preventing abuse, it has maintained that primary function. The reputation of "proper" claret and burgundy at the turn of the century was based on genuine excellence through state-of-the-art methods. Now, however, the Appellation can in some cases serve to shield mediocre wines from criticism. All a particular producer has to do, if he is permitted to use the Appellation, is to make sure he remains faithful to the relevant laws. Such laws, being conservative rather than progressive, do little to encourage improvement and can serve to stifle innovation. At the top end of the AOC category are the Cru-classifications for the Chateaux of the Bordeaux region and the finest estates of Burgundy. At this rarefied level, the small scale of output, the extremely personal ambience of each individual chateau or estate, plus the level of consumer sophistication, are generally sufficient to guarantee high production standards. Once again, the bottom line is the informed consumer.

Italy

Based on the French system, Italian wine is likewise divided between Vino da Tavola (Vin de table) and DOC—Denominazione de Origine Controllata. While the DOC appellation is, in itself, strictly controlled and therefore the market is hard to enter. There is yet another higher official stratum in the form of the DOCG—Denominazione de Origine Controllata e Garantita.

Legislation by Italian Minister Goria also provides for an equivalent of France's Vin de Pays category. The Indicazione da Geografica Tipica permits producers who are making good quality wines, but who have been prevented from achieving DOC status, to place their wines in a more desirable niche than the common category. The reforms of the Italian system during the 1990s were long overdue. The respect for Italian wines had been falling. The perception was that the large "industrial" scale producers had been sitting back on their right to use the DOC appellation and getting good prices for their rather "indifferent wine."

Market Shares

The market for standard wines retains the largest share of the still wine sector, representing about 47% of EU consumption and 50% of production. However, it is this area of the wine market which has been worst affected by the pattern of reduced consumption and the creeping encroachment of alternative beverages, such as beer or soft-drinks in countries and regions where wine had traditionally been the staple. In France, there is the reduction of consumption of table wines, and the concomitant decrease in production of table wines.

However, in Italy, table-wines continued to be a dominant part in the market share in both production and consumption. Table wines were over 70% of the wine consumed. However, DOC & DOCG wines represent an increasing share of production and are currently accounting for approximately 29% of total production.

The great bulk of Germany's production has traditionally been premium wine. The relative popularity of red, white or rosé wines varies greatly from region to region and from country to country (refer to Table 4:1). In Germany, the percentage of wine consumed as white-wine has decreased by approximately 50%, and now is only 33% of market share.

Of UK's consumption, table wines formed 21.5% by volume sales. Also, of the market, red wine was about 39%, and white wine comprised 47%. In the US, the still wines market share has grown dramatically and its market share is currently 90%. Table 4:1 shows how the market divides among the major European players and demonstrates the largest percentage market shares.

Wines	France	Italy	Germany	UK	US
Still	82	86	82	91	90
Red	55	43	43	39	36
White	13	37	33	47	40
Rosé	14	6	7	5	15
Sparkling	11	13	15	5	6
Champagne	5	0	0	2	1
Others	6	13	15	3	3
Fortified Vermouth, etc.)	6	1	2	4	4

Table 4:1 Wine Market Shares by Sector, in Percentage of Volume Sales
Source: Estimated from Country Sector Briefings.

UK consumption of champagne made a great leap during the apparent prosperity of the past few decades. The UK's traditional fondness for fortified wines has been dwindling since 1985, as demonstrated by statistics for sherry and port sales, where annual volume figures fell considerably. There was a slight rallying in the port sector owing to the improved marketing of new lighter styles including white ports, but the traditional heavy ruby ports have not done well. The decline in demand for vermouth and other flavored wines in UK is documented by the fact that total imports of these wines have declined by more than 50%.

Vermouths and aromatics continue a tradition, which was current in the middle ages of flavoring table wines with herbs and spices, although they now form a legally distinct bracket from table wines. The term Vermouth comes from the German word for Wormwood: "Wermut"—the flowers of this bitter herb have long been renowned for curative properties. Longevity was a promise of this drink. People who had a moderate practice of drinking it appear to live longer. The Longevity which had been attributed to the wormwood and other herbs is now generally recognized as simply being due to the wine—the grape and not the weed. Nevertheless, the herbs, bolstered by the extra alcohol used in fortification, succeed in rendering palatable though unsuccessful wines. The market share of Vermouths and aromatics is very small, due in part to the demise of "cocktail hour" and partly to the general drift away from higher alcohol content beverages.

The demand for wine coolers, the mixtures of light wine, fruit-juices, carbonated mineral water and flavorings, settled down (after a brief boom in the mid-eighties) and these types of alcoholic drinks failed to make much impression on the European market. Following the passing of the fashion for wine coolers in the US and Western Europe in the early 1990s, wine-based flavored alcoholic beverages (FABs) experienced a decline in popularity in most major markets.

Low alcohol wines (those not exceeding 5.5% by volume) and alcohol-free wines (not more than 0.05% alcohol by volume) gained ground, although from very small beginnings. Of these, around 58% are alcohol-free, 36% de-alcoholized and 6% low-alcohol. Imports from European countries, other than Italy, fell sharply and consistently after these beverages enjoyed the brief period of fashion. Therefore, producers and oenologists are no longer devoting time or trouble to the objective of producing a drink which resembles wine, but contains little or no alcohol.

Grape-Must

Another category of vinicultural product, although not a finished article as such, deserves brief mention, it is grape-must. The grape-must is defined under EC regulations as: the liquid product obtained naturally or by physical processes from fresh grapes. Grape-must has a permitted actual alcoholic maximum strength of 1%. This can be used in the production of wine by allowing fermentation to continue or it can be further processed to make concentrated must, which is used for export, notably to UK and Ireland for the production of British and Irish wines. Due to the general tendency towards over-production, various other uses of must have been considered, for instance using it to replace sucrose in the process of wine-enrichment. Its use in cattle feed has also been explored.

The above described distinctions between various wine products are the categories that have evolved over time and are universally accepted. These categories of product comprise the various markets for the global industry and the business of wine.

Chapter 5

PRODUCTION

Wine is fundamentally an agricultural product. The industry's production base has its roots in the land, roots which form a wide-spreading tangle, drawing sustenance from an enormous number and variety of sources.

One important element in the production process for wine is the ratio existing between quantity and quality of grape yields and the quality of a wine. Table 5:1 shows the costs of producing three levels of Bordeaux, but the results are similar for other wines as well. The first is "great wine" in quantities of 27 hecto-liters per hectare, with traditional planting density of 10,000 vines per hectare, using 50% new barrels each year and allowing for the unavoidable loss of 20% of the volume of wine during racking and fining, and from evaporation in barrel. The second is "good" wine in quantities of 45 hecto-liters per hectare, with wider-spaced vines at 6,600 per hectare, 20% new barrels, and 20% loss by volume. The third is minimum-cost wine in quantities of 63 hecto-liters per hectare derived from widely-spaced vines at only 2,600 per hectare (a common practice in California, but actually not permitted in Bordeaux), with storage in vats, and a loss of only 7% by volume.

The prices in Table 5:1 show only production costs. Land values, bottling costs, financing costs, transportation, variable pest control, and anything else are not included. These figures were originally calculated by famed Bordeaux shipper Peter Sichel (stipulated in constant US dollars, base 2003 and later updated to 2013). The hl/ha is hectoliter per hectare. Notice that these production costs result in the high-quality wine costing over twice as much as the medium quality and 8 times that of the ordinary wine.

Many growers would maintain that this quantity-quality ratio is the crucial element. The "smaller the yield, the better the grape" is an axiom which has been enshrined in the regulations of the French Appellation Controlée system, as well in regulations of Italy. Neither California nor Germany employs any such restrictions, which suggests that quality can be protected by mechanisms other than simple yield restriction. Although, even in California, which has spearheaded technological innovation in wine production, there is an increasing tendency among growers to minimize the use of complex processes and to revert back to the basics of soil, vine and grape.

Cost Heads	Production Costs (US$ per hectoliter)		
	Great Wine 27 hl/ha*	Good Wine 45 hl/ha	Ordinary Wine 63hl/ha
Viticultural costs	757	292	125
Storage costs	126	77	4.5
Loss from evaporation, racking, fining (20% in cask, 7% in vat)	151	56	8.75
Labor costs, racking and fining	40	40	4.5
Total cost	1075	469	139
Total production cost per bottle	**8.27**	**3.60**	**1.06**

Table 5:1: Production Costs for Bordeaux Wines

The grape harvest, generally commencing in early autumn, has changed very little. The decision as to when the harvest should commence is based upon the sugar and acid balance of the grapes, as well as upon their tannin levels and skin color of the grapes. As the grapes ripen, their sugar content begins to overtake their acidity. Choosing the right moment of ripeness is of utmost importance, and there is an optimum time for harvesting each particular type of wine.

In any winery, each month can be characterized by a particular activity. There may be slight variations in the period of year in which each activity is performed, due to regional differences of a winery in the northern hemisphere.

Table 5:2 shows the schedule of a typical winemaker in the northern hemisphere.

Figure 5:1 shows typical annual variation in labor intensity for French vineyards.

The monthly variations in costs follow a similar trend, as labor intensity in a typical French vineyard varies. Of course, the costs are different in California, because automated harvest techniques have been widely adopted in the US, somewhat reducing the total number of labor hours.

A good wine grower will take great care to ensure his work-force does not damage the fruit, since this would increase the danger of oxidation and infections carried by insects and microbes and would adversely affect his chances of selling his fruit (and, of course, the ultimate quality of the wine).

The harvest is then processed locally either by the producer or by the co-operative in a plant, which necessarily has been standing idle for the greater part of the year.

Month	Vineyard	Winery
January	Vines are pruned.	The wine is aged in barrels or vats. Previous vintages are prepared for sale. Equipment maintenance, etc.
February	Late pruning. New grafts are prepared. Equipment maintenance, etc.	Racking (moving wine into clean barrels) begins.
March	Final pruning. Sap begins to rise. Soil is worked to aerate and uncover base of vines.	Racking should be close to complete. Topping off continues. As the weather warms, malolactic fermentation may start or be induced. End of previous vintage bottling, etc.
April	General vineyard maintenance.	General maintenance.
May	Frost watch. Soil is worked again to turn under weeds. Remove suckers. First spraying against mold and mildew.	Shipping of previous vintage and preparing for next racking.
June	The vines flower. Much of the quantity of the vintage will be determined at this stage. Shoots are thinned and tied. Second spraying.	Second racking. Older wines are racked. As weather warms barrel maintenance becomes crucial.
July	Tiny grapes begin to develop. Vines sprayed with Bordeaux mixture. Turn the weeds into the soil again. Keep shoots trimmed.	Winery is closed down in times of heat. Steps are taken to prevent bacterial growth in winery.
August	Color begins to change in black grapes. Trimming and weeding. Preparation for harvest.	Everything is cleaned and inspected for the coming harvest.
September	Final harvest preparations made. Earliest harvesting begins.	Ensure that all vats and barrels are water tight.
October	Most vintages start late September and continue into early October. Once the grapes are picked and the whites are pressed, the grape skins are spread on the vineyard and turned into the soil in preparation of the winter.	Stemming, crushing and in some cases pressing. The new wine begins to ferment. Last year's wine is racked and moved to the aging cellar.

Month	Vineyard	Winery
November	Shoots are cut and collected to burn. Vineyard is plowed and soil heaped on the base of the vines.	Young wines are now finished with fining and filtering, and are then bottled. Older vintages may also be bottled. Wines that will be aged are still fermenting in contact with their skins.
December	Some vineyards the soil needs to be replaced after rains. Pruning starts about halfway through the month.	The end of fermentation for the hearty reds. Bottling of young and older wines is completed. Wines for aging are moved from vat to barrel after fining and possible filtering.

Table 5:2 Typical Yearly Schedule of a Winemaker in the Northern Hemisphere
Source: www.professionalchef.com

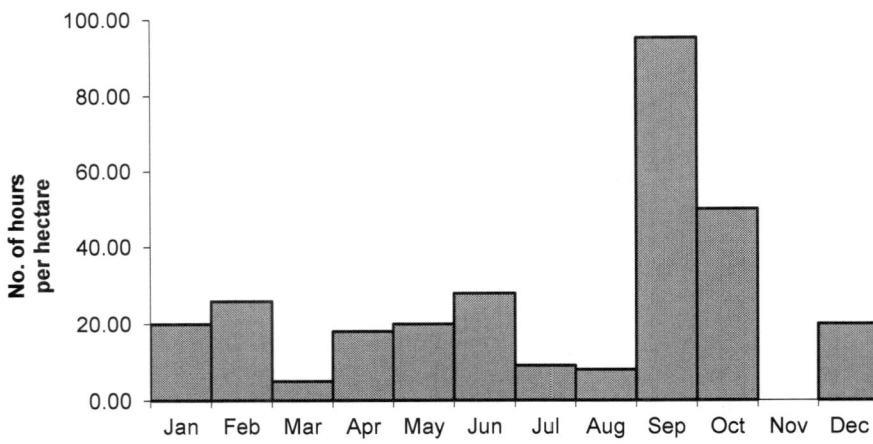

Figure 5:1: Typical Annual Variation in Labor Intensity for Vineyard (*Sep-Oct: Harvest months)
Source: Evaluserve estimates.

The basic process of wine production has not changed in any radical sense since the earliest times. Changes that have occurred are actually refinements of the process. For example, a discovery of prime importance was that sulfur could be used to preserve wine and prevent wild fermentation of the grape-must and secondary fermentation in the bottle.

The antiseptic qualities of sulfur have never been surpassed in the wine-making process, although it has in some cases been overused. There is less need to use excessive quantities of sulfur due to advances in the use of modern equipment. The materials and construction of this equipment, a better understanding of bacteriology, and general standards of hygiene during vinification and storage have also played a role. Decay through contamination or oxidation is now a much less common occurrence.

The increased use of stainless steel fermentation vats and shorter times that the wine remains in casks means that there is less need for preservatives such as sulfur. The preservatives inherently present in wine are alcohol, tannins and low acidity, which are now sufficient to preserve the lighter, fruitier wines which have become popular.

Overview of the Process of Making Wine

The following is a detailed description of the practices employed in making wine. For some readers, this will be interesting, for others it may be more than they wish to know.

For white wines, particularly in view of current tastes, it is desirable to minimize skin contact by pressing the grapes as soon as possible after picking. The first step is to crush the grapes with just sufficient force to break their skins. This gives rise to what is known as free-run juice, which naturally begins to escape immediately. Many wineries now employ de-juicing mechanisms, the most sophisticated of which, using carbon dioxide gas under pressure, can remove up to 70% of the juice before the actual pressing, with minimum risk of oxidation.

In the case of certain more robust white wines, the white grapes will be left to macerate at a low temperature for 24 hours before pressing, so that quantities of the tannins in the skins and other flavors will pass into the juice. The better quality rosé wines are also produced in this fashion, by allowing brief contact with a certain proportion of red grape skins.

Stems are generally included in the crush, partly to make the mass easier to handle, and to tease apart between first and second pressings. It is necessary, however to ensure that the press is not operating at such a pressure as to extract the bitter juices from the stems and the seeds of the grapes.

With white wines and rosés, the juice alone is fermented. In the case of red wines, the skins remain in the crush throughout fermentation, since the tannins and colors contained in these skins are of prime importance for the finished red wine. De-stemming is optional. Some wine-producers (notably those of Beaujolais, Rhône and Chile) prefer to leave the stems in throughout the fermentation process. This results in lower acidity levels and astringency. While some wine-makers maintain that the stems fulfill an essential role in aerating the mass, others claim that leaving stems are a waste of valuable space in the vat.

A method used prior to vat-fermentation in some areas (notably Beaujolais), to ensure proper extraction of the tannins and other elements from the skins, is called Carbonic Maceration. While there are various ways of achieving this, the basic characteristic of Carbonic Maceration is that the uncrushed grapes are loaded into a closed tank where their own weight will cause the skins of the bottom layers to break and thus begin fermentation. The resulting build-up of carbon dioxide gas within the closed tank forces the natural yeasts through the skins of the grapes, which are higher up in the tank, allowing them to ferment internally before bursting open. After about 48 hours, sufficient essential extracts from the skins will have passed into the juice for the mass to be pressed, leaving the juice to be further fermented in vats.

Another method used in the production of bulk red wines for the extraction of color prior to fermentation is called thermotic extraction. In this process, the crushed grapes are sulfated and placed in vats using pressurized nitrogen, which prevents fermentation from taking place. Heat is then applied (87 degrees centigrade) for approximately 40 minutes, which successfully draws out all the color. The resultant mass is then centrifuged and the juice is stored until it is processed into wine.

Fermentation

In simple terms, this stage in the vinification process is where the yeasts begin to consume the sugars which are present in the grape-must, and convert them into ethyl-alcohol and carbon dioxide. Different wineries have different attitudes concerning the wild yeasts present in the crop itself. There is a movement in the US, led by producers in California, to use only the yeasts naturally present. Others employ a process of re-centrifuging or flash-pasteurizing the juice to ensure an even distribution of the yeast which, in certain cases, may even have been genetically engineered to suit specific requirements. As a general rule, most wineries start the fermentation process by means of a considerable inoculation of a yeast strain chosen with regard to the proposed temperature at which the grape-must is to ferment.

A bi-product of the fermentation process is a considerable release of energy in the form of heat. A recent refinement has been the development of a cold fermentation process for white wines. It has always been known that an excess of heat, both from external conditions and from the fermentation process itself, causes flabby whites which lack acidity. In Europe, the only solution had previously been to produce fine white wines in small casks in the coldest cellars available. Newer technology with cold fermentation has become common practice. The huge fermentation vats are chilled and insulated with varying degrees of sophistication. In areas such as Australia and

California, light wines with extensive fruit flavors are now produced using long fermentation at very low temperatures. While the New World producers use temperatures as low as 8 degrees centigrade, in France 18 degrees is still considered cold.

The move toward cold fermentation has fostered the need for further research into alternative strains of yeast, since many will frequently cease functioning at lower temperatures, causing the fermentation process to stick. Fermentation of white wines generally takes between ten to fifteen days, while red wines are fermented in the vat for a period of between nine and twenty days.

In cases of red wines, where carbonic maceration is not employed, the bubbling of carbon dioxide gas in the fermentation vat causes all the various pieces of skins, pips and stalks to rise up and form a crusty cap on the liquid surface. Because this vegetable matter is decaying gradually, it is prone to getting too hot and to attract bacteria. It is essential to prevent such infections by regularly pushing the cap down to the bottom. There are many methods employed, such as simply employing men with poles to push the cap back under, the use of grilles just beneath the level of the fermenting liquid, or the more complex mechanical use of horizontally rotating vats.

When red wine is completely, or almost completely, fermented, the bulk of the liquid is siphoned from the vat into barrels or another tank. This is the vin de goutte. The remaining liquid and solids are gently pressed to produce the vin de presse which, naturally, contains higher levels of the essential elements from the now softened skins. A stronger pressing will yield a small quantity of wine, but this is generally too astringent to be used for anything more than giving flavor to other blends.

Of the processes permitted during fermentation of both red and white wines, perhaps the most contentious is must improvement or capitalization which involves the addition of refined sugar to the must in order to increase its potential alcohol content. There are very detailed rules governing the use of capitalization. For instance, the quantities of sugar permitted (and hence the level by which potential alcohol may be increased) must be strictly correlative to the actual potential alcoholic content of the wine to be capitalized. Besides the benefit of increasing the amount of alcohol (a preservative), the addition of sugar can also be used to reduce acidity.

This process is not permitted in certain areas of Europe while, in others, growers are only allowed under EU policies (attempts to match consumption to production) to use concentrated grape-must to fortify wine. Grape-must, of course, unlike sugar or grape juice, has the disadvantage of containing all the elements of the grape and consequently cannot serve to reduce acidity.

While capitalization is heavily regulated, there is little doubt that it is widely practiced when it ought not to be and, in an age where technology has come so far and where alcohol itself seems to be a less and less desirable feature of wine, the need for the process may be called into question. The producers of California after all, as we have already seen, voluntarily refrain from capitalization in any form.

Malolactic fermentation, on the other hand, is a process which has always naturally occurred in the case of some wines but which is now actively encouraged by producers, especially in the production of good red wines. It is a secondary, non-alcoholic fermentation, occasioned not by yeasts but by bacteria, which act upon the malic acid in the wine and turn it into milder lactic acid. This process serves to decrease the total acidity of a wine, to soften its edges and to generally increase the wine's complexity. The process is used predominantly in red wines, although it may also be employed in the production of white wines, where acidity is particularly high, such as Chablis, the Loire and Switzerland.

Sediments

The resultant young wines, both white and red, which emerge from the fermentation process, will require various degrees of processing to remove solids and particles. Racking is used to eliminate large-scale sediment and is effected by simply leaving the wine to stand for some time before siphoning into another barrel. This process is repeated at intervals of between three and six months, over a period of two years in the case of quality wines. This time-honored method of the European Vigneron is being increasingly adopted by the quality wine producers in California.

Smaller particles in suspension may be removed by fining, a traditional method involving pouring over the surface of the wine a substance such as whipped egg-white or gelatin. This layer of material will then slowly sink to the bottom, like a fine net, taking most impurities with it.

A problem, or a perceived problem, with white wine is the formation of tartaric acid crystals which, although harmless, may give the wine a bad appearance. This is most easily obviated by chilling the wine to just above the freezing point for several days and introducing tartaric acid crystals to attract the acid in the wine and bond with it.

The above-mentioned are the gentler options, chiefly reserved for fine wines. There are several more industrial and rather more drastic procedures available to the wine producer. Centrifuging is a very efficient method of removing impurities from wine. However, it can have an adverse effect on the wine's constitution, if used too enthusiastically. Filtration is effective. However it can be taken to extremes. Forcing wine under pressure through filters as fine as 0.45 microns succeeds in removing elements such as yeast and even bacteria, but it can also eliminate much of the wine's natural flavor.

The Equipment of the Modern Winery

The Press

A vertical press is generally acknowledged to produce the highest grade of the most pure juice. The traditional vertical press is one that has a plate which screws down onto the crush. However, such models are somewhat slow and labor intensive. The modern alternatives are either the industrial grade Coq-press, which provides a continuous stream of juice and ejects an equally continuous stream of cake. Such presses cannot be used for quality wine production and so the majority of the better wineries tend to use either the Vaslin horizontal basket press, which is similar in principle to the traditional type, but capable of faster turn-over, or the Willmes bladder press, which uses a large, inflatable bag to squeeze the grapes against an outer casing of fine mesh.

In the business of wine making, traditional fermenting vats of wood are rarely used now. Their shape, cost, and the problems inherent in keeping them clean, have led to their being supplanted. One option is the concrete tank which can be tailored to fit the available space in the winery, and which, when lined with epoxy resin, is very easy to sterilize. Since concrete is a poor conductor of heat, the importance of temperature-control has increased and attention has turned to stainless steel, which now dominates the modern winery.

Stainless steel, in addition to being decay-proof, is hygienic and a perfect heat conductor. Stainless steel also reduces the space demands, since one vat can, in the course of the year, fulfill several functions as a fermentation vat or storage facility.

Wood still plays a role. In the case of certain super-premium wines, oak casks are sometimes used for the fermentation process; however, for the aging process, oak has always been the sine qua non of a fine wine. In California, oak lore and snobbery is employed, and "tastings" are sometimes conducted from various batches of one particular wine that have been aged in oak from a number of different forests in France.

The benefits derived from oak are undeniable, when it is used judiciously. The wine enjoys a very gradual transfer of oxygen through the staves of the barrel, but more importantly, it absorbs a range of complex flavors such as the tannins and vanillin which pass into the wine from the wood. Provided the wine is of a type with sufficient character, it can be enhanced and the added nuances can greatly enhance it. Oak, particularly from certain regions, and old barrels which have already been used to store especially fine wines, are extremely sought-after and fetch high prices.

Aging

There are two specific types of aging in the business of wine making: oxidative and reductive. The former is that which occurs when the wine is kept in the cask; the latter is the aging process that occurs in the bottle. Bottle aging is known as reductive, because of the reduction of the quantity of oxygen the wine comes into contact with and the consequent slowing of chemical reactions. There is no set rule as to the optimum time wines should spend in either of these processes, but generally a combination of the two is required over a period of several years in the case of fine wines.

A California winery has been experimenting with another aging process. Winemakers have long known that wine recovered from sunken ships has a unique taste and the ocean has something to do with the process of aging. Mira Winery of St. Helena, California, placed bottles of wine in steel mesh cages and then submerged them offshore in an undisclosed location back in February 2013. After several months, the bottles were recovered and the wine judged against bottles from the same lot that was not "ocean aged." There have been similar experiments with ocean aging of wine in Europe. All that can reasonably be said is that the wine has very noticeable differences, a unique taste, but so far the judgment is that the wine cannot be said to be better or worse.

The Laboratory

Chemical analysis of wine to check levels of major constituents such as alcohol or sulfur is widely practiced. In most cases, this is required in order to comply with consumer safety regulations. At the same time, there are more complex methods of analysis available, such as gas chromatography and nuclear magnetic resonance. Such sophisticated equipment is capable of tracing up to 250 different elements, traces of which are present in varying amounts in different wines and which contribute significantly to their tastes.

The fact is that a fine wine is such an almost mystical combination of trace elements, often working against each other in combining and transforming the taste. This might imply that there is little point attempting to synthesize or regulate the infinite number of processes involved. Part of the pleasure in the consumption of wine, for many consumers, is the knowledge that wine essentially derives from nature and the land. Even if oenologists succeed in isolating every significant nuance of flavor and cloning the finest of wines in the laboratory, it is somewhat doubtful that people would purchase a synthetic product, if it is known to be derived in a laboratory.

Analysis can be used to determine whether certain processes should be employed during the production of a wine. However, there is a growing tendency toward traditional, natural methods and the minimizing of handling of a wine. For example, racking is preferable to centrifuging or filtration because it is a gentler process and less disruptive to the chemical structure of the wine. Certain technological innovations will remain of great value to the wine producer, and the popularity of high-tech, aseptic wineries that were common in the 1970s have decreased considerably. Such industrial processes tend to produce industrial "characterless wines" and the consumers' demand for such wines is decreasing.

The modern producer in the business of wine making uses a well-equipped winery and can employ the technological advantages to monitor the natural processes within the soil, the grapes, and the fermentation vat. Current philosophy, however, encourages the grower to respond to analytical data in a way that is in harmony with the natural processes of fermentation, rather than by employing harsh chemical or physical methods deriving from the laboratory.

Chapter 6

HISTORY AND DEVELOPMENT OF THE DISTRIBUTION SYSTEM

As with most products, globalization has been the central force for change, particularly in distribution systems. Over the past couple of decades, there have been major advances in distributional logistics, such as newer cost-effective means of transport in all the major market areas, including by road, rail, ocean and air. In terms of industrial distribution, these advances have reduced the importance of geographical proximity where international trade is concerned. Thus, a product or service that finds favor with a specific stratum of the market, for example in California, now stands a better chance of success with the parallel market stratum in London than it may with a different market stratum within the US. In this international business environment, it is understandable that we are witnessing a world-wide convergence of markets, with continually increasing concentration into larger global enterprises.

Evolution of Distribution

Until the mid-sixties, wine distribution was a highly complex structure and as fragmented as the production side of the industry, with its preponderance of small individual growers (Figure 6:1). This complex hierarchy persists to this day, particularly in the upper echelons of Bordeaux that is the most hide-bound of the major producing regions. However, there have been a number of attempts toward streamlining.

Traditionally, each link in the distribution chain has worked on a small scale and on one specialized aspect of the process. The wine grower produces wine with his own equipment on his own premises, or alternatively sells the grapes from his vineyards to the local cooperative. In rural areas, a good proportion of the wine, particularly table-wine, would be absorbed into the cellars of the local residents and get no further in the distribution chain. In the case of wine that was destined for shipment outside the local area, the process involved the stages as shown in Figure 6:2, where dashed lines indicate less frequent channels.

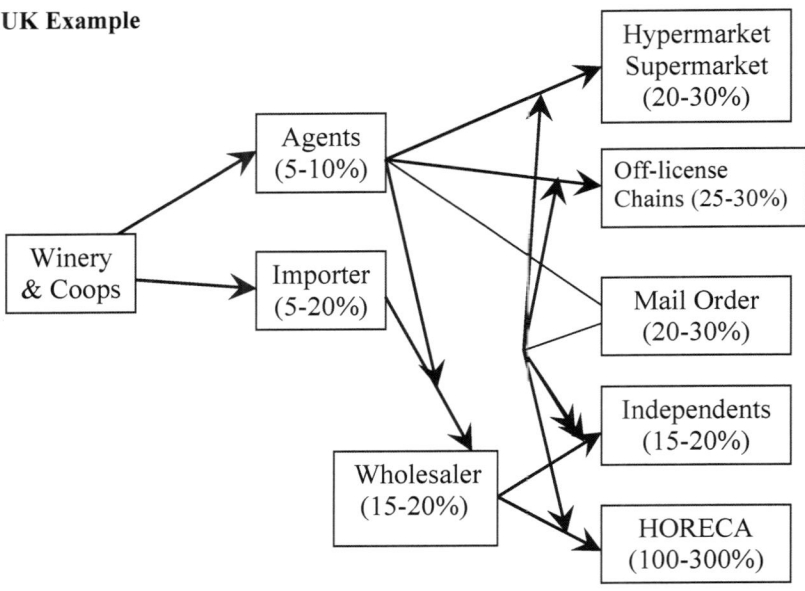

Figure 6:1 European Wine Distribution Systems & Mark-up
Source: Trade Estimates; United Line Estimates; Euromonitor.

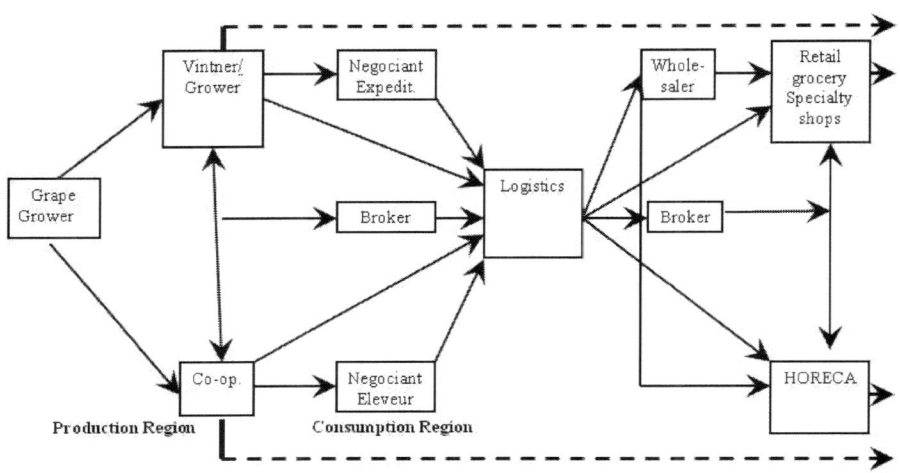

Figure 6:2 Traditional Business Flow – Before 1960

After vinification, the wine entered the province of a local broker, or courtier, before going to the local merchant (négociant). In this model, the broker never actually becomes the owner or handler of the wine, but fulfills an auxiliary role as mediator and adviser between the producer and the merchant. The function of the courtier is to cultivate an intimate knowledge of the region and of the wine being produced by individual growers. When a deal has been struck between producer and négociant, it is the duty of the courtier to see that the terms of the agreement are adhered to and fulfilled and that the quality of the wine supplied matches the samples.

For these services, the courtier is paid a commission of a small percentage, say 2% of the value of any contract, although a further cash payment amounting to another 3% would be common in many areas. If the broker is doing his job properly, by maximizing quality and minimizing cost for the négociant, then he merits his fee. If he is not doing his job, the onus should be on his employers to be more demanding or more discriminating. Even today, there exist many good courtiers who do a fine job in sifting through the thousands of producers clamoring to sell. However, many local brokers remain in business for reasons other than their own efficiency. The complexities of the French legal and fiscal system mean that growers have had little incentive to cut out these middle men (courtier and negociant) and to sell their wine direct. Despite the fact that for many top producers this would be eminently possible, they would thereby be classed as négociants and lose the handsome tax advantages and grant-aid they enjoy as exclusively agricultural producers. Another disincentive to deal directly, and hence another reason for the continuation of the courtier (especially in Bordeaux), is that there is considerable mistrust and class division between the top growers (frequently of the nobility) and the négociants (traditionally of the bourgeoisie). Therefore, there existed good reasons for the courtier's role in this distribution system.

The Quai de Chartrons was the traditional site of the great Bordeaux merchant houses. Most of these were established in the 18th century by expatriates who were forbidden to set themselves up within the old city boundaries. They established their little "ghetto" on the dockside of the Garonne into the centre of the claret trade. These were the Germans, Scots, Scandinavians and Britons that had the advantage of direct links with the export market and understood how the process of blending could turn fine Bordeaux into the heady claret beloved by the English gentry. The ascendancy of this tightly-knit and often inter-bred coterie of merchants continued for centuries, but the hold they had over the ultra-conservative system may ultimately have led to their own undoing.

Top growers in most other areas of France have learned to adapt to the changing market and to deal directly. In Bordeaux, however, there are few who have followed this pattern (with notable exceptions such as Baron Philippe Rothschild). Most have been happy to let the status quo continue, which is perhaps understandable given how top Bordeaux wines can become a commodity for international investment and speculation.

Greed, however, often reaps its own reward as was the case during 1972 and 1973. A much vaunted harvest proved to be less than mediocre and also coincided with the oil crisis. A large number of long-established négociants found themselves locked into exclusive deals with growers and forced to continue purchasing what amounted to over-priced wine. They were unable to re-sell this wine at a profit. The result was that many of the most famous merchant houses of Bordeaux —names such as Nathaniel Johnston, Barton and Gustier, Eschenauer, Mahler Besse and Cruse—came to grief during this period. Those that survived had to look at alternative strategies in a changing market. Such a disastrous scenario repeated itself with the extremely variable quality of the 1991 vintage (following severe frosts in April and a poor summer) coming in the wake of the superb bumper harvests of the previous three years. This time, there was the added problem of a worldwide economic recession restricting demand. The négociants, who paid premium prices to the producers, were now finding it difficult to pass-on the original costs to their customers. Moreover, as a result of the recession, large volumes of stock were being returned to France unsold.

The function of the négociant is to serve the wishes of the purchaser and to locate what the market demands. Traditionally, the job of the negociant éleveur was to assemble large quantities of stock that he would then age in cask before bottling and selling. However, since then, the general increase in direct sales, and the fact that producers profited by tax relief and EU subsidies for aging their own wine and investing in new bottling plants, has meant that there is now much less work for the négociant éleveur. Despite the fact that a reputable negociant is liable to do a better job of aging and bottling than some of the smaller domains, many people are now unwilling to buy wine unless their suspicions have been allayed by the guarantee that the wine has been bottled at source (on the propriété).

To remain a merchant in the classic model requires stocking a very good range of wines at very competitive prices. A good négociant indubitably has the resources and the skill required for the blending of generic wines such as Bordeaux Rouge, but dur to the rise of the the supermarkets' discount priced own-labels, the négociant margins are being squeezed too tight for many to survive. Therefore, they tend to concentrate on the top end of the market in the Crus classes, which still remain buoyant. Understandably, the abundance of quality wine at rather low prices has had a corresponding effect on sales of vin-de-table, which is now an even less desirable product.

In the case of vin-de-table, the traditional distribution procedure involved what was known as a negociant expéditeur, someone who would often sell without even storing the product. This function is similar to that of the export broker, and many négociants have now evolved into essentially merchant-brokers.

The bottling stage would be where the wine was blended, stabilized and packaged and where it assumed the identity (including any name-branding) by which the consumer was ultimately to recognize it. Until the 1960s, retailers were specialist wine shops and groceries, restaurants, hotels and cafes. The overall tendency was toward specialization at every step along the way from producer to consumer and was dictated by several factors. The various processes, such as stabilization, blending and aging of an essentially quite delicate product, require much expertise. Even transportation presents challenges. Over and above these considerations and the strict administrative and fiscal regulations to which the wine trade is subject meant that all parties had to know what they were doing, so as to cope with the red tape and to avoid the penalties of the law.

From the 1960s onward, however, the market changed dramatically, due to general social trends as well as those more specifically to do with the wine trade. There have been changes in packaging, marketing, consumer preferences, distribution and retailing.

Packaging

Packaging and its design began to play an increasingly important role, both in terms of product differentiation and also in terms of a concept, which had previously been unrealizable cost cutting. Economies of distribution had not been a possibility, while the wine-distribution chain remained a mercantile structure. However, the newer approach to distribution was more industrial by nature and hence, allowed greater scope for money-saving technologies and economies of scale.

From the early 1960s onward, the sale of wine on draught became much less common. This was due largely to new legislation that freed the removal of wine from bond and thus made it simpler for companies to do their own bottling, should they so wish. This gave more power to the distributors and retailers in the consumer region where the wine was to be sold (Figure 6:3).

In this distribution model, bulk transport of wine was now not only simpler administratively, but was becoming simpler in practical terms. Previously, barrels were used, but now the insulated container (the Safrap) and the tanker had achieved an almost total monopoly on long-distance hauling of bulk wine by water, rail and road.

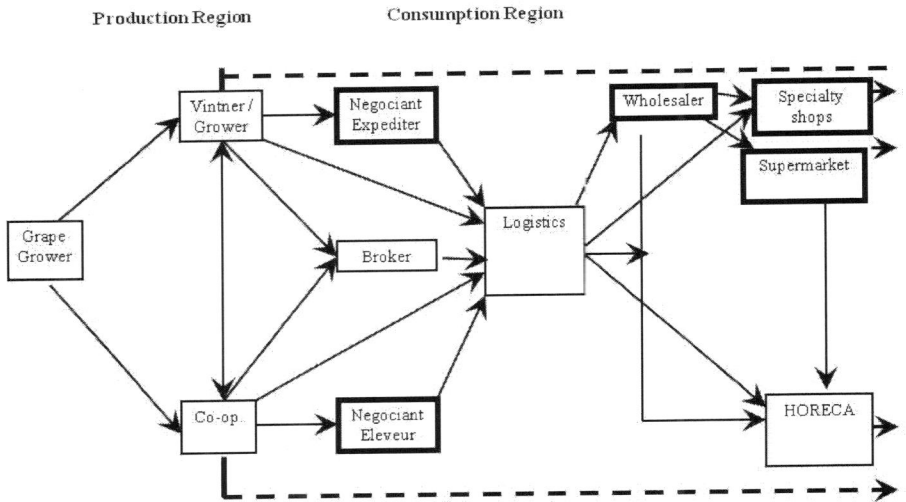

Figure 6:3 Negotiating Power Moves to the Wholesalers and the Supermarkets 1960-70

Formerly, within France itself, transport costs for French wine had been very high, not only because the wine was already encased in a great deal of heavy glass, but also because the concept of the "verre consigné" (return-deposit bottle) meant that the return trip for the packaging had also to be paid for. The new ascendancy of the bottler-distributor operating at the place of sale was challenged in the seventies by the advent of the plastic bottle. This idea flourished briefly, until consumers either got tired of the novelty and of the adverse effect such packaging had on the flavor of the wine and/or the consumers simply started to trade-up to premium product. Next came non-returnable, lighter glass and bag-in-box packs, which enabled the merchant at source to regain some share in the added value chain. Simultaneously, improvements in palletization techniques reduced handling and breakage costs, which benefited those AOC producers wishing to bottle their own wine at source.

The mid 1980s saw the arrival of the "tetrapak," a foiled-cardboard carton. This has the enormous advantages of being virtually unbreakable, as light as plastic, but without affecting flavor, and of being an eminently rational "brick" shape, which means that no space is wasted in transit or storage. Wine was establishing itself as a commodity as convenient and readily-available as the fast foods and TV dinners, which were luring people out of the cafes and restaurants where previously much wine had traditionally been consumed. Some would maintain that the wine box was a major element in the demystification of wine and that it opened up the market to people for whom a corkscrew was an unknown and esoteric instrument. However, statistics seem to suggest that the box failed to attract many new wine-drinkers, mainly because the required initial outlay was so high (higher indeed than the equivalent quantity of wine in conventional packaging).

The wine-box no doubt contributed to increased consumption of wine in the UK and elsewhere, but more on the part of regular wine drinkers who were beguiled by the hype about how convenient and economical wine-boxes were. The rather inflated claims as to how long wine would keep in a box were, in the case of most wine-drinkers, something of an academic point, particularly as the drinker was freed from the restraining factor of seeing the level going down.

Bag-in-box wine presently accounts for about 9% of the UK's still wine retail market. It is estimated to increase further, benefiting from the trend of greater wine drinking at home. Wine boxes have been available in the UK for over 20 years. Initially, the contents were arguably of indifferent quality, but standards have improved, as has packaging technology, so that wine really is kept fresher for longer. The UK consumer has embraced the sheer practicality of being able to pour a single glass, while retaining product consistency, at a price very close to the bottled equivalent.

Changes in Retail Distribution

The new techniques, regulations and forms of packaging have given rise to diversification in the retailing of wine. The proprietors of the old draught wine shops, freed from the traditional administrative demands, found themselves able to branch out into small grocery businesses and to give shelf-space to as many bottles of wine as customers demanded.

Other specialized wine shops have been gradually disappearing in face of increased competition from chain stores, co-ops, supermarkets and hyper-markets that now offer wine as simply one of a broad range of products (as illustrated in Figure 6:4).

By 1980, sales had increased at the big stores in France and accounted for 45% of sales for home consumption (around 15 million hl of which one-half were "own brand" lines developed by individual chains and stores). In 2011, supermarket/hypermarket wine sales in France constituted two-thirds of household wine purchases (less than a quarter of sales were specialists and discounters combined).

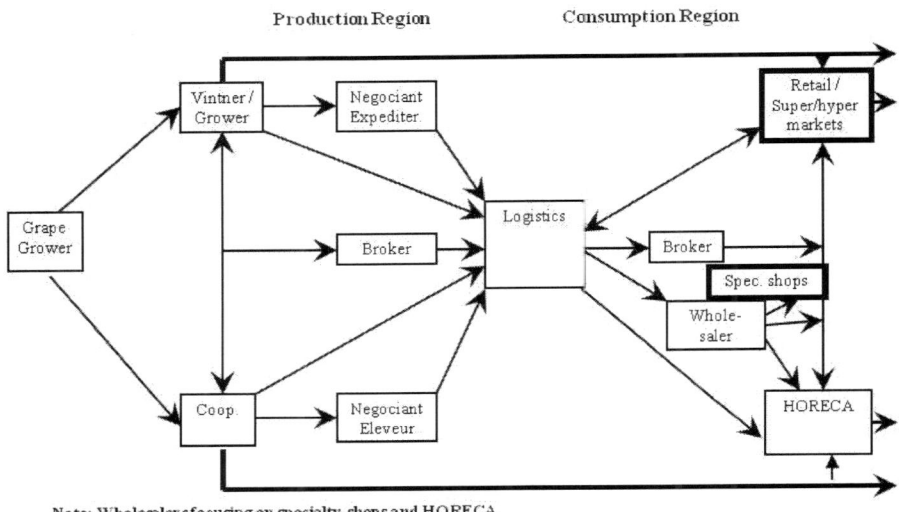

Note: Wholesalers focusing on specialty-shops and HORECA

Figure 6:4 Super & Hypermarkets Integrate Backward

Modern Retail Distribution of Wine in France

By 2005, supermarkets/hypermarkets had substantially increased their share of off-trade global volume sales in all regions, as consumers' 21st century "accelerated lifestyles" encouraged them to prioritize convenience in their shopping patterns. In the period of 2006 through 2011, the distribution pattern appears to have stabilized and reached a plateau, as illustrated in Table 6:1. Interestingly, the global phenomenon of Internet retailing of wine has increased but remains a very small percent of sales.

Wholesalers and importers make up France's wine distribution system. Wholesalers frequently sell to specialized wine stores, food stores, restaurants and institutions. Importers sell to supermarkets. Mail order sales are generally made directly by the producer.

Percentage off-trade	2006	2007	2008	2009	2010	2011
Store-Based Retailing	96.3	96.1	96.0	95.9	95.8	95.7
Grocery Retailers	94.9	94.6	94.6	94.4	94.3	94.2
Discounters	9.3	9.3	9.5	9.7	9.6	9.5
Food/drink/tobacco specialists	19.3	19.1	19.4	19.6	19.4	19.3
Hypermarkets	17.3	17.9	18.1	18.5	18.7	19.0
Small Grocery Retailers	17.6	17.5	17.0	16.2	16.2	15.9
Convenience Stores	2.2	2.3	2.3	2.4	2.4	2.4
Forecourt Retailers	1.0	1.0	1.0	1.0	0.9	0.8
Independent Small Grocers	14.4	14.2	13.7	12.8	13.0	12.7
Supermarkets	27.8	27.6	27.8	27.9	28.1	28.4
Other Grocery Retailers	3.6	3.3	2.9	2.5	2.3	2.2
Non-Grocery Retailers	1.5	1.5	1.5	1.5	1.5	1.5
Non-Store Retailing	3.7	3.9	4.0	4.1	4.2	4.3
Direct Selling	1.2	1.2	1.3	1.3	1.2	1.2
Homeshopping	1.1	1.0	1.0	1.0	0.9	0.9
Internet Retailing	1.4	1.6	1.7	1.8	2.0	2.2
Vending	0.0	0.0	0.0	0.0	0.0	0.0
Total	100.0	100.0	100.0	100.0	100.0	100.0

Table 6:1 Global Wine - Percent Breakdown of Global Wine Off-Trade Sales by Distribution Channel
Source: Euromonitor, 2012.

Table 6:2 shows the breakdown of total wine sales by distribution channel. It illustrates just how far the large-scale stores have increased their domination in the retail market. This advance has been primarily at the expense of small retail specialists in wine. The supermarkets and hypermarkets account for over two-thirds of all wine sales. These outlets benefit from being integrated into large buying groups that can exploit significant economies of scale. Specialist retailers are increasingly operating in a niche market. Specialists accounted for only about 9% of volume sales.

People who buy wine from specialist retailers are doing so mainly for special occasions, as gifts or when they believe that they need expert advice. Discounters, by their very nature, appeal largely to the price-conscious customers. Therefore, discounters' volume of sales is higher, but their share in terms of net revenues is not as great.

The mail order channel for high quality wines was established in the early 1980s, aimed at a small group of wealthy consumers, and its market share remains quite marginal.

Distribution Channel	Percentage
Supermarkets/Hypermarkets	66.4
Discounter Stores	15.5
Specialist Stores	8.8
Direct Sales	6.6
Independent food stores/grocery retailers	1.8
Convenience and variety stores	0.9

Table 6:2 Breakdown of Wine Sales by Distribution Channel-France (% Volume).
Source: Euro stats.

The Development of Direct Sales by Producers
It is now the powerful large-volume retail businesses who are determining the packaging, prices, delivery dates and payment schedules. This development of direct sales to retailers and end-users by producers has had profound implications on the supply side. The changes have been made possible partly through the development of smaller stainless steel tanks and techniques, such as the use of inert gases to prevent air getting to the surface of the wine while it is in storage, thus greatly reducing danger of oxidation. This last technique has freed the producer from the need to get his wine into bottles at the earliest opportunity. Because the producer can afford the delay, he is no longer under pressure to accept the offer of the first merchant who bids, but can wait until a more advantageous offer is presented.

Decrease in HORECA Distribution (hotels, restaurants, cafés)
Besides the much-reduced role of the specialist wine shop, the past two decades have witnessed a marked decrease in the role of Hotels, Restaurants and Cafes in the distribution chain for Europe as a whole. In France, this explains the general trend towards lower consumption of wine, and partly because of the tendency to eat-out less frequently than in former times. Particularly among the young consumers, the popularity of fast-food outlets, where wine is not often served, has contributed to the decreased consumption of wine.

Distribution in the United Kingdom
There are several factors that distinguish the British market and distribution system. The UK for all practical purposes is a non-producer, and the vast majority of wine consumed in the country is imported. Consumer-sophistication has risen swiftly in the relatively short time. The buoyant sales have coin-

cided with the retail revolution towards one-stop shopping in supermarkets and hypermarkets.

Table 6:3 shows the UK wine imports by the relative ranking of country origins. The import of quality French wine was increasing its market share. Indeed, this quality bias continued in all price segments above the bottle price of £4.75. French wines exports in 2012 showed a steady growth in volume with 15 million hl (showing an increase of 5% from 2011). Even higher figures were recorded in terms of value with 7.83 billion Euros, up 9% over 2011.

-   Champagne: 7% in volume and 29% in value
-   Sparkling: 4% in volume and 3% in value
-   AOP: 38% in volume and 50% in value
-   IGP Wines: 25% in volume and 10% in value
-   Vins de France: 18% in volume and 4% in value

Compared to the average figures over the past five years, the overall exports in 2012 had increased by 8% in volume and by 20% in value.

Ranking by Country
France
Australia
USA
Italy
Germany
S. Africa
Spain
Portugal

Table 6:3 UK Wine Imports ranked by Origin
Source: USDA Foreign Agricultural Service.

There are two types of retailer licenses: the so-called "On" and "Off." An On-License authorizes an outlet to sell alcoholic beverages for consumption on the premises, whereas an Off-License authorizes an outlet to sell alcoholic beverages for consumption away from the premises. Off-trade sales constitute a major proportion of wine sales today. Sales of standard wines heavily dominate the off-trade, which accounts for around 70% of total wine sales by volume.

Changes in the British Market over the Past Three Decades

Wine exported to the UK used to be brought into the country by London agency houses that sold to wholesale merchants, who would then act as distributors to specialist stores and the cosmopolitan restaurants. Understandably, in essentially a country that did not produce wine, the product was in earlier decades not an everyday commodity.

Later, the small wholesaler, who had previously been able to buy a few hogsheads of claret and bottle them by hand with his own name-label, began to be squeezed out of the markets. The revolution in transportation was primarily responsible. The Safrap container and the road tanker contained more than small wholesalers could accommodate. The small wholesaler was therefore forced into shipping bottles with the extra expense incurred due to the weight of glass. The forty-foot container (capable of carrying 1,200 cases) became the economic unit below which business was uneconomical. The brewers in the 1960s were making strenuous efforts to expand further into the wine and spirits markets and takeover the wholesalers who had previously acted as agents for the supply of their off-license outlets.

In the cities, the brewers knew that people were drinking more wine, so they proceeded to try and corner the market in the same manner they had managed to flood the beer market: with an anonymous, bland, but stable product. Their chief weapon in this field was branding. To the unsophisticated customer, branding made wine more accessible and enabled the customer to know what they were purchasing. Advertising costs increased for the breweries, but proved a worthwhile investment.

Meanwhile, the small independent merchant, who was still endeavoring to supply wines with some cachet, was being further squeezed by Britain's joining the EU. This meant that the appellation contrôlée system and laws were now accepted, and the trade of spurious wines was killed off. The effect was to increase the tendency towards bottling at source and the abolition of resale-price maintenance. The joining of the UK with the EU opened the opportunity for supermarkets to become the major force. As in all cases, where trade between countries is open and the rules uniform, the advantage goes to the largest business operations.

People wanted quality and individuality in what they bought, ate and drank, and that now included wine in the UK. Supermarket chains were quick to respond to demand. For example, it was Sainsbury's who set the pace, when they launched a massive discount campaign in 1978 that led to a major surge in the quantity of demand. Within two years, Sainsbury's increased their own-label by 37 wines. Since then, the supermarkets have continued to market their wines with phenomenal success and now sell several million bottles per week. Sainsbury's operates not only as a buyer, but also as product manager, exercising design input, if not actually from the vine, then at least from the bottling stage. They pride themselves on an extremely flexible purchasing strategy, being able to cope with huge shipments of generic wines, such as German Liebfraumilch, as well as small-scale shipments for the prestige end of their spectrum.

Sainsbury's continues to operate its online website sales of wine with success. Indeed, the technology has progress in the highly competitive supermarket virtual environment to include apps for your mobile phone. The supermarket sector today accounts for over two-thirds of total UK wine sales, and the off license chains have had drastic face-lifts in order to compete with the price and the convenience offered by the rivals.

The Merchant Vintners Association, companies such as Adams, Tanners, Cullens, Yapps, and Lay & Wheeler located in the provinces, has increased marketing in the London area. Paradoxically, the supermarkets have educated the wine consumer so effectively that she is now more often looking towards the specialist outlet for wine of high character and individual service. However, it is unlikely that the large stores will lose any significant market in competition with the specialist retailer. Nonetheless, some of the small well-run individual businesses will continue to prosper, by providing the personal touch both in terms of their ambience and of the type of wines they sell.

In conclusion, the wine market in the UK, having grown at an average rate of about 6.8% per annum for the past quarter century, remains sufficiently buoyant for it to be the most coveted target for producers both in Europe and the New World. Table 6:4 illustrates the breakdown of proportional cost of a single bottle of wine to the British consumer.

Expenses	% of Cost
Duty	21
Retailer's profit	21
VAT	13
Storage and Interest	13
Producer's Profit	11
Cultivation/Harvesting	9
Bottling	7
Shipping/distribution	5

Table 6:4 Analysis of the Cost of Wine
Source: Based on independent data.

Italy

In 2011, Italy was ranked as the largest wine producer in the world in terms of volume in millions of hectoliters, due to its 2010/2011 harvests, squeaking past France. In 2013, Italy remains the world's largest wine exporter in volume.

As has already been noted, the Italian wine industry is extremely fragmented with a half-million individual producers, making the average holding of only 1.3 hectares. On-trade sales, which includes wine sales made at outlets, where consumption of alcohol is allowed on the premises, increased over the last few years, in both volume and value terms (approximately two-thirds of consumption). In the off-trade sales, almost half of wine sales still go direct from producer to consumer. Two main types of direct sales can be identified: door-to-door in Italy and direct-from-source. Door-to-door sales of wine are actually increasing, whereas purchases direct-from-source recorded sharp decline in sales. Most bulk wine is sold direct-from-source, resulting in the overall decline in direct sales.

There are approximately 400,000 grocery outlets and retail food shops in Italy, most of whom will sell wine of one type or another. Almost all major retail chains have a separate area specially designed for imported products, such as Californian Cabernet, Argentinean Malbec, South African Pinotage and Chardonnay from Australia. In this area, price is not the main influence on the purchase decision, with branding playing a much more important role.

The popularity of wine bars, especially among young people continues to increase, driving growth in on-trade sales. However, the number of wine bars in Italy remains relatively low, reportedly about 1,200 bars, when compared to the 13,200 pubs and beer houses. These types of establishments account for a significant share of wine consumption, although other alcoholic drinks take precedence in these pub and beer establishments. All together, the 106,000 bars, cafés, pubs, beer houses and wine bars account for about 25% of on-trade consumption of wine. The Italians mostly drink wine during meals, and therefore the nearly 25,000 pizzerias and 47,000 restaurants and trattorias take the lion's share of on-trade consumption, which amounts to two-thirds of the total.

Table 6:5 shows the relative breakdown of on-trade volume sales, in terms of percentages and by distribution format.

Outlet	% of volume sales
Standard restaurants	26
Bar, pubs, beer-houses, wine bars	25
Hotels	21
Pizzerias	11
Trattorias	10
Fine Dining Restaurants	7

Table 6:5 Breakdown of On-trade Volume Sales by Distribution Format (% Volume)
Source: Euro Stats.

Packaging in Italy

While the 75cl glass bottle (750 ml capacity) is still by far the single most dominant packaging medium in Italy, a relatively high percentage of wine is sold in "bulk" form (i.e. in demi-johns, casks and unlabeled bottles of 1.5 and 2 liters). Still wine sales are evenly split between packaged and unpackaged (or bulk packaged) formats. Much of bulk packaged still wine is used in the lower price bracket of the HORECA sector, although some is purchased in this way for domestic use in homes where wine is regularly taken with meals. However, as elsewhere in Europe, there has been a marked shift from the consumption of less quantity of wine and towards an increase in consumption of higher quality wine. Of the 45% of total of wine sold in glass bottles, half is now bought in the 75 cl size.

Of new forms of packaging, the Tetrapak "brik" is the most significant. Caviro is the major producer of wine in this form of packaging, Wine in brik was first launched at the beginning of the 1980s, creating a new format and changing the competitive environment. Today its two major products, Tavernello and Castellino, are by far the most well-known brands on the market and boast a 64% volume share of the table wine segment. One of Caviro's main competitors is the Venetian producer Cielo, whose products include Terre di Ghiaia, a wine packaged in tetra-brik with an IGT denomination. Other rivals include San Matteo and Gruppo Coltiva (brands such as Bricco, Beldì and Osteria del Gallo). In 2010, the company that owns Tavernello and Castellino, Caviro, experienced a change in their segment of the competitive market. The change was a merger of Coltiva, GIV and Cantine Riunite brands. The merged brands have a total market share similar to that of Caviro.

Sparkling wines are chiefly purchased for special occasions, which Italians are prone to celebrating publicly in bars and restaurants. Consequently, the HORECA sector handles around 40% of sales of sparkling wines and champagnes. Unlike table wines, it is not possible to buy these wines direct from the producer, so the remaining 60% is accounted for by off-trade with about one third of these sales by super-markets.

Germany

The German wine market divides fairly evenly between imports and home-produced wine. German red wine is quite rare, and some Germans would maintain that red is rarely palatable. Most red wine consumed in Germany has to be imported and comes mainly from Italy, France and Spain. White table wine and wine for the production of sekt comprise about one fifth and one sixth respectively of total imports. White quality wine and table wine account for about 8% and 25% of the total wine imports respectively.

As has been noted in an earlier chapter of this book, wine production in West Germany is conducted by a large number of small producers, some of whom are part-time and many of whom bottle their own produce. There are as many as 67,000 vineyards. Consequently, much the same as Italy, a significant proportion of German wine goes directly from the producer to the consumer. Of the domestic wine production, close to 40% is sold directly by the producer or producer cooperative to the consumer. There is a traditional fondness among German wine-drinkers to have their "own vineyard" that they visit once a year. It is perhaps a matter of German pride and mark of status — "your own vineyard."

The area of retailing that is being squeezed, as elsewhere, is the specialist wine retailer; although they do still maintain a presence (less than 5%, mainly in the quality wine sector). Imported wines are increasingly marketed through low-priced food discount chains. Discounters, of which the best known is Aldi, are similar to supermarkets in terms of size, but make it their policy to compete primarily on the basis of price. Vintners and cooperatives sell their wines at about 20% below the prices in specialized stores.

Packaging in Germany

About 94% of German wines are in glass bottles, of which about 27% are returnable. Forty-nine percent of all the wine sold is in three-quarter liter bottles, which is the favorite bottling size for Germany. The industry has made a small effort to packaging alternatives and also tested PET (plastic) bottles, but came to the conclusion that PET is not a packaging alternative for wine in Germany. An alternative to the glass bottle is the five liter bag-in-the-box system, which is also frequently used for French wines.

Summary

There have been major changes in distributional logistics over the past three decades. Partly due to newer less expensive transportation methods that allows for much higher volume and cost saving packaging. The lower trade barriers within the EU have contributed to distributional changes within Europe.

Consumer preferences have been changing, due to the global marketing strategies and sophisticated modern advertising campaigns. Overall, geographical distances are of much less importancem since the advances in technologies has resulted in what is commonly referred to as the globalization of business. The consequence is not only a trend toward similarity, but it is a continuing movement toward industry concentration through mergers and acquisitions of smaller firms.

Chapter 7

THE MARKETING OF WINE

Most everything in the world that involves human activity is some form of business; and when money and wine come together, it is no different. One can be forgiven for thinking of wine as a romantic, unchangeable institution, but this is not reality. Wine has always been susceptible to the influences of the market, in the same way as any other commodity. Wine must be produced with consumer taste and fashion in mind. As far back as the late Mediaeval period, when the proprietors of the Champagne region found they could not ripen Pinot Noir sufficiently to produce a wine as red as that of Burgundy, they decided to test market their rosé as the latest fashion. Soon it was the most popular trend at court. Subsequently, in order to compete, the growers of Burgundy were reduced to straining out as much of the red pigment as they could from their beautifully ripe Pinot Noir grapes. Similarly, the innovation in Champagne by Dom Perignon illustrates how wine can be as suitable for development and adaptation to consumer demand as any other product.

The modern marketing of wine used to be regarded, until recently, as being a dangerous step toward the erosion of traditional heritage and standards, particularly by successful small wineries and old established family-run concerns. The old image of wine as a drink designed for a restricted market, such as the nobility, may have led to a certain degree of inflexibility. Australia, in the 1960s is an interesting example. For many decades, Australian wine had been produced predominantly for the UK. In many cases, the wines from Australia, at that time, were not of high quality. Nevertheless, the pattern of restricted demand was just as much as it was for the Grand and Premier Cru wines of France. In the 1960s, a change in thinking developed, caused by a number of factors, such as the aspirations of a new generation of oenologists, the change in prejudices regarding wine drinking, and the advent of new packaging, such as the wine box. As a consequence, wine became a high-volume product for sale to the mass market.

In other key markets, there was a consumers' movement that regarded wine as a beverage, creating an increased demand for mid and low quality wines. Since then, many of these previous beverage-wine consumers have now "graduated" and become today's consumers of fine wines. The market was experiencing a profound change. A number of producers and some countries were unprepared for this consumer shift toward higher quality product. There were some notable exceptions, such as Mondovi and Sichel and the Australian growers who kept part of their production capacity devoted to quality varietal wine. However, not enough attention was being paid to consumer trends and forecasts. In the 1990s, it became evident that the wine industry would need to incorporate strategic marketing into the overall agenda.

The 1990 Symposium on Wine and Vine Economy held in Hungary, and the two subsequent Wine Conferences in 2000 held in Australia and England, have served to open the eyes of many in the industry that the old attitude was no longer applicable. The position of consumers had changed. Therefore, the wine industry has had to change its traditional approach. The business strategy of backward-integration is putting wine distributors and marketers in a better position to influence the traditionally production-based industry. The advent of EU single market legislation in 1992 has led to further amalgamations, including joint ventures and acquisitions among distributors and retailers. There arose a need for an integrated policy on wine, from producer to consumer, based on consumer demand.

The Essence of Wine Marketing

Wine marketing, particularly in terms of fine wines, is more than a quantitative process of matching supply and demand: it is the art of matching the resources of an organization to the customer's actual qualitative needs and wants. This can only be achieved by providing satisfaction to the clients. However, in the increasingly competitive global market, it is no longer sufficient to rely on the historical factors of production technology and product quality. In order to ensure that appropriate products reach the desired consumers, a considerable amount of commercial acumen is now required. Retailers are now much more knowledgeable about shelf space margins, and the product life cycles of a slow-moving lines or brands.

The modern marketing mix is a complex of factors that have to be present in the right proportions and harmony in order to attain success. The required factors include such a proper understanding of consumer behavior, the development and maintenance of distribution and pricing strategies that will enable the company to grow and remain competitive in the marketplace.

There has been a dearth of documented information about marketing in the wine industry. Most of this material has stressed production and sales, with very little focus on market research based on consumer behavior. However this has been changing. During the past two decades, information has been more forthcoming.

Understanding consumer demand in the creation of marketing strategy, it is appropriate to look in more detail at the factors which contribute to the consumer's purchase decision.

The Consumer

A key aspect to effective wine marketing is identifying the difficulty that potential consumers may encounter when purchasing wine in the retail sector, which has been exacerbated by the rise in France of the Vins de Pays, the creation of numerous new Appellations Contrôlées, and by some questionable promotions. Complications are also due to the increased effectiveness of New World exports, which have further diluted the attention of the potential purchaser.

Wine consumers can be divided into target markets. At the top is the connoisseur, people who make it their business, or at least their hobby, to know about wine. Such people, informed by wine journals and discussions, will usually know beforehand what they wish to purchase and generally favor the specialty retailer, the auction or to purchase directly from the winery. These wine purchasers will not normally purchase a bottle of wine for a dinner party.

Similarly assured in their purchasing habits are the beverage wine consumers who tend to regard wine as a simple commodity, and know from long experience what they like These purchasers mostly favor the supermarket environment, and often purchase private label products, switching allegiance from their narrow preferences only when a particularly tempting promotional price is offered.

These two categories are often immune to innovative marketing. The real target areas are what have been defined as the "Aspirational Wine Consumer" and the "New Wine Drinker." These are consumers who are target segments in the wine market and offer growth opportunities to the industry. It is the Aspirational Wine Consumer who is the most anxious to make the correct purchase, and therefore the most susceptible to good marketing strategies. The intentions and objective of this sector also mean that the prices paid by this group tend to be in the middle to higher ranges.

For the consumer who is not absolutely sure of the characteristics of the wine she is looking for, the act of buying a bottle of wine can be a worrisome event. Even the admission of uncertainty, implicit in spending time looking at wine on a shelf, may be something the consumer is embarrassed about. The relative anonymity of the supermarket has helped to mitigate this factor. Similarly, the atmosphere in a specialty wine shop needs to provide a relaxed, knowledgeable yet tactful approach on the part of staff. This approach has become more commonplace in the wine stores. Aspirational Wine Consumers are people who search for signs to allay their fears of the risks perceived in the act of buying a bottle of wine and for assurances that what they purchase will properly fulfill their needs.

Many consumers buy wine to impress their dinner guests, enhance a social occasion or simply to make a meal more enjoyable. They fear damage to their reputation and lowering of self-esteem, if they purchase a poor or inappropriate wine. These customers require assurance that what they purchase is most appropriate. Frequently beguiled by the higher price-labels, these are the Aspirational Wine Consumers who are anxious to be assured that the price will be reflected in the quality of the product.

The New Wine Drinker is young and unsophisticated and one which seems to be dwindling rapidly in the countries of traditionally high consumption. This segment of the market has in the past been largely influenced by price and novelty.

Consumer Risk Reduction Strategies and How Marketers can Exploit the Perceptions

There are certain deeply held beliefs which affect purchasing patterns, such as the bias towards French wines being considered the most sophisticated, based on the consumer's perspective as either dauntingly complex or as the only possible choice for certain prestige occasions. German wines, on the other hand, are viewed as less complicated, more reliable and versatile; many consumers are comfortable with Riesling or Liebfraumilch.

Branding

Brand loyalty has always played a crucial role in the wine industry. This can take the form either of loyalty to a particular distributor or specific label or as loyalty to a region or even a generic type. It has only been since the legal challenge of using the names of viticultural regions as wine generics that the leverage potential of the regional name has been appreciated. Now, adherence to a regional fine wine denomination, viewed by consumers as quasi-brands, has become an increasingly important factor.

Wine advertising has also become much more important in recent years, because it is a form of brand recognition and "consumer training." However, the growing strength of the anti-alcohol lobbies as well as governmental agencies has meant that an outright ban on the advertising of wine, beer and spirits may be a possibility in some countries. There are some restrictions in Germany and the UK, while the restrictions in Scandinavia and the Netherlands for television and radio advertising are more severe. In the US, television and radio advertising has had a voluntary restraint on advertising of all alcohols, except beer, for over a half century. Only occasionally have the advertisers broken their promises and launched such advertising campaigns. Such campaigns have been brief because they always arouse public clamor for new laws banning all such advertisements. The majority of Americans believe that such advertisements influence the "under aged viewers" to seek alcoholic drinks.

Varietals of wines are another form of quasi-brand, and have become more important in recent years. Varietal loyalty is resistant to advertising and has a paradoxically liberating effect on buying patterns, since this loyalty permits the consumer to enjoy an anxiety-free crossover between brands. The New World producers owe much of their market penetration to the success of varietal wines, but now we see that many European producers are following this example.

Global Trends in Marketing

Manufacturers are now much more aware of the important role played by branding activities in an increasingly competitive global environment. Mass market retailing has brought wines to a wider audience and offered a greater choice at competitive prices. Premium wine producers are also investing in marketing activities aimed at strengthening their position in the market and increasing consumer awareness for their products.

New promotional activities have increased during the past few years, in the EU, North America, Japan, and in emerging markets of Eastern Asia and Central and Eastern Europe. These included qualitative studies; educational programs; customer loyalty discounts; promotions offering souvenir wine glasses, newsletters, and wine tasting parties; the Internet and Social Media. Specialty store outlets, that have been losing market share to supermarkets and hypermarkets, are increasingly engaging in these types of promotional activities. Additionally, some of these stores have begun using social media and online ordering. The online selling of wine is still in infancy; but with changes in rules for national postal services, this channel is expected to see some growth in the years to come. Due to restrictions on certain forms of advertising in many countries, sponsorship is also being used as a promotional tool.

Marketing Trends in Major Wine Markets

One of the consequences of the emergence of brand significance in France has been the rapid growth in media expenditures in that market. SOPEXA, the French marketing organization for the agricultural industry, has been active in regions such as Cotes du Rhône and Bordeaux. Advertising expenditures for wine, excluding that from trade associations, increased over 7% in that past five years. The most popular media remained print advertising, billboards and radio, accounting for 53%, 37%, and 9% respectively. Brands such as Vieux Papes and Blaissac benefited from major billboard campaigns and Malesan from a campaign in print. Wine sales also benefit from events that provide global exposure to a country. For example, French wines prospered when the country hosted the 1998 Football World Cup and champagne sales experienced a strong boost in anticipation of millennium celebrations.

Marketing activities for wine in Germany are mainly through heavy television and print advertising. The popularity of public television in Germany remains high; magazines and radio tie for second place with respect to popularity. New trends have also emerged in the promotion of wines. Tie-in advertising has been employed with wines advertised in conjunction with Knorr Hollandaise Sauce, a special during the asparagus season, which is very popular in Germany. Similarly, Langguth promoted its wines in conjunction with FROSTA frozen dinners. In Germany, in recent years, there has been a marked increase in the advertising of sparkling wines, which have accounted for as much as 62% of total promotional expenditures.

Likewise in Italy, there has been an increase in advertising activities in the wine segment. In the past, brand strategies have been important for Tavernello and Castellino with their box wines, but now there is an increase in promotional spending among bottled wine producers. In the south of Italy, where promotional activities are less restrictive, promotional activities for sparkling wines have increased 15%, with 75% of total advertising expenditures on TV commercials.

In the UK, price promotions have helped drive strong growth in both sparkling wine and Champagne. The most important media for advertising remains with newspapers, magazines and television. Companies also publicize the awards they have won, in an attempt to reaffirm the image of quality for their wines. Sponsorship of events, such as the Wimbledon Tennis Championship and leading television programs, also help in promoting brand images. Nonetheless, in the UK, total advertising expenditure has declined in recent years, of which the leading brand Piat D'Or accounted for almost 10%. Piat D'Or spent approximately 6% to 7% of the retail product price on advertising.

In the US, leading brands have experienced significant sales growth. E. & J. Gallo increased its market share to 27.3% of the wine market and this was largely achieved through a single brand oriented marketing strategy. Consumer awareness had been established through television and print advertising. Constellation brands, an E. & J. Gallo brand, also spent nearly $420 million on marketing and advertising over the past few years.

The Upsurge of Discounters

Discounters, a relatively new channel for wine sales in the global marketplace, capitalize on economies of scale. Discounters offer an alternative to supermarkets, hypermarkets and wholesalers, as they appeal to price-conscious customers. In certain developed markets, for example, France, Germany and the US, discounters are becoming increasingly commonplace. Consumers are moving towards this channel for their wine purchases. In Germany, for example, sales by the discounter channel increased rapidly, and in France, the market share was as high as 15.5%.

On a less fundamental level of allegiances, than those exhibited towards country or region of origin, the wine consumer is influenced by several other factors, which the marketer can also usefully employ in efforts to attract more customers. These include recommendation through publicity by journalists, specialty packaging and labeling.

The "Recommendation"

Informal recommendations are an important factor in many wine purchasing decisions. People feel more secure if they have the word of a trusted friend that a certain wine is worth drinking. Such informal publicity is, of course, beyond the scope of any marketing strategy. However, if such recommendation can be formalized and put into the mouths of wine journalists and the staff of the specialized retailers (both groups whose opinions are studied and sought after by connoisseurs and Aspirational Wine Consumers alike), the quality of a product no longer guarantees its salability. Assuming that the product is of good quality, skilled and personable marketers are able to develop influential relationships with journalists and retailers in order to ensure that they present a positive image of the products.

Packaging

Packaging is another factor that influences the potential purchaser. In wine marketing, packaging and labels assume undeniable significance. Packaging is a most important method of product differentiation in the wine industry. It forms an integral part of any wine's promotion and consumption. Wine packaging includes the front label, back label, bottle and bottle shape, and cask.

Manufacturers have been working to tailor the images of their products to appear youthful and trendy. Custom designed bottles and improvements in label printing and new technology have led to the introduction of packaging innovations designed to increase "on-shelf presence." In the US, innovations include shrink-labels, flex-graphic printing, new fonts and ink colors, stamped corks, flange tops and distinctive shapes.

Although the marketer is able to experiment with bottle shapes, variations of which are accepted and appreciated by a large number of consumers, the major tools for establishing shelf differentiation are labels and enhancements to the conventional glass bottle. Dressing, such as the Hessian wrapping, which did much to establish the Spanish wine Rioja in the UK market, or the heavy wax seals and lengths of ribbon on a number of product lines, can serve to enhance the image of a wine in the eyes of many consumers, particularly if these external extras form part of the recognized trade-mark of a respected brand or company.

Packaging by Format: Global Trends

Glass consolidated its position as the dominant packaging format in the global wine market over the period 1998 to 2003, capturing more than 70% of the market. And it continues to be the preferred container in the second decade of the 21st century. The popularity of glass is founded on its traditional association with high quality products that spurred the increase in global market share. This format benefited from a widespread trend towards upgrading to better quality, higher value products. Consequently, the 75cl glass bottles most often linked with high quality wine exerted an increasingly strong hold over global sales.

Cartons are the second most important form of packaging in global volume terms. They offer consumers excellent value, easy portability and storage, and the advantage of being able to reseal the product once it has been opened. As a result, they are particularly popular for regular purchases such as table wine. The format also appeared to gradually increase association with higher quality wine, due to the expanding variety of New World brands helping to improve the perceived quality of carton wines. However, the carton packaging share of global market was seriously eroded with the increasing success of bag-in-the-box wine.

One of the major developments in wine packaging in recent years has been the success of the bag-in-box format. Sales of bag-in-box products have increased and account for nearly 6% of the global wine market. The format offers producers and consumers easier transportation. Also, due to a tap mechanism, bag-in-box wine can be stored longer than bottled products once it is opened, allowing consumers to drink it in small amounts over a long period of time without the product losing its quality.

Other packaging formats declined, while plastic remained flat. Both formats were unable to generate sales in the fast growing premium segment of the wine market, because of the association with inferior quality wine.

Packaging by Format: Regional Trends

Glass proved an increasingly significant packaging format in every regional market, except Latin America, Africa and the Middle East. In some markets, such as France, glass is perceived as a hygienic material. The fact that it is transparent lends it a further advantage. Increasing consumer sophistication led to rising sales of glass bottles that are widely associated with higher quality wine. The most popular size remains the 75 cl bottle. Cartons accounted for an increase in the share of Eastern European volume sales. Cartons are not a significant packaging presence in Western Europe, with the exception of the Italian market where the carton became associated with quality almost by default, as consumers increasingly favored this format for bulk wine products.

Bag-in-box wine is increasingly significant in Western Europe, spurred by its growing popularity in certain Scandinavian markets. The format also showed growth in more traditional markets, such as France, where it is most often used for everyday consumption, and consequently, it is the package of choice for mostly table and country wine. However, the greater size and maturity of such markets, and their long-standing traditions, mean that novel formats are less capable of making a significant impact on market share. Growth of bag-in-box products in other regional markets, such as Eastern Europe, Latin America and Africa, has been constrained, as such boxes are representative of inexpensive hypermarket products. The market share of these containers ranges from low single digit percentage in Denmark to a high of over 50% in Sweden.

In some regions, a decline in volume share suffered by glass was driven by the expansion of the region's consumer base to include lower income consumers. For example, plastic became a significant format in South Africa and Latin America, due to the sheer size of the lower income groups. However, elsewhere the image of low quality associated with plastic proved detrimental to sales.

Traditional Corks vs. Emerging Formats
Traditional corks remain the dominant form of closure for glass bottles in the global wine market, accounting for around 87% of bottles sold. Of the remaining, approximately 7% of bottles are sold with plastic stoppers and 6% with screw-caps. Many manufacturers and retailers are keen to promote the advantages of using non-cork formats, arguing that cork carries the risk of oxidation and flavor tainting. Use of the "non-cork cork" is expected to increase.

Nevertheless, consumers strongly associate traditional cork closures with high quality products, and screw-caps, with definitely inexpensive and inferior wine. For this reason, in global terms, screw-caps, which taste-tests reveal to be of equal merit to corks in maintaining freshness and flavor in wine, are used only in an insignificant minority of budget wines.

The US and the UK do not have a relatively long-established custom of wine consumption, and these countries have seen wine sales grow in recent years. As a result, the amount of cheap wines sold in the UK is an important factor in the popularity of synthetic closures. Also, it is notable that significant and prestigious brands have proven increasingly willing to employ non-cork formats.

Labeling

It is the label, however, which is most important as a product feature in marketing, not only as a method of product differentiation but as an important element in communication between marketer and customer. Label appeal has to be carefully gauged to fit the taste of the segment being targeted, taking into account a broad range of subliminal effects such as coloring, cognateness and graphics, which influence the potential customer even before the customer is close enough to read what the label actually has written on it. These range from the mild colors of reassuring pastels and pictorial landscapes on the Sainsbury's private brand, through the alluringly minimalist bikini-style strip on certain Italian wines, and to the dourly formal labels common for Bordeaux (with the obligatory picture of the Chateau (either real or invented)). All of these designs, to be effective, need to fulfill a specific image impression aimed at the targeted customer market. For example, modern innovative and distinctive labels are more attractive to the younger target market, in contrast to the older market that prefers more traditional styles of packaging. Innovations include 360 degree shrink-labels and very distinctive shapes of labels, such as Sebastiani's triangular label for Vendange. The tendency towardstoo high a degree of modernism in labeling usually backfires on the marketer. The majority of consumers still want to be reassured that the product they are buying has its roots firmly fixed in reliable tradition.

The importance of labeling cannot be overstressed. It is the first step in the seduction of the potential customer and it is considered worthy of a major investment by wine marketers. Professional designers are now the real stars of the packaging realm, and companies such as the specialist label-designers Dom Tecma, in France, commands very high fees that sales statistics prove are merited. A few years ago, for example, the Pradel Company decided to modernize their renowned range of wines from the Côtes de Provence. They enlisted the services of a local graphic artist and the results were disastrous. The label produced, with its inappropriate mauve background, had heavy connotations of Beaujolais Nouveau and immediately served to reduce sales of the product by an astounding 25%. Conversely, Dom Tecma's Managing Director, D Charbonnel, has suggested that successful modernization of a product can increase sales by 30%.

At the same time, many consumers of quality wine regard labels as one of their most important sources of information, for specific products they are considering and as part of their wine education. The use of back labels is increasingly popular. Once the customer's attention has been attracted by the front label and they are satisfied that a particular bottle may meet their needs, a large percentage of label-readers will then turn the bottle around to glean more detailed information, as to the wine's nature and history of origin. The importance and influence of wines receiving awards, is also important

Branding and Supply Chain Management in France

One of the leading distributors of Vin de Pays in France is a company by the name of Chantovent, established in 1953. Bernard Queyssalier, a managing director, is one of the leading proponents of the doctrine of the consolidated approach to wine marketing, seeing the need for the establishment of an integrated chain from vineyard to consumer to ensure quality at source and a proper strategy of brand marketing up to the point of sale. Queyssalier had certain, very clear objectives and put these into practice with notable success. By establishing strategic alliances with growers and monitoring global consumer trends, the company was able to better match producer supply to consumer demand. Through the company's relationship with an investment finance syndicate in Minervois, the company was able to bring about improvements in the types of varietals grown and machinery used by the producers that were a part of the supply chain.

With the launch of Vins de Pays in France, there was, on the part of many marketers, a rush towards price cutting. Queyssalier, however, through careful reading of the trends (particularly the trend away from beverage wine-drinking), realized that consumers were prepared to pay for premium wine in order to ensure that they would obtain a quality product. Chantovent's La Payse brand, launched in 1970, was the first experiment in the supply chain management concept.

Queyssalier recognized the need for a merchandising strategy and also saw the advantages of reducing much of the anarchistic complications that had resulted from the creation of many new categories and appellations. Without proposing a reduction in product lines offered, Queyssalier saw the need to simplify the process for the consumer. These wines, of which Chantovent's Vin Des Cathares was the prototype, were produced from a blend of varietals that ensured a good aroma and an emphasis on fruity flavors that were popular at with consumers. These wines were marketed and packaged in a way that was both reassuring and approachable for the consumer. Some critics maintain that the creation of branded blends, reminiscent of AOC wines, has contributed to consumer confusion about grades of wine and to the diminution of demand. However, the converse argument is that, by ensuring quality at all levels, a certain stability was be reintroduced into the premium segment.

Branding in Western Europe and the United States

The wine industry is extremely fragmented and brands have mushroomed globally. Brands serve to combine different products, often from a particular region, under a single label. Retailers and producers have increasingly recognized the strategic importance of private label brands. Major supermarket chains frequently use private labels in order to build brand loyalty. In the UK, for example, 50% of retail wine sales are estimated to be private label products. Retailers have concentrated on developing the low to medium priced wine segment by providing a wider range of affordable products.

Unlike other countries, most private label brands in France use fantasy brands in order to overcome consumer prejudice regarding the quality of wines. An example of these fantasy brands is Pierre Chanau Auchan Sélection de la Cave Match, Despite the growing sophistication of consumers, the market share for table wine is larger than for quality wine. Therefore, the opportunity exists to cater to consumer perceptions through labeling.

In a market such as Italy, it is difficult for a wine producer to impose a single brand name for all of the products in a product line. This has resulted in the launch of new products under brands indicative or representative of the region of origin for the wine. For example, in 2002, Zonin launched the new product line Terre Mediterranée, which consisted of several wines from the Mediterranean area, including different brand names such as Negroamaro, Nero d'Avola, Primitivo and Aglianico.

In the UK, branded wines have continued to be an important segment of growth. The top 10 branded still wines grew by an impressive 21% in market share, compared to 6% for the wine market as a whole. Brands are becoming increasingly dominant, as they have the largest marketing budgets. The Hardy's product line includes a number of different labels, such as Stamp and Nottage Hill, and these experienced significant growth in recent years. In the retail segment, the buying power of grocers such as Tesco and Sainsbury's has enabled them to source quality wine from the producers and sell the wine at otherwise lower prices under their own private labels.

The wine industry in the US is also highly fragmented. Ten years ago, there were more than 750 wineries in California with a large number of products. Many of the small wineries had only a small market share. As evidence of growing consolidation in the wine market, the top 10 wineries in the US sold nearly 76% of the wines. The remaining 700 plus wineries accounted for approximately 24% collectively. Large-scale wineries, such as Gallo, have established dominance through the application of brand strategies. The US wine industry is much more brand-orientated than the wine industries of most other countries.

Reassurance and Guarantees

The method employed to reassure customers and to attract first-time buyers with the objective of winning their loyalty is the use of the "signature:" the name of the merchant offering a particular product line. This serves as an effective umbrella guarantee. Branding is becoming increasingly prevalent in regions such as Bordeaux and Côtes du Rhône. While Burgundy remains more popular with traditionalists, this has not stopped other companies from encroaching and establishing their own brands, such as Piat de Beaujolais from Piat. Another major success has been achieved by the SVF (Société des Vins de France) with their Classique line, which offers a wide range of wines from all over France guaranteed by the highly recognizable brand banner at the top of the label.

The Internationals

Very few wine brands have national market shares in excess of 3%, whereas the spirits market is characterized by market shares of between 15% and 80% for brand leaders.

There are three primary obstacles to competition for the Internationals in the prime target wine markets such as the US, Canada and the UK. First, wine retailers will always have easy access at highly competitive prices to basic products. In the past, there was resistance among them to accept the brand concept with price premiums over similar quality designation wines. The size of the market is changing this perspective, as supply chain management and economies of scale provide a competitive advantage for the larger companies. Second, there exists extreme difficulty in creating communications systems influential enough to alter the acquired habits of consumers in these markets. Thirdly, the key to market penetration is product differentiation, but legislation has made it very difficult to market innovative products. Consequently, the strategy of the Internationals has largely been to simply operate as distributors and, in some cases, as producers rather than marketing directly to consumers.

In the UK, all major independent retail chains were acquired by major publicly owned companies. This concentration of distribution is occurring globally, with the exception of countries where alcohol distribution is controlled by Government agencies. This control has been a contention since the establishment of the EU single market.

Private Label Marketing Based on the UK Model

After branded wine had succeeded in breaking down resistance to wine as a beverage in the UK, the supermarkets managed to further popularize wine and, at the same time, preserve the alluring hint of mystique through product differentiation. British supermarkets, such as Waitrose, offer clientele premium wine exclusively, in their supermarket chains. Sainsbury's positions wine on shelves to one side of the exit with minimal through traffic, where customers can browse at their leisure. Clear, concise labeling has been used by Sainsbury's to good advantage, exploiting the traditionally romantic image of wine by using appealing artwork of rustic scenes printed on parchment style paper.

Price is one of the factors which initially enabled the supermarkets to establish themselves so securely in the wine market. Their ability to undercut the competition is still a competitive advantage. Moreover, promotional offers are a regular feature in most supermarkets employed both as publicity with outside billboards and store-window posters. But point-of-purchase displays are also used in the store itself, usually positioned at the entrance to the wine section as a means of attracting new customers.

Having done much to educate the public about wine has resulted in a marked increase in consumption in the UK, but the supermarkets may now be finding that a segment of consumers is drifting away. For example, there is no longer any social stigma in serving own-label wines at a dinner-party. The Aspirational Consumer may not wish to accept that she is simply one of the masses and may decide to patronize the small independent retailer in search of exclusivity. In response, Sainsbury's decided to offer customers the option to trade up without leaving the premises by means of the introduction of their Vintage Selection range. The labels of these wines have in common a small gold rosette which subtly proclaims their added premium. As a matter of interest, the demand has increased for retail chains, such as Sainsbury's, to offer wines from prestigious producers looking for a retail placement of their Vintage Selection product lines. Table 7.1 shows the cost structure for differently priced wines.

Direct Marketing

Direct marketing emerged as a significant distribution channel since the 1990s. Because consumer lifestyles have changed globally, direct marketing has changed. There are two types of direct marketing: door-to-door and direct from producer. Most bulk wine is sold direct from the supplier. While there is an undeniable trend towards consolidation and globalization of wine distribution and marketing, there is also a breakaway faction of small suppliers who have created niche markets by employing the direct marketing approach through the medium of mail order. Direct marketing is of particular interest to the small winery supplying the connoisseur or Aspirational Consumer. Direct marketing appeals are made to consumers who take an active interest in wine and who may well have visited vineyards, even if not the actual vineyard from whom they purchase. Clearly, when potential customers are taking the trouble to visit a vineyard, this is an ideal opening for a direct marketing strategy. Personal contact between producer and customer is a key factor for marketing and an opportunity to develop the sustainable bond of consumer loyalty.

Cost Structure	Table Wine	Premium Wine
Grape	9-12	13-16
Vinification	16-19	18-23
Bottling	2	1
Labeling	4	2
Marketing	0-1	0-1
Margin	0-10	0-14
Agent	4-8	7-11
Duty	15	7
Transport	10	5
Retail	17-18	20-23
Vat	13	13
Total	£4.99	£10.99

Table 7:1 UK Cost Structure for Differently Priced Wines – Illustration of Value Adding Activities

The direct marketing strategy varies in importance across countries. For example, producer direct sales constitute a major form of distribution in Australia's premier wine-producing regions. Australian wineries are using wine tourism to provide opportunities to build brand loyalty at the winery. In Germany, this accounts for about 18% of sales and it is the third most important distribution outlet for wine. In the UK, direct sales from wineries have also grown. France instituted direct sales through mail order for high quality wines in the early 1980s, but this has been only a marginally successful channel.

Wine is commonly promoted through participation in trade shows and wine fairs. There is also a tendency to introduce leaflets and direct mail pieces which provide information on the origin of particular wines, the grapes, as well as recommendations from wine critics. Wine fairs are an effective promotion tool, since advertising of alcoholic beverages is restricted in some European countries. Wine tasting sessions help increase the popularity of the featured wines. For example, Cantine Cooperative Riunite organized wine tasting events in order to increase the popularity of its Lambrusco products. SOPEXA of France promotes the image of the "French style of living" and

"French cooking" through what are referred to as "French weeks," and also holds wine-waiter contests in foreign restaurants. The French ministry has supported the two largest professional trade shows in the US: the Wine and Spirit Wholesaler Association and VINEXPO.

Wine tourism is seen as a brand differentiator. It enables wineries to meet customers face-to-face and provides an opportunity to raise the profile of their products in the customer's mind. Customers may then develop a long-term relationship with a product that they have sampled at the place of its origin. Winery direct sales are especially important to smaller wineries that do not receive the same level of support from retailers as the larger competitors. Moreover, winery direct provide increased profit margins due to the absence of transportation costs or a channel intermediary.

The other major means of gathering names of potential customers is through the press, either through publicity in the wine columns or by advertisements. The small wineries, since they tend to be the most innovative, are best to attract the attention of wine journalists looking for interesting copy, a fact that works to the financial advantage of the small grower.

It is ironic that this return to the personalized approach, the establishment of a long-term relationship between producer and customer, has been as much a result of new technology as the globalization of distribution. What makes it possible for the busy producer to maintain personal relationships with clients is the database system. Computer software is used to make detailed customer information accessible and actionable, by producing individualized targeted direct mailings. Customer response can, with equal ease, be evaluated to provide information for determining current and future market trends.

E-Business and the Internet

Internet retailing is concerned primarily with those commercial services that are aimed at private individuals or consumers, rather than at corporations. Since the launch of the Internet in the 1990s, this medium has assumed global significance for most industries. Internet sales have been increasing in some countries, for example, in the UK with supermarket online sales. Nevertheless, the online sales in many countries remain a small share of wine distribution. Even in the most developed major markets, where the Internet is used extensively in many industries, the online sales of wine may have potential for further growth. To some extent, the low level of online sales as a percentage of total sales stemmed from legal restrictions prohibiting the sale of alcohol through anything other than specific government sanctioned channels, thereby thwarting Internet sales. However, there has been some relaxing of these restrictions and the Internet is gaining ground.

In addition, the Internet channel provides avenues for advertising and attracting potential consumers. The Internet offers high value as a promotional medium, and it has played an important role in distribution as well. Manufacturers are currently using dedicated websites as interactive advertising opportunities, as well as for brand building and raising product awareness. In a bid to capitalize this direct means of selling wine, retailers and producers have sought alliances that can provide competitive advantage in the industry. The Internet also allows smaller regional companies to reach a wider range of consumers and counter increasing competition from the supermarket and hypermarket channels. It is an effective means of reaching consumers and provides added value, because it can provide a wealth of information about all aspects of wine.

Internet's Social Media Channels

The Internet offers consumers another bridge to knowledge and a very convenient place to glean advice about what wines go with particular foods or occasions. The Internet marketing channel is undoubtedly a positive asset. In years past, marketing campaigns created spikes of activity followed by lulls in attention. Social media is the newest area of marketing and it has changed the dynamics considerably, because it allowing brands to create a continuous way to connect with consumers without dips in activity between large promotions. The Facebook and Twitter avenues are of increasing importance. Marketing firms are providing encouragement and even management to exploit this Social Media as a pathway and a means to consistently reach new consumers of particular brands, through the efforts of consumers already familiar with the product.

An example is the Lodi Winegrape Commission that decided it wanted to bridge the gap between the actual quality of Lodi wine and consumers' perceptions. That meant developing messages for creating an emotional connection with wine consumers and then backing it up with facts about wine produced in Lodi, California. The marketing team for the wine commission decided to provide the opportunity for consumers to have a one-on-one experience with winery owners and growers. The Lodi region is the largest and most productive winegrowing region in the US, but also has many small scale farmers who are responsible for every part of the wine production process. This allows for activities that can provide close contact with consumers who can experience every aspect of wine production. LoCA is the name chosen for the Lodi viticultural area. The message of LoCA (an abbreviation for Lodi, Calif.) also means "crazy" in Spanish. It was seen to imply a fun environment for the consumers to experience; the concept that LoCA is an ideal place for wine and people to meet. The Lodi Wine Commission has had real success with its social media strategy that it began in 2011.

In conclusion, whatever the style of an operation, a major company or a boutique winery, a modern marketing strategy is an indispensable necessity in the global environment. We have examined some of the problems faced by the industry and identified consumer trends; the increasing concentration of companies in production, wholesaling and retail outlets; the changing legal requirements, as well as government regulations and changes in taxation that make it difficult to compete in the global economy. Companies must have strategic objectives and sophisticated marketing plans with well executed strategy. It is necessary to have a keen knowledge of the market and be able to adapt as quickly and appropriately to the changing market environment. In the past, there was a time when the rustic grower could simply continue to produce wine as his father and grandfather did before him, clinging to a blind faith that what he produced would eventually be sold in the market place by an agent. That time is now past. It is gone forever, much like delivery by horse and buggy and communications by snail-mail.

Chapter 8

WINE COMPANIES AND HOW THEY COMPETE: EXAMPLES

The wine industry is composed of many distinct elements. These all have their common source in the vineyards of the world, but the multiplicity of routes by which the products reach the consumer are so numerous and fluid that to give an overall view inevitably results in some degree of simplification (described in our chapter on distribution). However, by examining the industry's development, it is possible to track the elements involved in competitive practices. We can identify the major areas of competition and illuminate the competitive initiatives that are shaping the marketplace in the business of wine.

Outside the traditional but dwindling sector of the western European market, there are very few places where wine is considered a day-to-day necessity. In most areas of the globe, wine is perceived only as a less frequent indulgence—more as a luxury product. In other words, drinking wine is something people may want to add to their life experience, but it is not necessarily considered a product of necessity for frequent everyday consumption. Consequently, selling wine requires more sophisticated marketing strategies than the more ordinary consumer products.

Wine is a product where the marketing is especially sensitive to fashions and to consumer trends that now have an international cross-cultural influence. Therefore, competition between providers is a series of changing and competing initiatives. Moreover, competition in the business of wine involves various corporate organizational strategies.

The Development of Strategies: Active and Reactive

The wine industry in the past has been slow to react to changes in demand, resulting in cyclical oversupply or undersupply. These changes are not the result of the agricultural cycle, but the result of actual changes in the variables of demand. Undersupply can be illustrated by the scarcity during the mid-nineties of chardonnay in the US. The undersupply followed the sudden vogue enjoyed by wines made with that particular grape. This type of change in demand should have resulted in a quicker response by producers, but it did not. The reason is partly due to a degree of traditionalist resistance to change that is felt in many old-established wine-growing areas, and also to the intractable problem of just how much time and money is required to initiate new vineyards or to change the varietals grown in existing ones.

With the increasing industry concentration through mergers and general movements toward fuller integration, there is now much more of a tendency among major companies to carefully track trends and to plan corporate strategies, to be in a position to react quickly to changes in demand. However, there is a rather large section of the wine industry that still relies on a kind of herd instinct and it responds reactively to external forces only when the situation absolutely proves painful. An informative illustration of this was the old advertising campaign by Anivit, where after years of dwindling consumption, finally producers were prepared to group together and attempt to counter the problem by promulgating an industry message—"a little wine makes all the difference to a meal."

The industry is, as we have seen, enormously complex, but can be broadly divided into the three broad product categories: super-premium, premium and standard wines. Each of these primary product categories demands a distinct marketing strategy. Each company needs to develop its own particular and distinct business model that matches the appropriate strategy for each product that they market, whether they deal exclusively in one particular category or have a variety of product.

The profit-to-volume ratio between the three broad categories involves specific major elements for successful strategies to be implemented for each of the categories. As competitive pressure increases on the wine market overall, many companies have been looking to integrate either backward into production or forward into retailing, or even horizontally by means of diversifying. Which route any particular company chooses is determined by their long tradition, experience with their existing business model, and their ability to incorporate strategic planning for marketing and organizational change.

Super-Premium and Premium Wines

During early 1990s, common wine was rapidly becoming a shrinking market. The real growth area was premium wine, the buoyancy of which started to spill over into the super-premium segment of the market. The super-premium category had traditionally been considered of minor concern to most participants in the wine industry. Among the absolute top-flight producers, notably the Chateaux of Bordeaux and the Domaines of Burgundy, competition was practically an alien concept, because the market is always ready and able to swallow the small volumes of super-premium Grands Vins available. According to Gilles Aguettant D'Aubignon of Chateau Mouton-Rothschild, it can take merely two or three hours to sell to the clamoring négociants the entire Premier Cru vintage of about 300,000 bottles.

The procedure for selling super-premium French vintages follows the classic triangular pattern of Producer-Broker-Merchant. Wine is sold via the brokers (the courtiers) to the merchants (the négociants) according to a strictly regulated allocation system. The demand constantly outstripping supply, there is little genuine competition involved until the wine comes into the realm of the négociants.

Strategic Considerations
The vast arrays of wines are not super-premium. All other wines, including premium, comprise the major markets of competition in the business of wine. Nonetheless, because the consumer has increasingly demanded higher quality wines, the premium category is quite competitive. A glance at the critical factors in competitive strategy indicates how many considerations are involved.

- Monitoring distributor
- Brand breation
- Critical advertising
- Differentiate packaging
- Protect brand reputation
- Contact with retail buyers
- Private labeling
- Importer alliance
- Price points
- Distribution alliance & acquisition
- Retail alliances
- Ensure distributor margins
- Protect consumer loyalty

This system is advantageous to the growers, since virtually none of them is large enough to market their own product on a worldwide basis, but also because the négociants must honor their obligation to buy their allocation whether it is a particularly good year or a bad one.

This is not to say that the classed-growth producers can afford to be complacent. If a vintage is poor, less of the wine produced will be classified as Grand Vin and the prices will be lower. So, while the great Chateaux have little to worry about in terms of external competition, there is still huge pressure on them to maintain the quality and the distinctiveness of their super-premium wine. Therefore, it is clearly of utmost importance to employ the best people one can afford, and thus, competition to employ and retain the most renowned Cellarmen available is intense. It is also increasingly important to maintain comprehensive laboratory facilities to assist in quality control. Such technological methods are seen by the traditional Chateaux, not as a replacement for human judgment, but merely as a guarantee against the possibility of human error. When one's reputation is of such crucial importance, it would be foolish not to protect it by all means possible.

The procedure for selling the Grands Vins to the merchants is open to manipulation by the growers, which is one of the few ways the Chateaux can strive to increase income. On the average, 60% of any vintage is forward sold, en primeur (i.e., prior to bottling). The sale is in two stages (tranches). If the market looks set to remain unexcited by the vintage and consequently stable, then the first tranche offered by the growers will be large. Conversely, if expectations of the vintage have made the market eager, then the first tranche will be extremely small, in order to simply whet the appetite of the buyers who will then be ready to pay much higher prices for the second tranche.

Once the Grand Vin has been sold, it is out of the grower's control. However, there are ways of unofficially monitoring its progress. A code exists by which it is made plain to négociants that excessive profiteering or selling-on of wine, without proper aging, will result in their being struck off the allocations list. Auctions also present a forum in which the Chateaux can profitably maintain a presence, not only to enhance their own image, but also in order to attempt to avert inflationary trends—such as what provoked the crash of 1974. In the words of Gilles Aguettant D'Aubignon of Chateau Mouton Rothschild, "We have no desire to see our wine becoming a speculative commodity."

The presence of a Chateau's representative at an exclusive auction, for example at Sotheby's in London, can serve as good public-relations and image-enhancement. Other opportunities for public relations activity have been somewhat curtailed by restrictions on advertising and promotion, prompted by the anti-alcohol lobbies of several European countries. Baron Philippe de Rothschild SA, for instance, used to sponsor sporting events such as regattas. These events are now closed to them. However, a collection of paintings belonging to the family—one of which is reproduced each year on their label—is on permanent tour to various prestigious galleries around the world. This type of activity provides an avenue of strategic competitive advantage.

While the majority of super-premium wine presently comes from the very traditional areas of Europe, wines from elsewhere are beginning to achieve similarly exalted reputations. This is the case of Cloudy Bay Sauvignon from New Zealand, which has been as much in demand as some of the greatest Premier Cru wines of France. In the US, too, there has been increasing interest in super-premium wine. As early as the late 1970s, Baron Philippe de Rothschild SA proffered a strategy where he entered a joint venture with Mondavi in California's Napa Valley. Starting with the 1980 vintage, together they began building an entirely new segment in the American market—producing vintages which retailed for much higher prices. Initially the rest of the industry thought they were foolish, but this opinion proved wrong. Over the years, many of the smaller wineries have followed suit with what are termed "boutique" wines, which carry similarly high premiums. Mondavi controls approximately 9,800 acres of vineyards in winegrowing regions of California, including Napa Valley, Lodi, Mendocino County, Monterey County, San Luis Obispo County, Santa Maria Valley, Santa Barbara County and Sonoma County. In addition, the company's joint ventures control over 1,725 acres of vineyards in the winegrowing regions of Chile, Italy and California.

In Bordeaux and Burgundy, a Chateau-bottled classed-growth wine must be produced only from grapes grown within the grounds of the named Chateau. In the case of the New World super-premium wines, this convenient form of exclusivity is not present. However, as the reputations of these new contenders in the super-premium field become established, who is to say that any one particular vineyard in Hawke's Bay or Napa Valley should not one day enjoy the cachet accorded to Chateau-Latour or Romanée-Conti? Such cachet has made the great Chateaux prime targets for acquisition. In France, the banks and insurance companies showed considerable interest in wine real estate as have many international buyers from America, Britain, Japan and elsewhere.

The Value of a Superior Brand

The desire of major companies, often outside the wine industry itself, to enhance their profile through the acquisition of prestigious vineyards has contributed to the skyrocketing prices in the real estate market. Competition for ownership of prime vineyards has been increasingly intense. There are a mere 1,000 hectares of really prime Bordeaux vineyard and these pieces of land rarely change hands. This is equally true of the vineyards of Burgundy. If a large institution has the patience to wait until a really first-rate Chateau of international renown comes onto the market, with sufficient money to buy it and a sufficiently long-term outlook, they can expect to reap very handsome rewards over the long-term. They will have acquired a unique product where 75% is traded in the extremely lucrative export market.

French investors in Bordeaux and Burgundy include large companies such as BNP Paribas, which has created its own subsidiary Paribas Domaines to handle its vineyard investments. French insurance companies such as Garantie Mutuelle des Fonctionnaires, the Compagnie du Midi and Assurance

Générale de France are represented in the area of vineyard holdings. The giant AGF is also the owner of Chateau Larose-Trintaudon, producer of an exceptional Cru Bourgeois and is one of the very few Chateaux to engage in advertising campaigns. The ownership strategies of these investment companies change over time.

The international strategies of acquisition are sometimes difficult to execute or may even be blocked by the French authorities. For example, when the Danish retailer, Flemming Karberg, attempted to integrate backward by acquiring Chateau Kirwan in St Emilion, the French Government resisted the purchase for more than two years. When the Japanese company Suntory wanted to take over Burgundy's famous Domaine Romanée Conti, the government stepped in to prohibit the transaction; and so in 2013, Domaine remains co-owned by the de Villaine and Leroy/Roch families. Nevertheless, one of the most important and successful entrants into the world of strategic acquisitions is China. Many Chinese companies have been on foreign acquisition buying sprees since the 2008 financial crisis.

For example, in 2011, Chinese companies acquired additional vineyards in France, Chile, the US, and Australia. In June of 2013, three prestigious Bordeaux wine chateaus, Bon Pasteur, Rolland-Mallet, and Bertineau St. Vincent, were acquired by Chinese companies. In fact, Christie's recently opened "Vineyards by Christie's" in China, an estate agency which serves as a discrete consultative service for clients looking to acquire vineyards in the world's most sought-after wine regions.

The importance of the name and image of a Chateau or Domaine has meant that the strategy of acquisitions and mergers very rarely lead to relaunches of the product under a different name. Actual profitability from the small output itself can, in certain circumstances, be less important than the image and prestige derived from ownership of a piece of history and vinicultural heritage. Moreover, the name of the Chateau can be used to reflect glory on other lines, such as is demonstrated by the policy of Rothschild with their Mouton Cadet. In such cases, however, great care must be taken not to devalue the flagship brand name or this strategy will backfire. While the prestige element is important, it usually takes more than the promise of glamorous connections to make major corporations, such as Allied Lyons, Nestle, Suntory, Kirin, Grand Met, Kobrand and Chandon, decide to make new investments in this elevated stratum of the wine industry. Trends in consumer behavior, profits in terms of return of investment and synergistic effects are part of the decision process. The trend toward the consumption of less, but better quality, wine points to the super-premium category as being an area of increasing potential profitability. So the desire for premium vineyard sites is based on more than sheer image-enhancement. These corporations see the likelihood of making considerable returns on their investments.

Shrewd investors, particularly those in countries where super-premium real estate now commands truly extraordinary prices, have increasingly been looking toward regions where prices have not yet reached such astronomical levels. The Loire and the Rhóne valleys in France have represented good potential investments. Likewise, some California areas around Napa Valley Monterey and Sonoma County, in particular, continue to offer some pockets of extremely high quality land for vineyards which, although expensive, is comparatively affordable, particularly for international buyers when the dollar decreases in exchanged value. Highly prestigious companies like Rothschild no longer consider it beneath their dignity to acquire vineyards in California. Similarly, Torres has done well by marrying their name to the superb wines produced in vineyards they have acquired in Chile.

Competitor's Strategies: The Internationals

Since the rise of the New World wine makers, the global wine industry has become increasingly internationalized and ferociously competitive. Size of the company is increasingly important for competitive strategy in the international marketplace, where huge retails chains need to be matched in size at the negotiation table and the supply chain. It is only over the past 25 years or so that this drive for size has dominated much of the corporate agenda, and there are still firms for whom growth has not been part of the strategic agenda. Today, a small number of large players dominate many newer markets, whereas the traditional mature markets in Western Europe see only small concentration of market shares.

As the wine industry has evolved from an artesian "home business" to global organizations serving every type of customer, rules of good business practice have also been increasingly recognized. The costs of grapes and wine produced decreases significantly with increased size of operations. Figure 8:1 illustrates and tracks the correlation of these costs for wine companies of various sizes (for small wine companies under $1 million annual, and along the way to those over $20 million).

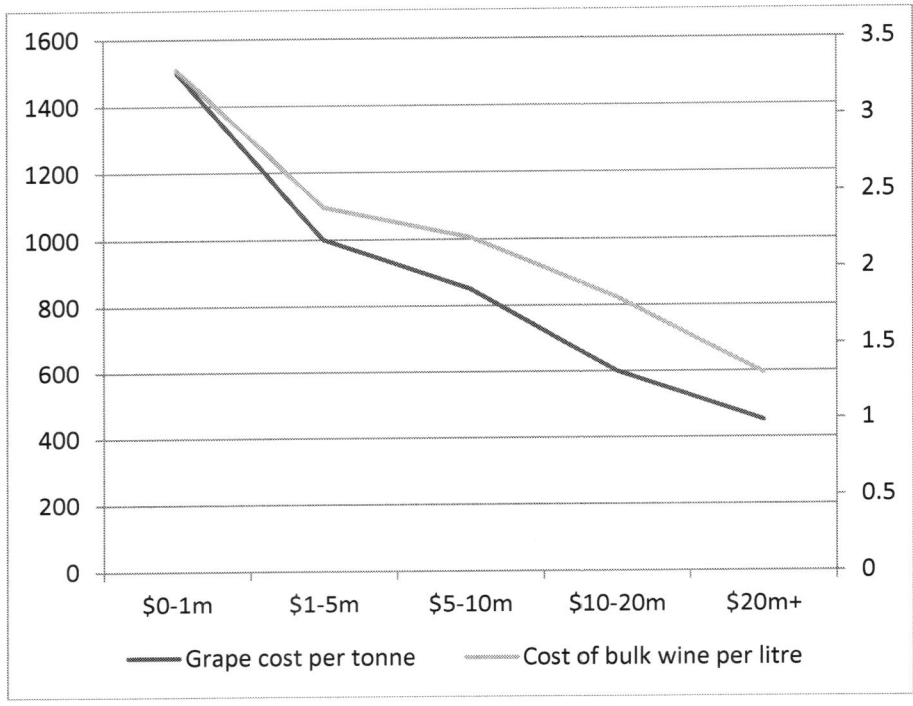

Figure 8:1 Cost of Wine Production
Source: Deloitte Report - Annual financial benchmarking survey for Australian Wine Industry.

Although the costs of grapes and wine produced falls dramatically with increased size of operations, the profitability of the firms do not automatically follow. The traditional industry savants have argued for years that the winery business is an "economic trap," where the performance ranges from poor to worse. It is interesting to note the very different strategies adopted depending of the size of the firm. Smaller wineries pursue niche markets for expensive wines and allow for profitable returns, despite the higher cost structure and much lower asset turnover. The medium-sized wineries are "caught in the middle"—not large enough to truly exploit size, but too large for only niche market strategies, having complex product ranges and costly organizations to manage. Yet, they don't have the ability to exploit economies of scale and cannot afford the focus and attention of a boutique winery. These conditions are stimulating for industry consolidation and acquisitions by the very large companies that can exploit economies of scale. Such competitive strategies are logical, particularly in light of the general process of escalating globalization.

Table 8:1 shows the results of a detailed statistical study of the effects of size (scale of operations) on the profitability of wine production.

	Winery Size (2005 revenue in $ millions)					
	$0-1m	$1-5m	$5-10m	$10-20m	$20m+	Listed
Revenues and expenses per case						
Revenue per case	$172.67	$107.40	$89.05	$73.25	$77.16	n/a
Gross margin per case	$84.14	$53.42	$36.66	$25.35	$28.08	n/a
Profit per case	$13.90	$2.99	-$3.71	-$0.61	$4.87	n/a
Advertising spend per-case	$5.24	$4.25	$3.69	$2.36	$4.05	n/a
Overhead per case	$14.25	$7.56	$9.64	$7.26	$2.82	n/a
Packaging cost per case	$23.74	$19.38	$16.16	$15.10	$15.34	n/a
Solvency ratios						
Current ratio	277%	322%	295%	277%	307%	184%
Debt to equity ratio	55%	85%	65%	80%	74%	73%
Debt to tangible assets	34%	38%	35%	41%	46%	48%
Efficiency ratios						
Inventory turnover	1.55	0.7	0.75	0.98	0.86	0.78
Fixed asset turnover	0.71	1.4	0.88	1.11	1.93	1.14
Asset turnover	0.28	0.6	0.86	0.38	0.55	0.32
Profitability ratios						
EBIT margin (average)	11.50%	8%	1.40%	4%	7.50%	15.90%
EBIT to assets	4.90%	1.20%	6.40%	4.10%	6.00%	5.90%
EBT to equity	8.80%	3%	-5.10%	-4.60%	7.50%	8.10%
EBT to net case sales	9.40%	6.40%	6.20%	1.60%	5.60%	16.60%

Table 8:1 Winery Size and Profitability
Source: Deloitte Report - Annual financial benchmarking survey for Australian Wine Industry.

Industry consolidation primarily takes place through three different types of acquisitions.

1.   Some premium wineries purchase or merge with direct rivals. For instance, Southcorp and Rosemount merged to become the leading Australian wine producer in 2001. However, this merger cannot be said to have been a successful and profitable strategy. Later in

2005, Southcorp was itself acquired by Foster's Group of Australia. In late 2011, Foster's Group itself was acquired by SABMiller.

2. Jug-wine producers began to acquire premium wineries in order to keep pace with changing consumer tastes. For example, Constellation Brands, a leading jug-wine supplier, purchased small premium wineries such as Franciscan Estates and Turner Road in 2001, to augment its portfolio and provide retailers with a broader selection. In 2005, they acquired Mondavi. In 2008, Constellation Brands acquired Beam Wines Estates and Fortune Brands that included several major brands such as Clos du Bois. Soon after, Constellation acquired additional premium companies in its portfolio, but divested Almaden Vineyards, Inglenook Winery, and Paul Masson winery.

3. Other alcoholic beverage firms have diversified into the premium wine business. For example, Foster's Group of Australia, as previously mentioned, purchased Beringer's Wine Estates of California for $1.47 billion in 2000, and subsequently Penfolds in 2005. Similarly, leading global distilled spirits firms such as Diageo acquired several premium wineries. Consolidation of all tiers of the business is continuing to define the landscape and is accelerating among suppliers, as well as among distributors.

The large corporate globalization of the world involves constant mergers and acquisitions. The top corporate management is always looking toward growing the size of the companies that they lead. As can be seen, the business of wine is certainly no exception. The strategy and pace of dynamic acquisitions is making it increasingly difficult for anyone to keep up with "who really owns which companies, and when the wineries are changing hands again."

In 2003, Constellation Brands and E & J Gallo were the largest volume wine companies, with volume shares of 2.3% and 2.4% respectively. However, in 2005/2006 Constellation Brands became the world leader, following its acquisition of Robert Mondavi, reaching 2.6% in terms of global wine volume. Both these companies, Constellation and Gallo, owe much of their strength from position in the large US market. In 2011, the entry of Accolade Wines became a new leader. This company was formed by the acquisition of Constellation Brands' Australian and UK wine businesses by Champ Private Equity of Australia. Subsequent to acquisition, the company of Champ renamed Constellation Wines Australia and Constellation Europe as "Accolade Wines" in mid-2011. Constellation had been stressed by attempts to restructure and reduce its high level of debt during the travails following the global economic "financial crisis."

In France, three firms, LVMH, Pernod Ricard and Vranken-Pommery, dominate. Australia is dominated by Foster's Group and Lion Nathan; and in the UK, it is Allied Domecq and Diageo.

In the following, we will take a closer look at some large and small firms in the industry, in order to better understand their strategies.

Understanding Size-Related Strategies

The initial size of the company determines strategic directions. Large companies often use acquisition to effectively execute long range marketing strategies. In 2012, there were 7,498 wineries in the US, but only 30 companies represented 90% of the domestic wine sold annually in the US (by volume). Professor Philip Howard of Michigan State University tracked 3,600 wines, and traced the production to more than 1,000 different firms, but many of these firms are found to be actually owned by one of the three largest parent companies: E. & J. Gallo, the Wine Group and Constellation Brands. In fact, these three parent companies together control the majority of wines, 51.5%.

An example of a very large wine company is E & J Gallo. Originally a simple producer of table-wines, this company has become the US giant. It is headquartered in California and Gallo's business dates back to 1933, when the two brothers Ernest and Julio Gallo founded the winery in Modesto, California. In 2013, it has become a thriving global wine company, reaching 100 countries with a variety of wine programs and a global brand portfolio that includes 65 wine brands. It is the largest wine company in US, with over 16,000 acres of vineyards across the state of California and 5,000 employees.

Gallo occupies approximately a quarter of the US table wine market and is the leading US wine exporter with wineries located in the Modesto, Livingston, Sonoma and Napa areas of California. Gallo's wine empire was built upon a base of inexpensive table wines. It was previously known for its inexpensive jug-wines and even cheap fortified varieties such as Thunderbird. In the 1980s and 1990s, Gallo followed consumption trends and moved aggressively into more expensive categories, particularly cork-finished varietals (wines made wholly or predominantly from a single type of grape, such as Merlot). Many of its products appeared in the marketplace under brand names other than Gallo, including the brands of Turning Leaf, Gossamer Bay, Indigo Hills, and Northern Sonoma. Gallo is also a market leader in sherry, vermouth, and port, marketed under the Gallo trade name. Gallo's other leading brands include André sparkling wine, E & J brandy, and Bartles & Jaymes wine coolers. Among its premium wines and imports are those of Gallo Family Vineyards Sonoma Reserve and Italian wine Ecco Domani.

Privately owned, Gallo had always avoided publicity in the 20th Century, unwilling to discuss its viticulture and winemaking, much less financial or marketing operations. However, in recent years with the advent of the 21st Century, and with the third generation now entrenched in the management of the business, the company switched gears becoming open to the outside world. Historically, Gallo developed its own brands instead of acquiring them; but in recent years, it has vigorously used acquisition strategies to raise the overall quality of its offerings and enlarge the enterprise. In 2002, it purchased Louis M. Martini Winery in the Napa Valley, California. Later that year, it also acquired the San Jose-based wine producer Mirassou Vineyards, one of the oldest wineries in California. The purchase includes the brand name and stocks, but no vineyards. Mirassou's product range included a Cabernet Sauvignon, a Merlot, a Pinot Noir, a Petite Syrah, a Riesling and a Zinfandel. In 2003, Gallo acquired Bridlewood Estate Winery of Santa Ynez, California, in a bankruptcy sale. E. & J. Gallo acquired William Hill Estate Winery in Napa Valley in 2007.

One of Gallo's hallmarks has been attention to divining quality. Gallo has always been at the head of the pack, technically, with vineyard and winery experiments. As early as 1947, Gallo began a research program to evaluate various viticulture techniques and pest control. Information from the program was often shared with Gallo growers, and the winery established what is believed to be the industry's first formal grower relations program. An enology research program was established in 1954, which included studies in cold fermentation, yeast and the impact of oak barrels on aging.

However, in the past, many of those experiments were not advanced for various reasons. Now, those experiments are seeing shelf space, as the third generation of the Gallo family manages the processes of winemaking and operates in the market. Gallo has a research center in Modesto that has programs in genetics, biochemistry, microbiology and sensory and flavor science. For example, it has isolated more than 400 distinct aroma compounds. Over the years, Gallo Winery Research Center has been responsible for many unaccredited developments in winemaking.

The company's success in the business of wine is also attributed to its long-established distribution network. In its early years, Gallo made contributions to promote the status of wine. Realizing that consumption would never rise while wine was relegated to a secondary position behind hard liquor, Gallo introduced the novel concept of salespeople who sold wine exclusively, a highly successful idea which was soon widely imitated. The company management recruited a team of zealous salespeople to push Gallo products and guarantee high visibility on store shelves. From the beginning, Gallo followed a strategy of expansion into new markets, only when existing markets were conquered. Twenty-five years later, Gallo brands were available nationwide, and the company's distribution system was regarded as its greatest competitive strength. Its size and superior distribution has also been a key ingredient in its success of serving the large US retailers.

Gallo made a splash in 2004, when it introduced Red Bicyclette wines from France and Da Vinci from Italy. In 2006, Gallo renamed and repackaged the "Gallo of Sonoma" brand, which is known as "Gallo Family Vineyards." It also distributes Black Swan wines from Australia in the US, in partnership with Brian McGuigan Wines of Australia. It has also established supply contracts with a South African wine producer. Now in 2013, the company US brands include the following: Gallo Family Vineyards, Barefoot Wine & Bubbly, MacMurray Ranch, Louis M. Martini Winery, Redwood Creek, Frei Brothers Reserve, Rancho Zabaco, Edna Valley Vineyard, André, Ballatore, Boone's Farm, Turning Leaf Vineyards, Peter Vella, Carlo Rossi, Apothic Red Winemaker's Blend, The Naked Grape, Bear Flag Wines and Bodega Elena de Mendoza. Gallo imports and markets wines from France, Chile, Germany, Italy, Australia, South Africa, New Zealand, Spain and Argentina.

Wine of Luxury Image and Strategy

The strategic alliance between the Louis Vuitton Group and Moët Hennessy took place in 1987 and resulted in the holding company LVMH, the world's largest group dealing with prestige products. Until this merger, Moët Hennessy had been chiefly concerned with pushing acquisition policy forward into distribution and the acquisition of brands such as Veuve Clicquot and Charles de Cazanove. In 1979, they had acquired the Dutch distributor Wilmering and Muller, and in 1980, the US company Schieffelin.

After the 1987 merger with Louis Vuitton, distribution agreements were struck with Guinness and the investor Agache, acquiring 33% of LVMH; and one year later, Moët acquired a 70% stake in an area of 150 hectares of quality sparkling wine production in Spain—Domaine Chandon. Since its creation in 1987, LVMH has focused on strong growth, guided by its brand development strategy. It is one of the largest companies in market capitalization and is regarded by some analysts as a financial miracle. Today LVMH is a world leader in luxury, possessing a unique portfolio of over 60 prestigious product brands. The group's product range includes five categories: Fashion & Leather, Wines & Spirits, Parfumes & Cosmetics, Watches and Jewelry and Selective Retailing. The list of its products identify with well-known luxury brands and the categories are very interesting.

- Fashion & Leather Goods: Louis Vuitton Malletier, Loewe, Berluti, Kenzo, Givenchy, Celine, Marc Jacobs, Fendi, Stefano Bi, Emilio Pucci, Thomas Pink, and Donna Karan

- Wines & Spirits: Chandon, Dom Perignon, Veuve Clicquot, Krug, Mercier, Ruinart, Chateau d'Yquem, Belvedere, Cloudy Bay, Cape Mentelle, Domaine Chandon California, Bodegas Chandon, and Hennessy
- Fragrances & Cosmetics: Parfums Christian Dior, Guerlain, Parfums Givenchy, Kenzo Parfums, Laflachère, BeneFit Cosmetics, Fresh, Make Up For Ever and Acqua di Parma

This is an interesting diversified portfolio of products, and it is a successful strategy, because of the unifying concept centering on luxury brands. The 2012 revenue for LVMH was about 28 billion Euros, and wine constituted 4.13 billion of it. A large share, approximately 15% of revenues is beverages, as can be seen in Figure 8:2. The Figure 8:3 illustrates the wine and spirits group revenues, volumes and geographic regions served during 2011 and 2012.

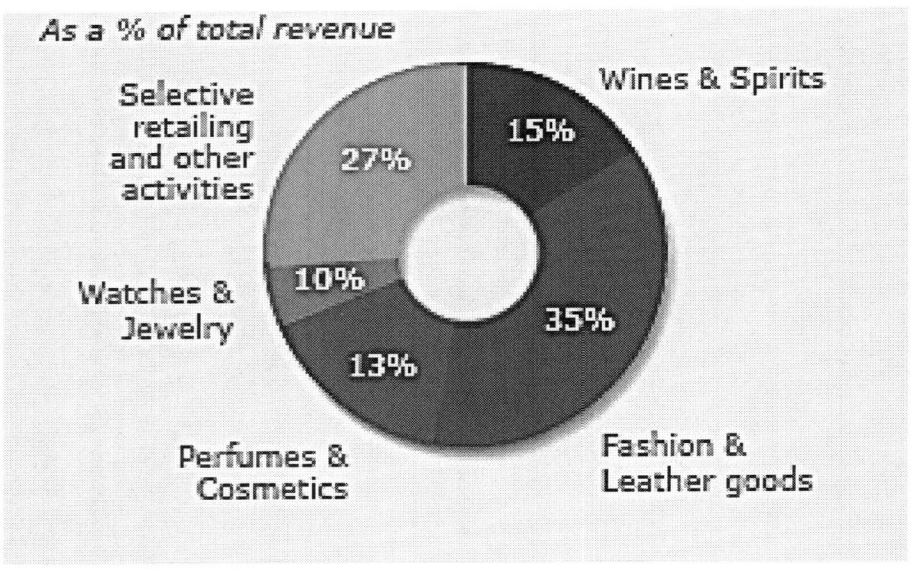

Figure 8:2 Revenues of LVMH by Business Group for 2012

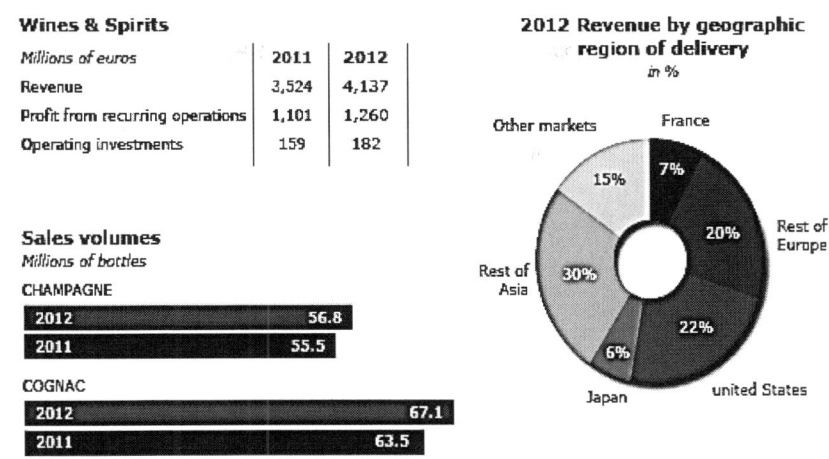

Wines & Spirits		
Millions of euros	2011	2012
Revenue	3,524	4,137
Profit from recurring operations	1,101	1,260
Operating investments	159	182

2012 Revenue by geographic region of delivery
in %

Other markets 15%
France 7%
Rest of Europe 20%
Rest of Asia 30%
united States 22%
Japan 6%

Sales volumes
Millions of bottles

CHAMPAGNE
2012 56.8
2011 55.5

COGNAC
2012 67.1
2011 63.5

Figure 8:3 Revenues of LVMH Wine and Spirits Group

Wines and Spirits business group focuses its growth on the high-end segments of the market. Number one in champagne worldwide, LVMH also has a business in sparkling and still wines from the most famous wine-producing regions of the world. The Group is the world's leader in cognac with Hennessy brand and is expanding its presence in the luxury spirits area. The portfolio of brands is served by a powerful international distribution network.

With the acquisition of the two successful champagne houses, Pomméry and Lanson from BSN for the sum of 613.7 million dollars in 1990, LVMH increased their share of the champagne market from 18.4% to 24%. The price they paid may seem high, being 39 times their net 1989 income, but LVMH's chairman judged that internationally-known champagne brands were such a limited commodity that it was a step worth taking.

LVMH acquired the champagne brand Pommerchy in 1991 and took over the champagne producer Krug in 1999. It bought the Newton and Mount Adam vineyards in 2001. In 2002, it sold the Pommery champagne brand. The champagne volumes and income continue to grow with price increases and new improvements in the product mix that increasingly favor only premium qualities and vintages. The well-known champagne brand Moët & Chandon is advancing in the non-traditional markets, such as Central Europe and China, and was achieving double-digit growth by 2006. The growth of its pink champagnes, Rosé Impérial and Nectar Rosé in the US, confirms the unquestionable position of Moët & Chandon in this segment.

In 2006, LVMH's Wines and Spirits business group continued to illustrate the creativity of its brands, particularly with the worldwide launch of Brut Rosé non vintage by Veuve Clicquot and a limited edition of Dom Pérignon—"A Bottle Named Desire." It launched a large-scaled advertising campaign on the US market for Hennessy cognac and a new communication campaign for the vodka Belvedere. In the second collaboration with Dom Pérignon, LVMH completed a publicity campaign for Dom Pérignon Rosé.

In 2013, the company is a market leader with an impressive arsenal of labels. The portfolio of brands is served by a powerful international distribution network. LVMH has more than 1,466 selective retail stores worldwide. The great competitive strategic platform enjoyed by LVMH is its luxury image rather than any unified retailing strategy. It would be rare to find the full range of the company's products on the same floor in any one of the major stores, let alone side by side on the hypermarket shelf.

Traditional Family-Owned Wine Businesses

Nearly all wine businesses began as privately owned family businesses. Most remained small, but some executed competitive strategies for large scale growth. There are a number of large firms, and in some cases, publicly held wine producers. Typically, most of these large entities produce lower-end wines at lower price-points. Although much consolidation already has taken place, the wine industry is still dominated by small, family-owned businesses that are intimately involved in the local, agrarian communities where they are located, particularly in Europe.

After the mid-1980s, once dominant on the international scene, the family-owned prosperous European winemakers faced challenges from New World competitors with bigger vineyards & marketing budgets, lower costs, modern production techniques and increasingly good quality. European family business owners continue to strive for the glorious past.

For example, Freixenet is a Spanish family-owned wine company. The company is the world's leading seller of traditional method Champenoise sparkling wine. Fleixenet is pronounced "fresh-eh-net." Spain is a traditional wine-making country. There is the Catolonia area in the north-east part of Spain, which has a long history in making wine with effervescence and is the birthplace of Cava. The term Cava means "cave" in Spanish. Cava is also a type of sparkling wine made in the champagne method, using local Spanish grape varieties. It is an alternative to French champagne, but less expensive.

Freixenet is one of the early Cava producers in Catalonia. Founded in 1861, Freixenet began to produce Cava in 1914. Since then, Cava has always been a thriving business for Freixenet and it was Freixenet that turned Cava from a homespun recipe to a well-established wine category in the global wine community. Sequential successful launches of new Cavas helped establish Freixenet as one of the world's leading sparkling wine-makers. Lower wages and production costs enabled Freixenet to price its Cava lower than

French premium champagne, making it an attractive and acceptable alternative to French champagne.

Freixenet has always been a wholly family-owned company. The family business, originally named Casa Sala, gained ground when the family's second generation launched the company into Cava production. In 1914, the company adopted a new name, Freixenet, and formally incorporated as Freixenet in 1928. It began to export wine in 1920s and its first overseas subsidiary was opened in the US at a site in New Jersey in 1935. Since then, its overseas market has been constantly growing.

In the second half of the 20th Century, Freixenet adopted successful marketing strategies and became Spain's leading cava producer. In the mid-1980s, Freixenet sought to extend its business into the still wine sector. In 1985, it acquired Rene Barbier in the Pinedes region. In the 2000s, Freixenet's business portfolio continued to extend into the French champagne market by buying Reims-based Henri Abel, one of the oldest of the region's champagne producers. By the early 2000s, the company's exports reached more than 150 countries. In 2003, it acquired Chandon Cava from the French luxury group LVMH. By 2005, Freixenet had succeeded in balancing its portfolio, with still wines representing some 40% of the group's sales, while remaining the world's leading seller of sparkling wines.

In recent years, Freixenet has been actively establishing wine producing presence in new areas such as Argentina, Chile and South Africa. Further business acquisitions and expansion may suggest a public offering, but as of 2013, the Ferrer family still keeps tight control of its company.

Another example of family owned European wine companies is Château Margaux. Tradition is the cornerstone of Château Margaux, designed by the architect Louis Combes in 1810. In some ways, Château Margaux reflects the recent history of the French wine industry. Once insular and hidebound, the industry gradually awakened in the 1980s and thereafter to the challenge of the well-made and cleverly marketed wines from places like Australia, California, South Africa and Chile. Producers gradually updated their equipment and winemaking techniques, and began thinking seriously about how to compete in global markets. Château Margaux is one of the five first-growth wine-producing properties in Bordeaux, along with Lafite-Rothschild, Mouton Rothschild, Latour and Haut-Brion, and thus one of the producers of the world's greatest and most sought-after red wines. Although protected by a classification system that dated from 1855, Château Margaux wines' quality fluctuates, and at the time that the Mentzelopoulos family acquired control of the estate, it was in shambles.

In 1977, the Mentzelopoulos family from Greece bought Château Margaux. The Mentzelopoulos family restored the chateau and its reputation in the wine industry. The first vintage in 1978 was seen as one of the best Bordeaux wines of the year. After the father died in 1980, 27-year-old daughter, Corinne, inherited the estate. She worked closely with the young enologist and also with the longtime managing director Paul Pontallier, to keep the best quality of their wines. They tore up and replanted about 30 acres of vineyard and rebuilt storage vats and cellars. The chateau itself was restored inside and out; and within a few years a succession of superlative vintages were brought forth. Château Margaux produces an average of 130,000 bottles per year of its first-wine Château Margaux. The process involves taking grapes that were discarded from the first wine and using them in producing another 130,000 bottles of its second wine, Pavillon Rouge du Château Margaux. In addition, the estate also produces 15,000 bottles of its wine Pavillon Blanc du Château Margaux. About 10% of the grape production, while qualified as Château Margaux, is sold in bulk to other wine merchants to be included in their generic wine, on condition that the source would not be released.

High price level and good vintages have generated good revenues. While price of French wines generally are falling, prices of first growth Bordeaux have been rising. The company's expenses are rather stable. About 70 people are employed in production and four in administrative functions. In terms of distribution, Château Margaux follows a time-honored tradition that Château owners entrust their distribution to wine brokers in the city of Bordeaux. While owners don't do marketing, the distribution channel works as a marketing tool. The scarcity of the product, and the few selected places where it could be obtained, create the allure of the quality product.

Over the years, the owner had been forced to sell off parts of her stake in the chateau to raise cash. Perhaps Ms. Mentzelopoulos' shrewdest move came in 2003. After the Agnelli family of Italy decided to sell a controlling stake that they had previously acquired in 1991, Ms. Mentzelopoulos was able to repurchase the Agnelli family's 75% share, giving her complete ownership. The estate currently stands at 98 hectares. Margaux has become a part of the overall "French luxury world." The company's competitive strategy has been to continue to focus on marketing its portfolio of products, which is a combination of the Château Margaux and those obtained by acquisition, to new markets overseas.

Innovation in Wine Marketing & Branding

As mentioned previously, modern marketing is relatively a new concept in the wine industry. The 1990s saw a clear transition from traditional supply-driven production to market-orientated types of business models. Ever since, the suppliers who were first to recognize these changes, in particular those from New World countries, have enjoyed tremendous growth.

High volume producers have systematic competitive marketing strategies. Large organizations with a wide portfolio of brands are able to adapt to new consumer tastes and build strength in new business sectors by using their far-reaching distribution networks in the world market. Significant budgets are invested in advertising campaigns.

However, in the segmented and complex wine industry, there are numerous wine producers that are competing innovatively in certain wine segments or in very specific markets. These focused competitors are either highly market-oriented and/or very creative in product development. These competitors have experienced substantial business growth. For example, the vineyard Yellow Tail succeeded by creating a new market in the US, and the success of Bonny Doon is largely attributed to its peculiar selection of wine varieties and anti-conventional label design. Innovation doesn't stop with production methods. The Bonny Doon winery has changed strategic competitive focus in recent years, moving toward higher-end, boutique vintages.

Yellow Tail is a vineyard based in Australia. It was owned by Casella Wines Pty Ltd., a family-owned business that began in the 1820s in Italy. In 1951, the Casella family moved to Australia for a better life. By the 1960s, the Casella family was selling wine in bulk.

The Yellow Tail brand was an incredible hit in the US market in 2000, launched under the leadership of Casella's new generation. At that time, the American wine industry was the third largest in world, worth $20 billion. But the customer base was stagnant, 31st in the world in terms of per capita consumption. Per capita US wine consumption is low by western European standards, although the number of wine consumers in the US.makes it a very large market. Figure 8:4 illustrates the sizeable per capita differences.

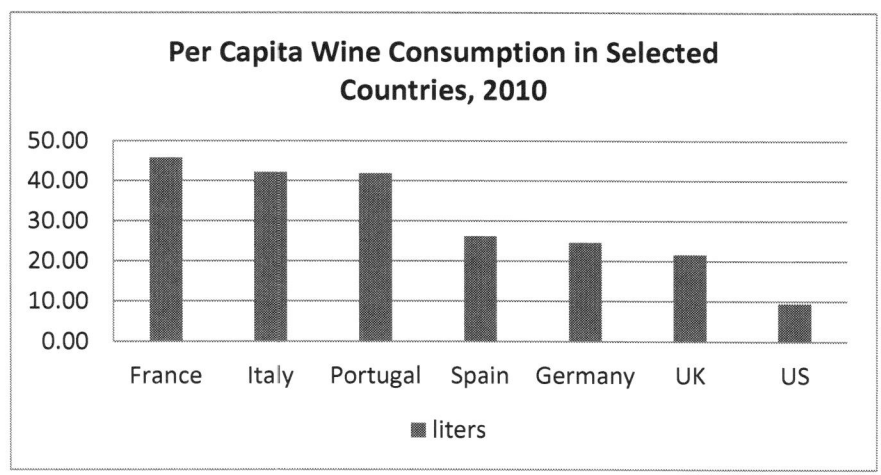

Figure 8:4 Per Capita Wine Consumption in Selected Countries
Source: www.wineinstitute.org

Twenty-five percent of US adults drink at least one glass of wine per month, even though 38% of US consumers do not drink any alcohol at all. American consumers have become value conscious, and those who do drink wine are choosing wines from non-traditional regions (i.e., non-Western European) that have greater perceived value.

In the late 1990s, the new general manager of Casella analyzed Americans' drinking preferences and spotted the emerging opportunity in the American market. The data showed there was a marked preference for wines that express the "toasty vanilla flavor that oak barrels release." This pushed many other wine makers to invest in the expensive oak barrel replacement. The taste of Yellow Tail is fruity, soft on the palette, sweetish, and great for those who didn't drink wine before. It uses the same bottle for red and white, keeping logistical costs at a lower level. Traditional wine makers highlight the oenological terminology, vintage year and aging qualities, which confuse the less sophisticated consumers. Yellow tail took a different approach to packaging and communicating with the public. The Yellow Tail label design is uncomplicated with the distinctive kangaroo and catchy colors of contrasting deep yellow and black. Casella Wines sold 200,000 cases of Yellow Tail wines in 2001 and 2.2 million the following year. Yellow Tail became the number one imported wine, outselling France and Italy, and the fastest growing imported wine in the history of the US market.

Yellow Tail's competitive marketing strategy was illustrated in the book "Blue Ocean," authored by two professors. The Blue Ocean refers to high profit growth at low risk, opportunity in new industries, untapped market demand and unknown market space. In late 2012, Yellow Tail launched a very innovative strategic arrangement with the digital music service Spotify to offer 14 wine-inspired playlists curated by 15 Australian celebrities and media identities (enjoy the music as you wine and dine).

A Subversive Californian Winemaker

Since its founding in 1983, in the tiny hamlet of Bonny Doon in California near Santa Cruz, the winery named after the hamlet, has enjoyed enormous growth. The Bonny Doon winery grew quickly from 5,000 cases a year in 1994 to 200,000 cases a year in 1999. By 2005, Bonny Doon's revenues approached $27 million. The founder, Randall Grahm, had a strong interest in the "ugly ducking" wine varietals, such as Mourvedre, Syrah, Grenache and Roussanne from the Rhone and Nebbiolo, Charbono and Dolcetto from Italy. He believed that the California wine industry, especially those in Napa and Sonoma, were overpriced and pretentious. The founder also believed in high value and inexpensive wines, and he often poked fun at wine critics and wineries that often caused people to reject the pretentiousness of wine.

Bonny Doon's wines differ from traditional California wines in two important ways. First, while most of the US market makes and sells chardonnay, carbernet and merlot, Bonny Doon offers Riesling, Malvasia, Refosco, Gewurztraminer, Rousanne, Sangiovese, Grenache, Zinfandel, Meunier, Charbono, Nebbiolo and Barbera. Secondly, while in the New World varietals are the preferred wines, Bonny Doon, in the Rhone tradition, sells many interesting blends. The penchant for relatively unknown grape varieties left Bonny Doon vulnerable to growers. For example, in 2002 Bonny Doon owned a vineyard near Soledad, California, that accounted for only 20% of the grapes used by Bonny Doon Vineyard. The other 80% of grapes that were required had to be bought from other growers. Nevertheless, the company survived the weakness.

Unique strategic positioning in the marketplace has always been a hallmark of Bonny Doon wines. Its labels are considered distinctive, with funny and even irreverent design accompanied by unusual prose. Bonny Doon has traditionally preferred small to medium-sized distributors. However, given consolidation within the wine distribution industry in the US, cooperation with large distributors is unavoidable. In addition to distribution through traditional channels, Bonny Doon also sells wine at tasting rooms and through its direct sales network.

The company management believes that winemakers should embrace the French concept of "terroir," which is the idea that a great wine is the product of soil, climate and weather and the winemaker's duty is to let the nature take in course. In 2006, Bonny Doon sold two of his leading wine brands to The Wine Group LLC, a management-owned wine company based in San Francisco. The sale of Big House and Cardinal Zin to the Wine Group includes the brand names, inventories, grape supply contracts and key brand icons. In the founder's explanation, the rapid growth of the Big House and Cardinal Zin brands in the last several years had stressed the company's resources and infrastructure to the max. The company sold its two brands with a view to allow it to focus on the production of bio-dynamically produced wines that fully represent the concept of "terroir." In 2008, the company sold their old tasting room and winery, moving Bonny Doon into new locations in Santa Cruz. Once again, we see the dynamic strategies taken by large and small producers and how these strategies interact to form the stratified landscape of global the business of wine.

New Player from Emerging Markets

While Argentina and Chile are attracting investments for wine-growing and wine-making, the country of China, until very recently, remained rather unknown to the global wine industry. However, this has changed, and China's rapid economic growth and promising consumer market are appealing to wine exporters who are trying to cover the losses stemmed from declining wine consumption in the traditional wine-drinking countries.

With lengthy business cycles and complexities of the wine industry, it will still take many years to build up a competitive industry in China. Nonetheless, China is witnessing a growing potential in its wine industry, where the top four domestic wine companies represent more than 50% of the total market share. Some of them have already established strategic international visions that are changing some segments of the wine industry.

For example, the company Yantai ChangYu Group Limited was the first industrialized winery in China, headquartered at the coastal city Yantai, Shandong Province. It was established in 1892 by a well-known overseas Chinese merchant, Chang Bishi.

The Chinese modern wine industry began with the ChangYu story. Over the century, ChangYu witnessed several changes in ownership. Its sales staff grew from 3 in 1989 to over 1500 in 2006 and 1600 in 2008. After 1994s ownership restructure and 2004s privatization, ChangYu was fully geared up for substantial growth. As China was moving away from producing "half-juice" wine towards serious wine making, ChangYu wines has been moving up the price ladder, with an increased focus on mid-range and high-end wines. For years, ChangYu has been leading the château-building boom in China. In 2001, it formed a strategic alliance with the well-known French wine group Castel. The cooperation took the form of two JVs: Castel-ChangYu Wine Co. Ltd., located in Lang Fang, Hebei, and Yantai ChangYu Wine Chateau Co. Ltd. In 2003, ChangYu-Castel Chateau launched the "barrel ordering" sales mode, which was new in the Chinese wine industry.

In 2006, ChangYu entered the ice wine business by cooperating with Canadian Aurora Ice Wine Co., which had successfully planted ice grape in China on more than 300 hectares of land in five years. The yield of global ice wine, restricted by climatic conditions, was confined to Canada and Germany. ChangYu's ice wine is targeted at the young, especially female consumers, as it was sweet in taste.

ChangYu created a chateau in New Zealand, named ChangYu Kely Estate of New Zealand, by partnering with Karikari Estate of New Zealand; it is a notable golf chateau. ChangYu was also collaborating with Karikari to build a wine distribution network in 100 golf courses in China. ChangYu Kely wine has been targeted at foreigners living in China. However, the prospect of other strategic market penetrations is considered.

In June 2007, ChangYu opened the AFIP Chateau in Beijing, which witnessed an investment by China, Italy, the US, France, and Portugal. Its target consumers are high-end personalities in political and business circles. The new chateau aimed to be a premium wine producing center, with an annual production of 1,000 tons, as well as a tourist and wine culture club. With the launch of the new chateau, ChangYu introduced in China a new sales and marketing mode:wine futures. ChangYu released 100 casks of 2006 AFIP wine futures, 20 of which were bought by TXB, one of the largest European wine distributors. The new Beijing Chateau also released cellar spaces for personal storage, owners of which were entitled to a cask of AFIP Chateau's best wine and long-term access to the storage space.

ChangYu's growth was fueled by its market-orientation and global vision, while ranking first in terms of market share among Chinese wineries, with an estimated 20% of the total volume. Its cooperation with big international wine groups enhanced its competitiveness in the fast-growing Chinese market and gave it access to knowledge for global operations. By 2006, ChangYu wine was sold in around 3,000 shopping malls, supermarkets, and stores in 14 European countries. In June 2006, ChangYu signed an exporting agreement with TXB. At the end of the year, 240,000 cases of ChangYu Jiebaina dry red wine had been ordered by TXB, which was the biggest single export order for Chinese wine. ChangYu Jiebaina also began to be served on Lufthansa's Asia-bound airlines. In the international marketplace, ChangYu targeted to be featured among the top 10 wineries in the world in 2008. After the global financial weaknesses of 2009, the company enjoyed significant growth in revenues and profits in 2010 and 2011, but 2012 brought revenues down by 11% (ChangYu financial reports).

In 2011 and 2012, Chinese wine interests moved to increase positions abroad and acquired more of the world's vineyards and wineries.

Summary

Competition in the business of wine is now a global phenomenon. Strategic competitive practices are becoming commonplace. These competitive initiatives are related to organizational size, the dwindling Western European market, the decline in European vineyards (imposed by EU directives), the philosophical position of individual vintners, and the changes in transformation and communications methods, but most importantly by the increasingly cross-cultural convergence and greater openness of international trade. These have been the changes shaping the worldwide marketplace, and the process of shifting ownership and control will continue as strategic investments react to the process of global competition.

Chapter 9

LEGISLATION AND POLITICAL ISSUES

The business of wine, like all businesses, is played according to "rules of the game" established by government laws and regulations, and sometimes a few additional policies of trade associations. For the reader interested in the rules of the game, this chapter details the legislative and political history of the EU and explains the current laws and policies that have controlled or influenced much of the industry.

Background to EU Legislation
The Stresa Conference of 1958, following the Treaty of Rome, confirmed the basic principles of the Common Agricultural policy and placed agriculture in a pan-European rather than narrowly national context. The principles established at that time are still the basis that forms the policies of today:

i.   Free circulation of agricultural products, guaranteed by a system of uniform prices and uniform guarantees to producers;
ii. Community preference, achieved by means of a common frontier with common customs duties on imports from non-member States;
iii. Financial solidarity and the assumption of responsibility by the Member States as a whole for the necessary expenditure on the agricultural policy, irrespective of levels of expenditure within individual States.

There were monumental problems in attempting to create a common set of policies for wine in an area that constituted half the entire global market. Traditionally, these countries had restricted or even prohibited imports of wine, while simultaneously striving to export their own small surplus of wines. The volume of surplus French wine was often small, because the average Frenchman was consuming a hearty 126 liters per year. These were relatively comfortable times for the wine-producer and returns were good. Perhaps for this reason the issue of wine-pricing was avoided for quite some time. The major problem was that the creation of the proposed common market in wine would bring together the two greatest wine-producing areas in the world, France and Italy, who had previously practiced a policy of almost complete mutual exclusion of the other's wines.

Moreover, Italy's total annual production had been steadily rising over the decade from 1948/49 to1958/59—leaping an astonishing 60% from 40.4 million to 67 million hl. Faith was placed in the steady increase of Italian consumption, the stability of the French market and a pronounced increase in consumption in the Benelux countries and the North. However, it was clear that enormous care would have to be taken, if the prosperous, well-regulated and lovingly-nurtured wine industry of France were not to be totally swamped by the overly fertile, Italian wine industry. Therefore, progress was slow. The first specific legislation on wine adopted by the Council of the Community was regulation number 24 of April 1962, which laid the foundations still operational today. These were:

i.   the institution of a viticultural land is registered based on a general vineyard census;
ii.   compulsory annual notification by producers of the quantities of wine and grape-must produced, and annual notification by producers and all merchants, except retailers, of stocks held;
iii. annual compilation of a forward estimate of resources and requirements;
iv.   adoption of rules covering "quality wines produced in specific regions" based on respect for traditional practice and covering the demarcation of the area of production, vine varieties, cultivation methods, wine-making methods, minimum natural alcoholic strength, yield per hectare, and analysis and assessment of organoleptic characteristics;
v.   establishment of a management committee to oversee the rules established by at least 54 votes of a total of 76 distributed as laid down in the Treaty of Rome for the Council of the Community.

After the initial batch of regulations were put into effect, there followed a very quiet period in the 1960s of eight years. During this time, the only forward motion consisted of some hesitant steps toward unification of the market by increasing the bilateral import quotas and extending them to all Member States. This long period of inactivity was largely a consequence of the difficulty of solving the enormous problem of reconciling France and Italy, a problem rendered even more prickly by the fact that France was under an obligation to import around 7 Mhl annually from her former colony, Algeria, until September 1970. In Italy during the same period, the massive expansion of wine-production had been largely defused by elements such as the economic revolution, which had provoked a huge exodus of labor from rural areas to the cities, and also the falling away of "promiscuous cultivation" in multi-crop vineyards that simply could not compete with the newly-planted single-crop variety.

Despite an increase in production-levels over this period from around 116 hl to 138 million hl and a rise in end-of-year stocks from 37m hl to 75m hl, consumption had risen almost proportionately. The imminent cessation of France's obligation to Algeria promised to free-up another significant market for surplus Italian wine. Therefore, on 22nd December 1969, the Council of the European Communities, after long and difficult negotiations—especially between France and Italy—thought the time was right finally to put into practice the common organization of the market in wine. In April 1970, it adopted two basic regulations: Number 816/70 laying down additional provisions for the common organization of the market in wine and Number 817/70 laying down special provisions with regard to higher quality wines produced in specified regions.

Since then, there have been hundreds of further Community regulations on wine prompted by the ups and downs of production and consumption, but also because all matters concerning vines and wine (with the exception of fraud) were withdrawn from the jurisdiction of individual Member States and became the exclusive prerogative of the European Community (and later the designation of the EU).

The optimistic analysis of the future of the wine industry, which formed the bedrock of the 1970 legislation, determined the range of mechanisms thought needful for the regulation of wine production and marketing. It was the more liberal approach of the Italians that took precedence over the interventionist French approach, and a compromise was eventually reached. New planting and replanting of vines was made subject only to rules of quality rather than to any quantitative limits, such as had previously been operating in France. Again, there were no binding rules covering the market of wine above the rules on wine-production. These rules on production were sufficiently loose permitting a continuation of practices in individual countries prior to the 1970 regulations. In effect, this meant that the French had tied their own hands to some extent in comparison with the rather more easy-going attitudes prevailing among her competitors.

A fairly spare structure of intervention mechanisms, namely distillation and storage aids, were deemed sufficient to be called upon should the need arise, and these rules applied only to common wine. It was presumably felt that production and consumption of quality wines would be self-regulating.

Chronology of the Fundamental Rules of the Legislation

Rules regarding viticulture: Vine varieties were to be classified as "recommended, authorized or provisionally authorized" for each of the various administrative units. A date was set after which grapes from varieties falling outside these three categories would be excluded or permitted only for distillation purposes. New planting, replanting and grubbing were to be declared annually to the competent authorities of the Member States.

Definitions of wine-types: It was declared that table wine had to have a minimum alcohol level of 8.5% and not exceed 15%. The lower limit was later raised to 9% with the exception of certain parts of Germany. The quality-wine category was also enshrined in legislation.

Wine Production: The Community was divided into zones (A, B, CI, CII, and CIII) form North to South. Minimum natural strengths were apportioned according to region and also the maximum permitted levels of enrichment were established (decreasing from 5% in the North to 2% in the South). Enriching with sugar was legally permitted only in zones where it was a traditional practice.

Pricing and intervention: Rules for determining guide prices and threshold prices that would activate the agreed upon system for intervention were defined as were methods for determining weekly market prices for table wines, in order to make possible the application of specific intervention measures to support prices. The guide-price is set each year and runs from September to August of the following year. It indicates the average wholesale price which has been adopted as its policy objective for a sector. When the market was depressed over a short term (3 months) or long term (9 months), then private storage assistance would be paid. In the case of persistent and serious surpluses, the distillation of table wine could be subsidized.

Trade with non EU Countries: Import statistics of wine from outside the EU were to be monitored and, besides additional customs payments on such wines, it was decreed that they should also comply with a reference-price. Conversely, aid was extended to exporters in the form of excise refunds.

Surveillance: It was decided that all the laws on declaration of harvests and stocks, oenological practices, methods of analysis, and labeling should be properly enforced and monitored.

Free movement: Full freedom of movement for wine was declared within these European countries. Qualitative restrictions and duties were prohibited in trade between Member States. The optimism already mentioned as the justification for the Council's establishing the above legislation proved ill founded. Bumper harvests in 1970, 1973 and 1974 caused a massive extra influx of wine from Italy to France, straining the newly established pricing system and the mechanism for distillation of surpluses. This resulted in a 1974 French growers' blockading of the port of Sete, which was the main conduit into France of Italian exports, and this provoked the first "wine war." France eventually decided to impose a tax on Italian imports, which was later withdrawn in 1976, as a result of action by the Community.

Agreements of 1976
A more or less blanket ban on the planting of new vineyards, especially in the area of common wines, was adopted as a first step to "rationalizing the market." Subsidies were simultaneously made available for grubbing-up and replanting with alternative crops. Aid for the establishment of wine-production facilities was likewise restricted. This package of measures was merely an interim expedient, but there were certain lasting benefits from the 1976 shake-up, such as the establishment of the principle that the authorities responsible for policing fraudulent practice in each of the Member States should be permitted to collaborate amongst themselves.

Even if the common market members were at this time still struggling to balance production and consumption, progress had been made in the field of fraud-prevention. Some of these instances of malpractice had become so deeply ingrained as to be almost institutionalized, such as the admixture of Algerian reds to so-called Burgundies exported to Britain. But in the unified system, these abuses could be more easily traced and stopped. Even today, it would be extremely naïve to suppose that nowhere in the EU are growers blending illegally or adding sugar when they shouldn't. But the consumer can at least take comfort in the fact that it has become increasingly difficult for wine-producers to be dishonest.

Deliberations of 1979
In 1979, after much deliberation, a complete overhaul was proposed. Genuine planning was begun for the wine-sector as a whole—from planting, through yields per hectare, to consumption. However, once again it was nature's bounty which rocked the boat. Exceptional harvests in 1979 and 1980 caused a serious crisis of overproduction. The minimum price mechanism included in the recent rules was not applied, partly because there had not been time for full discussions of the new proposals and partly because several countries recognized how expensive the implementation would prove under

the circumstances. Again, all that the member nations could do was to distill ever-larger quantities of wine, as an exceptional measure in response to exceptional surpluses. There was also a recurrence of the previous wine-war tactics, with the French fishing fleet once more rushing to help their vigneron brothers by blockading the port of Sete. Something major clearly had to be done to prevent these wine-wars from reoccurring.

The Reform of 1982

The attempt to bring France and Italy together into one financial market was proving too much for the mechanisms in place at the time. Furthermore, the imminent accession of Spain and Portugal into the Community was a problem for which they had not prepared.

The new principles decided upon in 1982 were the following:

i.   Community intervention price should not fall below 82% of the current guide price for table wine.
ii.   Provision is made for the automatic opening of optional "preventive distillation" from 1st Sept each year. The producers receiving 65% of the guide price.
iii. All producers may be required to distill a proportion of their production under certain conditions of market crisis—for which a reduced price of 60% of guide price (later further reduced to between 40% to 50%) will be received by the producer.
iv.   When compulsory distillation has to be resorted to, there is to be automatic opening of voluntary distillation at 82% of guide price. The total deriving from such voluntary distillation not to exceed 5 million hl, except where the Council deems it permissible.

Other provisions introduced later (31st March 1984) included the reduction of the aid available for the distillation of wine enriched with sucrose or subsidized must concentrate and the discontinuation of Community grants for short-term storage.

Also, the total ban on new planting was extended and is a rule which generally is more or less followed. However, the development of new techniques of cultivation has meant that wine-production per-hectare has been increasing every year by about 0.60% to 0.70%. In the light of the accession of Spain and Portugal with vineyards of large size but restricted yield, the Community saw the possibility of further huge production increases in the future.

Consequently, if the aims of the Community were to be achieved, more stringent measures such as the restriction of re-planting had to be imposed. At the same time, a progressive reduction was introduced in the quantities of table wine eligible for all forms of optional distillation and for long-term storage. In other words, the principle had been adopted that levels of guaranteed prices and market support measures were to be reduced for products in surplus. The Council in fact had little choice in the matter, as the Community budget simply could not go on supporting extremely high expenditures to finance the maintenance of its famous wine.

The chronic surplus, aggravated by swiftly diminishing demand from the two main traditional markets for table wine, France and Italy, followed by yet more record harvests, provoked the 1984 Dublin meeting of heads of Government, at which the wine sector was prominent on the agenda. Some drastic measures were decided upon. Besides an increase in the grubbing-up policy to reduce areas under vines, there was agreement that compulsory distillation should be increased when a serious imbalance occurred, such as when prices remained low for an extended period, or when stocks were in excess of four months of utilization, or when production exceeded consumption by 9%.

However, the mechanism designed in Dublin proved extremely difficult to administer and met with a high degree of resistance from growers whose profits it badly affected. The complexities of deciding how much wine had to be distilled in any particular region and from which growers it should be obtained—not to mention the sheer cost of the operation—demanded a cautious approach on the part of the authorities. In the first year the new rulings applied, surplus stocks amounted to approximately 30 to 35-million hl, but only 12m hl were "condemned" to compulsory distillation—from this figure the 6 million hl already sent voluntarily were to be deducted. Even when, in 1987, the Community decided to clamp down when faced with an excess of around 40 million hl (Spain now being included in the calculations), measures taken were insufficient to restore balance and the price of wine remained at the rock-bottom 82% of guide-price.

Since then, the wisdom of distillation has been called into question—notably by the French. One fundamental flaw is that the distillation of grape by-products is a costly and imperfect way of producing industrial alcohol. Another problem is that corruption undeniably persists. The fact that the EU intervention price is designed to protect wine from falling below a certain price inevitably tends to draw subsidy towards low-grade wine. Hence, some growers clearly see little incentive to produce better quality. Given also that the distilleries are frequently sited—as in the case of a number of Sicilian operations—in the caves themselves, it is plain to see that some unscrupulous producers were merely using Community money to buy plant for the distillation of wine, which served only one purpose—to net further Community money in subsidies

Refinement of the Early 1990s

In 1990, the Commission Regulation No.2676/90 was adopted, relating to the methods for the analysis of wine. It describes methods in the context of commercial transactions and control operations in order to establish the composition of the product and to check if it has been subjected to treatments in violation of the authorized oenological practices. The Commission Regulation number 3201/90 established detailed rules for the description and presentation of wines and grape-musts. Custom matters were regulated by the directive of October 1992, which defines the various categories of alcoholic beverages and prescribes the basis of calculating the excise duty. It introduces special provisions for certain regions of Spain and provides general exemption to alcohol that is not intended for consumption as a beverage. In November 1993, the Community adopted the Regulation 3199/93 on the mutual recognition of procedures for the complete denaturing of alcohol for the purposes of exemption from excise duty. And this was amended in 1995 by Commission Regulation No. 2546/95, which establishes the various formulations of denaturants in the Member States and the variations allowed in individual countries.

The Reform of 1999

Council Regulation No 1493/99 adopted on May 17, 1999, established a new common market organization for wine and provided simplification and transparency by replacing the previous twenty-three Council Regulations dealing with the wine sector. The measures adopted offered a positive impact on the competitive performance of the EU wine sector, in the context of an expanding global economy, and addressed the new situation in the sector in the immediate and medium term. The reform provided for transfers in competence from the Council to the Commission as well as from the Commission to Member States (which may delegate to producer organizations).

The reform had seven broad objectives:
- Improve the balance between supply and demand on the Community markets and allow producers to take advantage of expanding markets;
- Enable the sector to become more competitive in the longer term;
- Eliminate intervention, where it is considered an artificial outlet to surplus production;
- Maintain all traditional outlets for potable wine alcohol and vine-based products;
- Take regional diversity into account;
- Formalize the role of producer and sector organizations;
- Simplify current wine legislation.

The reform retained the existing ban on new vineyard plantings until 2010. However, the member-states were authorized to distribute new planting rights for a limited quantity of additional plantings, which were equivalent to 2% of the national areas under vines, and 1.5% of were divided between the producer countries as shown in Table 9:1.

The Commission was empowered to allocate additional rights from the Community reserve to those regions where there is additional need that could be met by the distribution of such rights. A new system of reserves of new planting and replanting rights facilitates transfers of replanting rights to enable the development of areas with a manifest need. The system addresses the situation of irregular planting and replanting, including sanctions where appropriate.

Country	Area (Hectares)
Austria	737
France	13,565
Germany	1,534
Greece	1,098
Italy	12,933
Luxembourg	18
Portugal	3,760
Spain	17,355
EU Reserve	17,000
Total	**68,000**

Table 9:1 Distribution of Newly Created Planting Rights Allocated to Member States
Source: Council Regulation (EC) No. 1493/99, on the Common Organization of the Market in Wine.

Replanting is necessary to allow the renewal of the European vineyard. Replanting rights can be attributed in the following situations:

- Grubbing-up of an equal surface on the same holding.
- Transfer coming from another holding in a same Member State, under conditions determined by the Member State.
- Replanting rights shall be used before the end of the 5th year after grubbing-up. However, a provision was included enabling Member States to extend the duration of replanting rights to up to 8 years.
- These rights can be used on predetermined surfaces and destina-

tions. The Member States can order to replant on the grubbed-up areas.

- The provision regarding planting rights applies to Member States whose production is greater than 25,000hl only.
- In order to avoid income losses, the replanting rights can be attributed before the grubbing-up (anticipated planting).

Restructuring: 2000 to 2004

Restructuring and conversion measures were introduced with the aim to adapt supply to the demand in both qualitative and quantitative ways. These concern the following actions:

- Converting vineyards toward other grapes varieties;
- Relocating vineyards;
- Improving the vineyards management techniques.

The measure does not concern replanting because of a normal end of the vineyard life cycle. Only regions in Member States that have compiled an inventory of the production potential may benefit from the system, and support may only be granted, if a restructuring and conversion plan was drawn up and approved by the Member State. These plans concern the vineyards whose production does not meet the market any longer, but where a conversion of vineyards towards other grapes varieties, or relocation of vineyards or improvement of management techniques can meet the new exigencies of the consumers. The support is of two kinds:

- Contribution to the actual costs of the restructuring and conversion not exceeding 50% of these costs (75% in Objective 1 regions).
- Compensation for loss of revenue resulting from implementation of the plans (no compensation where old and new vines coexist for a maximum of three years).

Inventory

An accurate picture of existing production potential is essential to ensure that the sector can be managed in the most effective way. Therefore, an inventory of production potential has been introduced and has two functions. First, the inventory is a precondition for Member States for the purpose of regularization and to gain access to the newly created planting rights. Second, regions of a Member State may only have access to restructuring and conversion aid, where the inventory was completed in those regions in 2001.

Market Mechanisms

The market mechanisms refocus their aims on maintaining all traditional outlets for wine and vine-based products, allow the Commission to address exceptional cases of serious structural surplus and/or quality problems, and ensure continuity of supply and the quality of wine reaching the market. A
number of obsolete mechanisms were removed, as was the possibility of
finding artificial outlets for unmarketable products.

Certain existing measures were retained as they remain necessary for
quality and technical reasons, namely, the distillation of by-products of winemaking as a quality measure, the distillation of dual purpose grapes and private storage aid. In addition, aids are still available for the use of grape musts
for increasing alcoholic strength (enrichment) as well as for processing. A
specific distillation of table wines and wines suitable for yielding table wines
was introduced, aimed at supporting outlets for potable wine alcohol. A "crisis" distillation measure, available on a voluntary basis, was introduced to
deal with exceptional cases of market disturbance and/or problems of quality.

Producer and Sector Organizations

The more recent reforms allowed member States to recognize producer organizations with certain aims. If Member States recognize such organizations, checks at regular intervals must be made and the Commission must be
notified of decisions on recognition or withdrawal. Member States may lay
down marketing rules for these organizations, provided that such rules do not
contravene Community law on free movement, competition or non-
discrimination. Rules set by Member States need to be reported to the Commission, if they regulate supply. Consumer interests must be taken into account in organizations' activities.

Trade with Third Countries

The existing provisions for export licenses and refunds, as well as import duties and tariff quotas, were maintained. In addition, grape-must from third
countries may not be vinified and the blending of Community wine with imported wine is forbidden, unless approved by the Council based on a Commission proposal.

Oenological Practices and Processes

The Council Regulation establishes the basic principles for authorized oenological practices and processes, which allow only defined product be put into
circulation. It restricts the use of wine lees and grape-marc for the production
of alcohol, spirits and piquet only, and disallowing its use in the production
of wine or other beverages. It also forbids the production of wine from raw
material of origin in third countries or blending with wine of origin in third

countries in the territory of the EU, with some exceptions, especially for the UK and Ireland.

Member States may continue to impose stricter conditions, in order to ensure the preservation of the essential characteristics of quality wines produced in specific areas, table wines described by a geographical indication, sparkling wines and liqueur wines.

The rules relating to the description, designation, presentation and protection of certain products aim at protecting the interests of the producer and consumer and the smooth operation of the internal market. It specifically restricts the use of misleading or confusing information in advertising and marketing a product. Labeling of products in circulation in the EU must be in accordance with the principles laid down by the reform.

Certain provisions pertaining to the labeling of wine sector products, which includes still, sparkling, semi-sparkling, aerated and liqueur wines and grape-must, were introduced later. These Regulations (2585/2001 and 2086/2002) include restrictions on the use of the word "wine." Another legislation relating to specific matters also came into effect in 2002. The amendments to Common Agricultural Policy (Wine) in 2004 (SI 2004/1046) provide for the enforcement of EU Regulations in England and Northern Ireland. They define new rules that need to be observed before a table wine originating in England may be described as a "regional wine." These also provide for the accreditation of organizers of organoleptic assessment panels to determine whether a table wine is of a satisfactory organoleptic standard for a regional wine.

The purpose of all this legislation and rules is the pursuit of some sort of market stability. It is easy to criticize the workings of the EU. It is an enormous and, consequently, sometimes rather ponderous organization. There are still things wrong with the way the wine business is organized (or disorganized). However, as we have seen, the problems involved are complex, and it would be unjust to allow criticisms to entirely eclipse the overall achievements of the EU legislation in attempts to assist the industry—the business of wine.

The wine market has undergone a significant change over the past four decades, moving away from high volume production of low quality wines toward providing better quality wines in smaller quantities for a more discriminating consumer. Of course, price and production of quality wines have always followed consumer demand. This characterizes the future market as well, and much of the EU legislation of recent years has been aimed at reducing the burdens of economic spikes and valleys.

Chapter 10

THE FUTURE OUTLOOK

The future of the wine industry is predicated on the interactions of economic fundamentals. We view the industry from the established trends or as economists might say, "the dynamic interactions of supply and demand over time." The future is always an unknown. Even the best prognosticators and economic experts cannot unquestionably foretell the future, but projections can be made using reasonable assumptions derived from prudent observations of trends. For example, the global market for the wine industry evidenced that consumption in volume terms would probably increase from about 220 million hector liters in 2002 to 235 million hector liters in 2007. This prompted a forecast for 2007. Later, the industry data for 2007 confirmed that this forecast was essentially on-target, and the global market had been growing at a 1.3% annual rate (Figure 10:1).

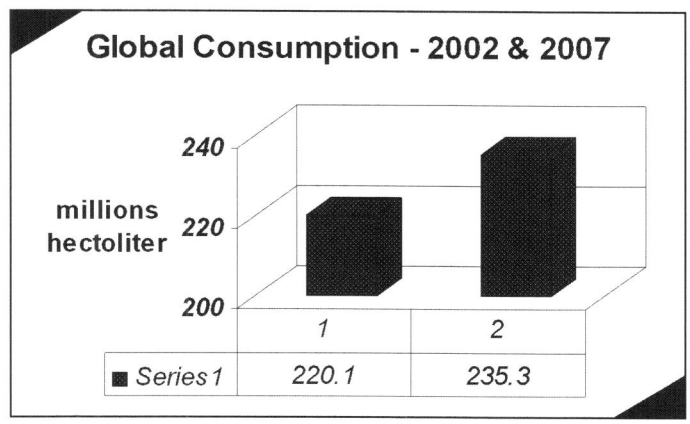

Figure 10:1 Previous Growth in Total Volume of Global Wine Consumption (2002-2007).
Source: Based on data from Vinexpo-IWSR/GDR.

Similar to the estimates of consumption in terms of volume, estimates were made for global wine sales in terms of US dollars for the same period. Global wine sales (including taxes) were estimated to have increased from $101.6

billion to $ 114.2 billion in constant dollar terms. The global sales forecast was a very reasonable approximation of the same period. However, later forecasts for 2009 proved wrong. The "financial crisis" and subsequent global economic downturn seriously changed the market for many commodities, including wine. Figure 10:2 shows that volume did not decrease, but revenue in terms of US dollar growth decreased with the onset of the economic disruptions initiated by the financial crisis.

However, using a currency such as USD ($) for tracking and projecting sales can easily confuse analysis and confound the results, because of the possibility of large changes in the exchange value of a currency. Changes in the exchange value have certainly been true in terms of the USD over the period 2002 to 2013. For example, the British pound (£) to the $ in 2002 was $1.60, and by 2007 it was $2.00—a significant fluctuation in relative valuation. The fluctuations have been even more volatile since the "financial crisis" of 2008-2009 and the subsequent aftermath of global monetary policies around the world. By the second quarter of 2013, the British pound (£) to the $ stood at 1.53. Even more confounding for comparison is the EU euro that has fluctuated from a high of $1.58 to a low of $1.21, and in the second and third quarter of 2013the euro hovered around $1.30 to $1.31.

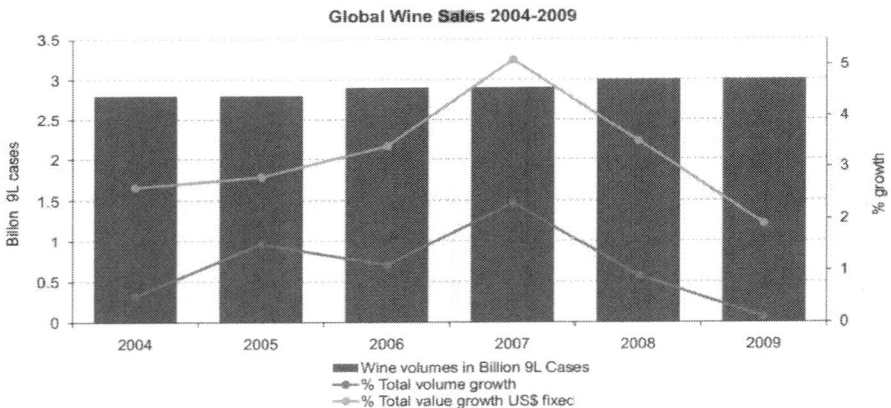

Figure 10:2 Global Wine Sales. Euro Stat

More recently, the data from 2007 through 2011 and an estimate of 2012 are depicted in Figure 10:3.

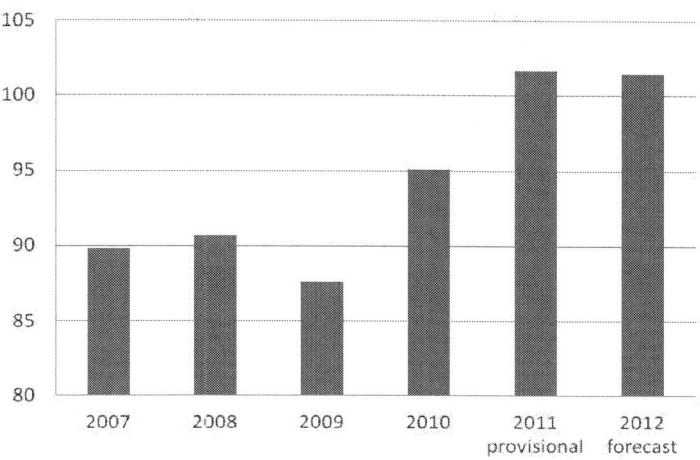

Figure 10:3 Trends of the Global Wine Market (export volumes), Mhl
Source: OIV, 2013.

Estimates of volume can be more reliable than monetary estimates. Figure 10:4 is an example of monetary estimates.

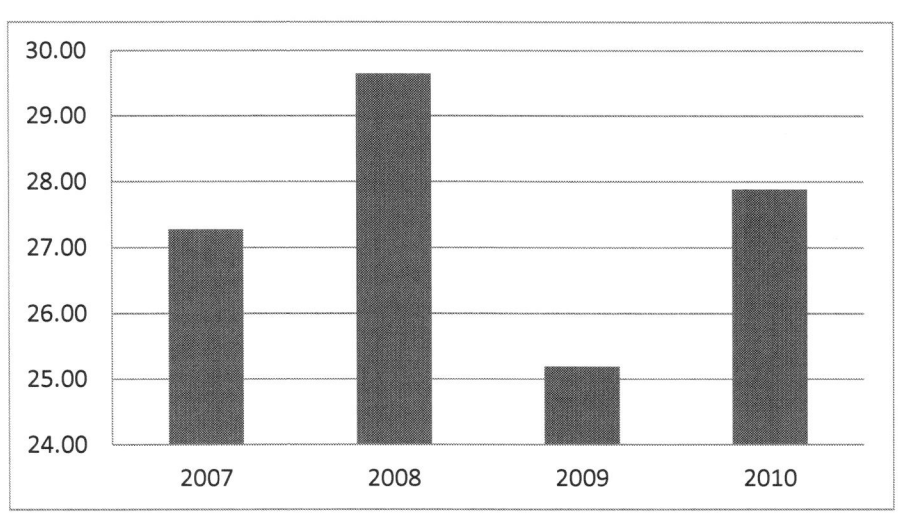

Figure 10:4 Trends of the Global Wine Market (total sum of all countries' exports), USD, billion
Source: OIV, 2013.

We know that the growth in wine volume consumption in the UK was increasing, and also increasing in terms of the £, but the value in terms of the $ could show an even higher growth rate during one period and a lower value during another simply because of volatility in exchange rates between currencies. This is why we must be careful when comparing statistics from different sources that may use different measures. Even when attempting to adjust for price constant-currency, there are problems when trying to compare such derived growth rates in global terms. Nevertheless, we can obtain some insight by comparing different country data using a single currency measure such as the British pound, EU Euro or USD.

According to research studies, the US, France and the UK emerge as the top three wine consumers. As to exports, Table 10:1 provides the growth rate in the total retail export sales in the major wine markets during the period 2007 to 2010 (as calculated in terms of USD).

USD billion	2007	2008	2009	2010
France	9.25	10.00	7.69	8.39
Germany	0.99	1.13	1.02	1.14
Italy	4.74	5.28	4.84	5.17
UK	0.38	0.41	0.49	0.65
US	0.90	0.96	0.88	1.10
Australia	2.49	2.15	1.82	1.96
Spain	2.40	2.86	2.29	2.45
Argentina	0.50	0.64	0.63	0.74
Switzerland	0.15	0.15	0.09	0.16
World Total	27.27	29.64	25.19	27.88

Table10:1: Wine Export Value, USD, billion
Source: faostat.fao.org

The UK and Germany look set to continue their upward trend. In the UK, the wine sales in 2010 were over 70% higher as compared to 2007. In the case of Germany, wine sales were approximately 15% higher as compared to 2007. In the US, the 2010 wine sales were about 22% higher as compared to the wine sales in 2007. Overall, the trend for red wine consumption is likely to continue to increase its market share. The market share of fortified wine and vermouth has overall been witnessing a declining trend for many years.

When forecasting, there are numerous variables to take into account, such as the effect of changing weather conditions on production, year by year; the potential effect on demand of various social issues: and government policies. Gathering and interpreting data and calculating adjustments is difficult; for example, in the productive areas of Russia and Eastern European states where production has been experiencing rather high growth rates (as much as 3% per year or more), therefore accounting for changes and forecasting is challenging.

The EU has been considered the primary "over producer." Consequently, the European governments and EU commission have pursued policies designed to reduce overall output. The trend towards consumption of less, but better quality, wine means that countries such as Italy are able to adapt to the changing market without any disastrous consequences for the vinicultural community. Italy has converted a number of its vineyards to smaller yields of better quality grapes, which has resulted in an average annual decline in total volume production, but with higher returns from sales.

The slow fall in consumption demand for wine in terms of volume within Western Europe was expected to continue a while longer. However, the general trend of consumption of higher quality (therefore higher priced) wine is also expected to continue, slowly. The possible exceptions are certain markets, such as the UK and Scandinavia that appear to remain in an overall upward trend, due to the increased acceptance of wine-consumption and substitution for other alcoholic drinks. All short and medium forecasts of trends are likely to be a bit off the mark, because of the EU situation where the EU leaders are attempting to forcefully maintain their single currency, the euro. A single monetary unit of account imposed on many regions of highly diverse cultures and economic endowments is a disablement to many of the national economies. Therefore, the next few years will be unpredictably confounded by the EU attempts at monetary policies, while attempting to balance fiscal policies between the diverse nations of different cultures and economic endowments.

In Eastern Europe, there has been significant growth in wine production, which despite slow growth in the Western European nations, is expected to continue, at least modestly. The overall Russian wine market is also expected to continue to grow as well. Growth in Eastern Europe will continue to be largely due to an increase in the main consumer group, ages 20 to 40, and the slowly growing, but increasingly affluent middle-income group. Table 10:2 depicts the change of wine markets in specific Eastern Europe countries from 2007 through 2010.

The countries that have enjoyed good vintages in recent years appear set to continue increasing the export potential of their wine. Examining the top five wine markets in the Eastern Europe, total wine production increased significantly from 2001 to 2007 (averaging around 1.4 million hl per year). Between 2007 and the final quarter of 2010, the growth continued in all these countries except Ukraine.

North Africa, Morocco and Tunisia have increased production by 14% and 13% annually. Algeria on the other hand decreased by 12.5% and will continue to decline in terms of wine production.

The wine-producing countries of the developing world, in Latin America especially, have been expanding domestic markets with their upward trend in volume production. Argentina is likely to be producing 4.3m hl more per year by the end of the decade (an annual growth rate of 2%), while Chile, whose export market in quality wines is quite buoyant, may grow significantly.

	2007	2010	Global Market Rank	% change
Russia	1,113,000	1,150,000	6	3%
Ukraine	220,100	205,000	24	-7%
Czech Republic	174,000	198,000	26	14%
Poland	69,300	79,000	32	14%
Slovakia	79,400	73,000	33	-8%

Table 10:2 Growth Rates in Major Wine Markets in Eastern Europe
Source: wineinstitute.org

Worldwide wine consumption is expected to increase only modestly in the future. The future scenario would seem to be one of increasing focus between the common wine and premium wine sectors. Producers who cannot or will not upgrade to the premium category will be competing for a dwindling number of low-priced consumers. Producers of premium brand wine who aim at the more modest price points (not-too-elevated) should be able to gain a consistent and growing section of the market. Producers in the super-premium arena will continue to attract a small clientele that is willing to pay increasingly high prices for the highest quality. As in all business, it's a matter of supply and demand. We have reviewed the supply conditions, and some of the consumer demands, but now we will consider the details in future implications of demand.

Demand
Consumer behaviors around the world are converging in many ways. The developed countries of the EU are a good example of this process of consumer convergence of product preferences and this is certainly true for the market of wine. The changes in consumption patterns are due to increasing globalization of marketing and the cultural cross-fertilization that arises from increasing contact. The growth of multinational business is a powerful force

for convergence of values and behaviors. Consumer researchers have been interested in tracking the consumption patterns in different parts of the world and determining the extent to which they are becoming similar. Shifts in wine consumption patterns in Europe are representative of this type of convergence. As traditional boundaries become blurred, consumer preferences for types of alcoholic beverages, particularly wine, are changing. The preferences appear to be driven by a growing acceptance of a cross-cultural influence and the effects of global marketing strategies. Researching such trends is interesting and useful to the business of wine, as it relates to the degree of socio-economic and cultural change over time. In particular, we find that the dissimilarity of wine consumption between Europeans has narrowed significantly between the northern and southern European countries. This is strong evidence for interpreting the changes brought about by cross-cultural influences in marketing and regional policies.

Products such as wine incorporate identification with their national origin, but they need not be standardized in order to have broad appeal across national or regional frontiers. Wine need not be adaptive or standardized for the purpose of marketing. Wine has experienced a slower global shift than culture-free or standardized life-style products, but over the long term there has been a definable trend. We can see shifts in all alcoholic beverage consumption patterns over the past half-century. Over time, as barriers to trade have decreased, the consumer preferences for wine have trended toward more similar consumptive patterns, with the Northern European countries increasing their consumption and the Southern European countries slowly decreasing their per-capita amount of wine consumption.

The Culture of Wine

Today, as throughout history, wine is not only associated with cuisine, but also a ritual part of many social gatherings. The drinking of wine facilitates social contact by stimulating a collective feeling of well-being. Drinking has a range of rituals that have different associations for drinkers, depending on their various cultural identities. Understandably, the consumption of wine has been more popular in the wine producing regions of Europe, and it was deeply integrated into these regional cultures. Nevertheless, the type and level of consumption changes as culture itself gradually changes.

Previously, cross-cultural analysis of consumption patterns has focused more on attitudes, values, and other normative aspects, rather than on the absolute quantity of alcoholic beverages consumed. However, the per-capita quantity of wine consumed is an important measure. People living in the Mediterranean region have been predominantly wine drinkers, while people who live in countries in Northern and Western Europe are primarily beer drinkers. Wine is consumed both at meals and by itself, while beer and especially spirits are mainly consumed apart from meals. These patterns of behavior remain largely intact, despite considerable recent shifts in the consumption of wine.

National drinking patterns have developed over a long period of time and, consequently, beverage consumption has been deeply ingrained into national cultures. This is especially true in the producing nations. The way beverages are used has influenced government policies and tax measures, which have also influenced changes in drinking patterns. In some countries, temperance movements have influenced governments to take measures to shift consumption toward beverages with a lower alcohol content. Here again, wine is a natural contender for superiority. Particularly in Finland, Sweden, and Norway, the governments sponsored various policies to change drinking patterns away from beverages of higher alcohol content toward lower content, through a number of different types of control measures. An example has been taxation levels, such as taxing hard-spirits higher than wine or beer. Similarly, Belgium, Denmark, and the UK have attempted to influence drinking patterns away from beverages of higher alcohol content through these same types of control and taxations measures. Furthermore, the EU has been responsible for pressuring the member nations to unify their taxation, and this has also encouraged increasing wine consumption in the Northern states.

Over the past half century, growing affluence, increased leisure time, greater travel, broader communication, and the development of common trade areas, have all conspired to modify previous national drinking patterns. Moreover, unequivocal evidence of trends in drinking patterns can be traced from the late 1970s and early 1980s, during the time when most countries experienced changes in their economies, demographics, and general societal attitudes. Patterns of alcoholic beverage consumption throughout most of the EU countries reflect an expression of the generally observed convergence in cultural and economic contexts. Historically traditional patterns of wine consumption were deeply rooted in national cultures, but global integration, and most certainly European integration, has resulted in changes that are easily observable. Although there are differences in the average annual consumption of total alcoholic beverages, as well as specifically in consumption of wine, the data show that countries are becoming more similar in their drinking habits.

Many aspects of cultural convergence appear to be a worldwide trend, and the evidence from European studies is quite interesting. The data presented here is based on a comparative study of alcoholic beverage consumption in 15 countries of the EU: Austria, Belgium, Denmark, Finland, France, Germany, Greece, Ireland, Italy, Luxembourg, Netherlands, Portugal, Spain, Sweden and the UK. In Northern Europe, the traditional beer consuming countries include Austria, Belgium, Denmark, Finland, Germany, Ireland,

Luxembourg, Netherlands, Sweden, and the UK. In Southern Europe, the countries in the Mediterranean region include France, Greece, Italy, Portugal and Spain, the traditional wine producing and largely wine-consuming countries. International per capita consumption data of total alcohol and, particularly wine consumption, are presented in ten year intervals from 1950 to 2010. Of course, to determine the extent of shifting patterns of wine consumption, it is necessary to examine not only wine, but also figures for total alcohol, beer, and wine, and then compare the patterns.

The 60-year-long data series is also used to make projections. This is an ordinary trend analysis, where it is assumed that future values are determined by the same combination of past values and similar data errors.

Consumption and Trends in Europe

One aspect of a drinking pattern is whether a population drinks a lot or a little. Another is the type of beverages consumed by the population. Although there are differences in the average annual consumption of total alcoholic beverages, as well as in consumption of the different types of beverages, the research shows that countries in the EU are becoming more similar in their drinking habits. The analysis discloses explicit and undeniable trends that are valuable for defining the future of the business of wine.

Table 10:3 displays actual international per capita consumption data of wine for the 15 countries from 1950 to 2010 (estimates in ten-year intervals). Home production of wine, tourist consumption, tax-free sales, and minor personal purchases across borders affect actual consumption figures. The data shows the total sales measured in liters within nations, and is divided by the total mid-year population of drinking age for each country. Consumption figures reflect a realistic national consumption pattern for each country.

Consumption increased rapidly during the early to mid-1960s in Europe. Much of the growth is attributable to recovery after World War II and to a growing number of people entering the market. In a number of countries, consumption began to level off in the mid-1970s; and during the 1980s, the previously higher consumption countries were actually experiencing declines on a per-capita basis. This established the beginning of the trend for greater homogeneity in per-capita consumption within and across these countries (Table 10:3).

The changing patterns of wine consumption are partly related to the effects of substituting wine for the previous custom of drinking hard-spirits. No single factor explains the pronounced shift away from hard-spirits to wine. However, several influences are evident. For example, the past economic conditions sometimes encouraged governments to search for revenue generators and, consequently, taxes increased in a number of countries, particularly on import products such as wine. However, more recently, changes have occurred that tend to equalize the price differences between these countries as the EU aligns the fiscal structures of Member States. Another factor is the aging population of these countries, which is believed to be contributing to reductions in overall per capita consumption of alcoholic beverages. Moreover, the long-term government control and taxation policies have sought to reduce consumption and shift drinking patterns of alcoholic beverages.

	1970	1975	1980	1985	1990	1995	2000	2005	2010
Austria	34.6	35.1	35.8	34.3	35.0	32.0	31.8	30.4	29.0
Belgium	14.2	17.8	20.6	22.7	24.9	25.0	20.0	19.3	21.1
Denmark	5.9	11.5	14.0	20.7	21.3	27.6	30.9	33.5	36.8
Finland	3.3	5.1	4.8	4.5	6.5	11.5	19.2	20.1	22.2
France	109.0	103.0	91.0	79.7	72.7	63.0	56.0	52.5	51.0
Germany	16.0	23.2	25.5	25.6	26.1	22.2	23.6	23.2	23.2
Greece	40.0	38.0	44.9	37.3	32.8	34.5	34.0	34.0	34.4
Ireland	3.3	4.2	4.7	6.1	8.7	19.1	33.2	33.0	38.2
Italy	113.0	103.0	92.9	75.0	62.5	55.7	51.0	48.0	44.3
Netherlands	5.2	10.3	12.9	15.0	14.5	16.6	18.8	19.0	22.0
Portugal	72.5	89.8	68.7	87.0	50.0	58.1	50.0	50.1	51.0
Spain	61.5	76.0	64.7	48.0	37.4	32.2	33.0	31.3	28.0
Sweden	6.4	8.3	9.5	11.6	12.3	12.6	15.3	15.9	20.6
United Kingdom	2.9	5.2	7.2	10.0	11.6	12.3	16.9	18.0	19.3

Table 10:3 Per Capita Consumption of Wine in 15 EU Countries 1970-2010
Source: J.B.B.S. Fall, Vol. 24, No.3.

As a result of the 2008-2009 financial-economic disruption and its aftermath, a considerable volatility in wine sales was experienced in most countries. Nevertheless, a long-term trend is quite apparent, which is largely related to the social issues, tax policy alterations and to the changing attitudes towards lifestyle and health. There has been significant increase in health consciousness and the benefits of drinking wine as opposed to hard spirits. At the same time, health information about over indulgence in quantity of alcohol consumption has decreased overall consumption in the southern countries traditionally associated with high levels of consumption. For a number of years, there has been a move to lower alcohol content beverages. The recent association of wine as a nutritionally healthy beverage is likely to continue to influence consumption choices favoring wine over other alcoholic beverages; and this is a factor in cultural changes in consumption.

The changes take place and become an amalgamation of individual behavior that exhibit synergistic responses to the increasingly homogeneous consumer behavior and present greater opportunity for larger scale companies. This brings advantages to larger scale international retailers and further contributes to the globalization of markets.

Wines Market Share

To some extent, the remarkable growth in consumption of wines in some areas and the decline in others during the last decade is a continuation of trends during the past half century. In most of the countries studied, a traditional beverage historically accounted for a significant share of the alcoholic beverage market. However, over the years, the market share of the traditional beverage has tended to decline. In 1960, beer accounted for over 50% of total alcohol consumed in six of the countries in northern Europe: Belgium, Denmark, Germany, Ireland, Luxembourg and the UK. However, over the long term, beer consumption declined, while wine consumption increased in all of these countries. A reverse-pattern is quite evident and significant among the countries in the south, where wine traditionally held the largest market share. In France, Greece, Italy, Portugal and Spain, the internal market for wine declined and the market share for beer increased in all five countries. The cross-cultural influences, perhaps largely due to global marketing, have been causing a convergence to greater similarities.

One of the reasons for the growth in wine consumption in the northern countries is that distilled beverages may be taken before or after a meal, but are not as commonly consumed during meals. Wine is more multidimensional in the sense that wine is perceived as a suitable drink with or without an accompanying meal. Wine consumption as a common daily practice has a long history in France, where drinking has been described as the national way of life. The French experience has in some sense been adopted, people in the northern countries now like to drink wine because it tastes good, has many varieties, is perceived as nutritionally valuable and a socially acceptable alcoholic drink. Although all alcoholic beverages can be misused, the negative effects are more highly associated with higher alcohol content beverages. Previous studies have shown that that hard liquor spirits consumption on a per capita basis was associated with a significant risk of cardiovascular mortality, while recent medical studies show that moderate consumption of wine is actually associated with prolonging life, facts that will help continue the trend toward higher wine consumption in regions were wine was not traditional. Similarly, there has been a remarkable and significant shift in the market share from fortified wines to pure wines. For example, the market shares of the stronger wines have decreased since the mid-1970s. In Denmark, market shares for fortified wine were over 20% in 1975, but they have declined to only 4% or less over the following two decades. There is a variation among the countries with respect to the level of wine consumption. Nonetheless, the pattern indicates that consumption differences have been converging, as clearly illustrated in Figure 10:5. There appears to be a movement toward a type of equilibrium between the countries of Europe. Indeed this convergence of consumption patterns for wine could be reached within the next fifteen years.

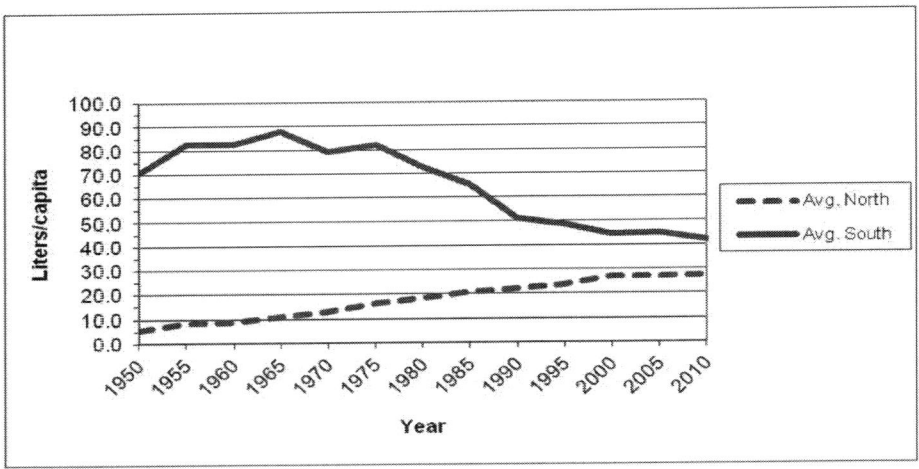

Figure 10:5 Time Series of Per-Capita Wine Consumption in Northern and Southern Europe

As we have noted, the degree of trade in wine varies significantly between countries. Moreover, as may be expected, countries in the southern region of Europe, with a climate suitable to viticulture, import much less, whereas northern European countries import much more wine. Based on statistical projections, using the time series methodology, aggregate wine consumption in the north of Europe is expected to continue to increase, while wine consumption in the south of Europe will similarly continue to moderately decline (Figure 10:3).

The pattern is clear and the reasons are understandable. Eight countries that were once only marginal wine drinking communities have significantly increased per-capita consumption of wine over the past half century. Conversely, the six countries that were formerly very high wine drinking countries have been continually evidencing the trend of decreasing consumption. Overall, these two patterns are mirror images of consumption behaviors approaching each other over time, with the northern most countries experiencing the largest percentage changes.

Table 10:4 shows the percentage changes in wine consumption by European countries from 1970 to 2010, and identifies the countries by rank order. Decreasing average consumption is indicated by a minus sign (-).

Rank	Country	1970–2010 Percent up or down
Increasing		
1	Ireland	960
2	Finland	573
3	U.K.	566
4	Denmark	511
5	Netherlands	323
6	Sweden	221
7	Germany	45
8	Belgium	48
Decreasing		
9	Italy	-61
10	France	-53
11	Spain	-54
12	Portugal	-30
13	Greece	-14
14	Austria	-16

Table 10:4 Percentage Change In Wine Consumption By Country
Source: J.B.B.S. Fall, Vol. 24, No.3.

A Deeper Look at China and the Global Wine Market

International competition within the wine industry has increased significantly. Here we will single out one country in particular, China, and focus on China's wine market and the role of its global competitive strategies, particularly with respect to the wine industry. In chapter 2 of this book, the history of China's vineyards was detailed. In this section of chapter 10, the concentration is on evaluating the growing Chinese wine industry and markets from a strategic perspective and considering what may be expected in the future. Phenomenal growth of the Chinese economy and the sheer size of its population inspired global wine suppliers to enter the Chinese market. The global wine suppliers entered with the hope of gaining a market stronghold in a rapidly growing national economy of 1.35 billion people. Similarly, China's wine producers have been expanding their own production and marketing of products from Chinese ventures. These cross trends between foreign wine imported into China and the Chinese production and marketing of their own wine ventures are explored in this chapter. We also examine implications that may be drawn from the economic factor-endowment-theory, as we examine China's competition and strategies under free-trade in an open global market.

Overview of China

China is a large nation in many ways, not only in territory, but also in terms of human resources—it has the largest population in the world. Furthermore, the economy has been consistently growing faster than any other national economy and the rate of growth has been at least twice the rate of the world average or higher. China is now the world's largest exporter and world leader in gross value of industrial output. China is huge in mining of iron, steel, aluminum, and coal. The largest producer of armaments, textiles, apparel, cement, chemicals, fertilizers, consumer products, food processing and transportation equipment, rail cars and locomotives, ships, aircraft equipment, and commercial space launch vehicles and satellites. Industry after industry, China is quickly becoming the largest market in the world. It is understandable that wine producers and suppliers from other nations would be greatly interested in what appears as the largest potential market in which to sell imported wines. Lifestyle and living standards have dramatically changed, following China's transition to a market-oriented economy. The national economy is not entirely free-market-determined, because the government establishes capital infrastructure in precisely planned specific geographic locations in order to foster enterprise strategically and advance its markets. The coordination of serious public infrastructure ahead of private capital decisions greatly supports rapid strategic development.

In terms of purchasing power parity, the GDP of China ranks second in the world behind the US and its rate of growth is around four times greater. In 2007, it was estimated that over 211 million Chinese already had middle-class living standards in terms of average personal income measures, and over 400 million Chinese thought themselves to be middle class. By 2012, other estimations put the middle-class at 300 million, almost the size of the entire population of the US. No other nation can claim as much, and these numbers are remarkable no matter how one calculates the population of middle-class consumers. Such market potential is certainly attractive and explains one of the reasons behind the vigorous competition for Chinese markets. However, it is the other billion Chinese not yet middle-class that comprises an even larger future market potential, and the market for wine is no exception.

Indeed wine sales have been increasing in China. Moreover, the rate of growth in sales is significant, as shown in Figure 10:6.

The global wine producers/suppliers have been exporting to China and satisfying the emerging middle-class desire for the cache of imported wine. At the same time, there has also been a significant domestic growth in production and marketing of Chinese wines. One begins to wonder about the future, and two questions come to mind. First, how much of this Chinese market will be claimed by imported wines and how much will eventually be dominated by the wine produced in China? Second, how much of the global wine marketplace will eventually be strategically taken over by the Chinese ownership?

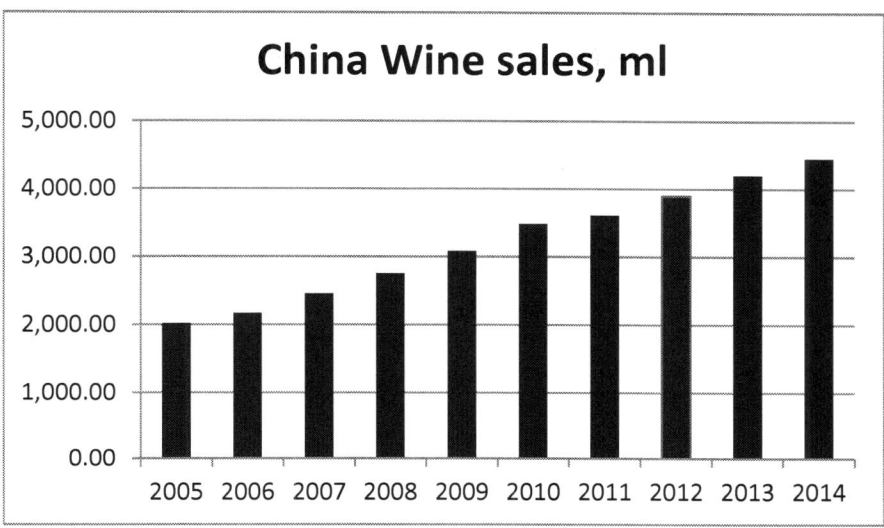

Figure 10:6 Wine Sales in China (millions of liters)
Source: Based on data from trade reports, and the years 2012-2014 are authors' estimates based on trade sources and national statistics.

The recent history of China's export-oriented industries is one of strategic domination. The label "made in China" is ubiquitous, and it is located on most of the world's manufactured products. Many of the industries in the Western developed nations have struggled to survive, and often succumbed under the competition from the products produced by the Chinese. Could this be the case with wine as well? Will the currently dominant global suppliers soon become disillusioned about their dream of the huge Chinese market? Will the penetration of a marketplace, based on the population of 1.35 billion Chinese, fail? Will the domination of the Chinese marketplace for French wine, end, and will the Chinese come to dominate the global wine industry? The likelihood of this scenario depends, not only on the Chinese consumers, but also on Chinese production and the strategic actions and interactions of all the wine industry's players.

Chinese Wine Production
China has been growing grapes for over two thousand years. However, the production and consumption of grape wine was not prevalent until rather recently. Remarkable growth in production has been evident since 2002. In fact, the production has exceeded expectations in industry forecasts year after year and is likely to continue (shown in Figure 10:7).

Hundreds of grape varieties are grown in China. The more important wine varieties include those of Chenin Blanc, Gewurztraminer, Sauvignon Blanc, Semillon, Chardonnay, Italian Riesling, White Riesling and Rkatsiteli for white wine, and Cabernet Sauvignon, Cabernet Franc, Merlot, French Blue, Muscat Hamburg, Pinot Noir, Syrah, Carignan and Saperavi for red wine production. China is fortunate in not having any phylloxera pest problems.

Most of the grape planting material used in China has been propagated through domestic cutting. From a competitive standpoint, China has the advantage of large wine fields that do not have the problems of pests found in most other wine producing countries, allowing China to expand production more quickly. As the overall economy has been growing rapidly, the Chinese preference for wine consumption has been growing rapidly. This domestic market for wine has spurred significant increases in wine production.

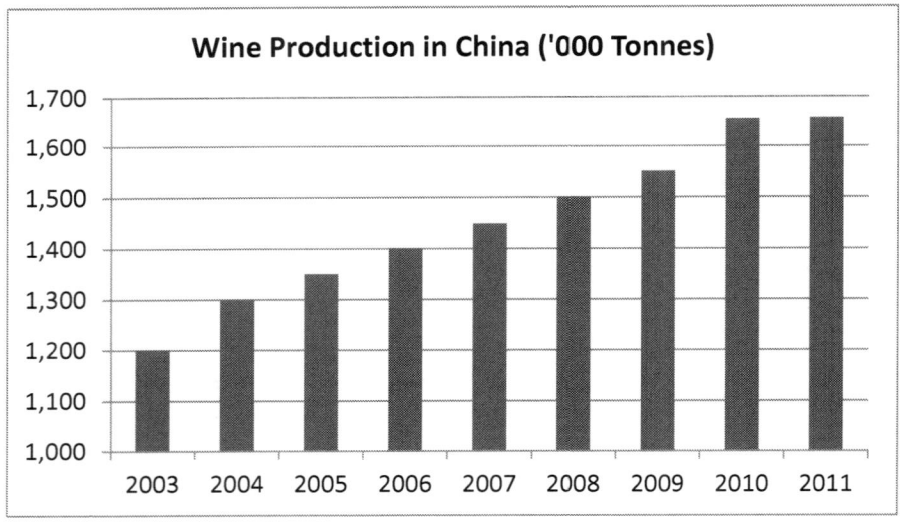

Figure 10:7: Wine Production in China, 2003-2011
Source: faostat.fao.org

There are hundreds of local wine companies established in 26 of the provinces. The five leading provinces contributed about two thirds of the total grape production in the country. Growth of Chinese vineyard production has continued throughout the provinces. As early as 2005, the vineyard acreage exceeded Australia, Chile and South Africa combined.

A five-year growth of vineyard acreage in China was the highest in the world, with more than a 113% increase. Furthermore, there is still a very significant opportunity to continue increasing the production of high quality wines. In 2010, China's wine production continued to grow and China became the world's fifth largest producer of wine in the world, as shown in Figure 10:8. Wine production in China increased over 20% from 2005 to 2011.

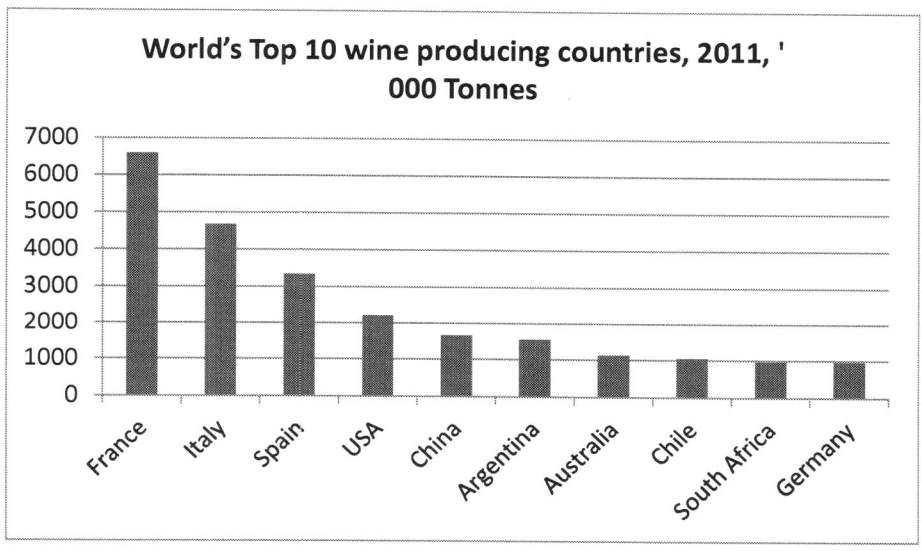

Figure 10:8 World's Top 10 Wine Producing Countries, 2011
Source: faostat.fao.org

China Wine Consumption
Even with the significant increases in wine production, the quantity of domestic supply has not entirely satisfied the domestic consumption demands of the Chinese people. Imported wine has filled the gap. Part of the increases in demand for grape wine was initially due to the government campaigns that encouraged consumers to switch from drinking rice-wine to drinking more grape-wine, in order to maintain the level of rice supply for food. Another factor was the rapid growth of a young urban middle-class who wanted to enjoy the same type of wines as the rest of the world. The sales of wine in China have increased consistently, as shown in Figure 10:9.

The correlation of increases in annual wine consumption, with the general increase in the overall economy, is remarkable. This statistical association highlights the change in wine consumption habits of modern China. Previously, the Chinese cultural habit was consuming distilled spirit drinks. The economic transition and exposure to international cultures have been partly responsible for increased wine consumption. Wine has become a compelling substitute for both beer and spirits in China. More people increasingly consume wine instead of the distilled spirits. The younger affluent Chinese wine drinkers demonstrate their independence and success by drinking expensive imported wine. By 2005, China became the world's fastest-growing wine market. A year later in 2006, the Chinese reached an important level of consumption; it accounted for 6% of the world wine market. By 2011, China reached 6.7%. This is significant when compared to the US that accounted for 11.7% of the wine market. For the industry, China had become an important market for wine.

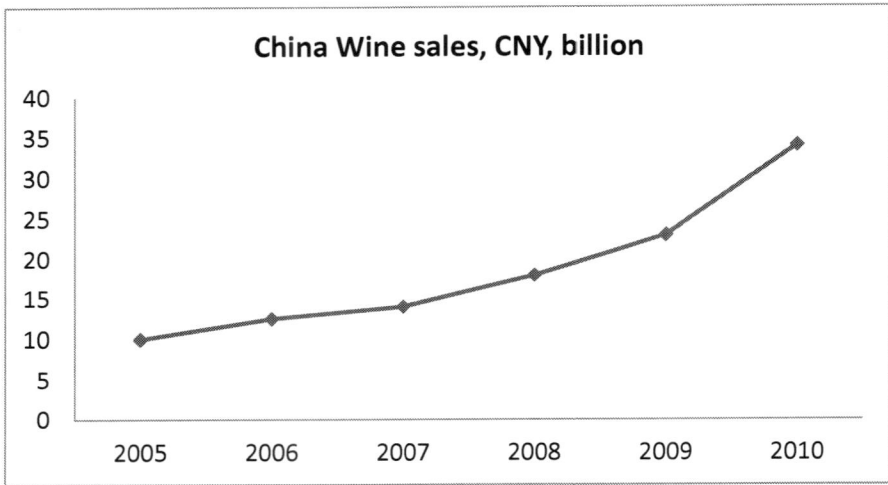

Figure 10:9: China Wine Sales, CNY, billion
Source: Five-year-plan of China's wine industry.

China's wine market is already fifth in the world markets, only behind France, the US and Italy and Germany in terms of total consumption. The Chinese will almost certainly develop into a much larger market for wine in the near future.

The Giant as Competitor
The large role of China in the global wine industry has been achieved in only a short time (most of the growth was in two and a half decades). Nevertheless, the Chinese economy still has significant room to expand. While the wine exporters to China envision ever increasing profits, many have been somewhat disappointed. The Chinese distribution is difficult and local producers and brand-holders have been out maneuvering the international participants. Chinese firms, with little wine tradition as a mental barrier, have shown an amazing creativity and consumer orientation. The Chinese will

continue to compete and have opportunities to expand into market segments previously dominated by other suppliers. For example, in 2008, China's own wine production increased 69.78% in one year. In 2012, they added another 19% over the 2011 figures in vines alone.

There is no doubt that China is now on track as a major force in the wine industry. Moreover, China has production advantages in numerous areas that may be impossible to counteract through market strategies alone. China has some of the largest agricultural land holdings, plentiful agricultural laborers, modern technology that is second to none, and a capital market with huge financial reserves.

In addition, Chinese management has assimilated the most skillful techniques in contemporary business strategies. This means that production, distribution and marketing are not limited to its geographic frontiers. The Chinese wine investors have already begun expanding around the world. For example, The Longhai International Trading Co. Ltd, a Chinese real estate group founded in 2001, acquired Chateau Latour Laguens, a wine property in the Entre-Deux-Mers region, southeast of Bordeaux. Latour Laguens makes wine in both the Bordeaux and Bordeaux Supérieur. The rationale behind such acquisitions was to master the technology of winemaking in France and to win widespread international recognition.

By 2011, there were another 18 acquisitions of French wine properties by Chinese. These included Château Richelieu (Fronsac), Château de Viaud (Lalande-de-Pomerol), Château Laulan Ducos (Médoc) and Château Chenu Lafitte (Cotes de Bourg), plus four more estates purchased by Cheng Qu (the billionaire Chinese owner of Château Chenu Lafitte). The additional Cheng Qu acquisitions were Château Branda (AOC Bordeaux), Château Grand Branet (AOC Cotes de Bordeaux), Château Laurette (AOC Sainte-Croix-du-Mont) and Château Thebot (AOC Bordeaux). The owner, Cheng Qu was also designing a huge "wine theme park" in his home province of Dalian.

The Yantai ChangYu Group Company Limited is an example of strategies in the business of wine. Yantai ChangYu is the largest wine production company in China, accounting for approximately a fifth of all sales. The company was the first Asian winery to be ranked as one of the top-10 wineries in the beverage industry. Some of the Chinese wines not only win awards, they are shrewdly positioned for export, and there is no reason to believe that the Chinese will not be able to continue to increase their position in the global wine markets.

Chinese business acumen and strategic competitiveness are reason to wonder if the potentially huge Chinese market will actually be the most important future market for foreign exporters. Alternatively, the Chinese could strategically maneuver in the foreign markets as they have done with other products many times before, and become the largest controlling owners of vineyards and wines around the world.

Examining the fundamental economic advantages, we see that it is not a question of whether the Chinese have an advantage in one single factor of production, but actually, they may have more advantages.

With a labor force of 795 million workers available, China has a deep and reasonably long lasting source of economic advantage in production and distribution. Another factor of production is arable land, and China has 1.11 million arable kilometers available within its own nation. This nation has real potential for greatly increasing wine production, and this would still amount to a small percentage of their overall agricultural production. The Chinese business leaders possess market expertise, and there is absolutely no shortage of technological knowledge and capability. Lastly, the factor of financial capital investment is not a problem for China to expand business; the nation has trillions of dollars' worth of excess financial reserves available. Moreover, China invests a remarkable 48% of the nation's GDP annually.

Outcome and the Future of China Wine

The wine business may not be a top priority of the Chinese political-economic leadership, but the nation has new billionaire entrepreneurs, and it has shrewd business executives that certainly appear to have the ability to win in most market competitions, and perhaps also in the wine industry, as they have done in many other industries. Europeans are already drinking French wine from Chinese companies, but many of these Euro consumers probably do not know it (more than 20 Bordeaux producers are now Chinese-owned). Nevertheless, exclusively Chinese brands are gaining explicit acceptance. For example, recently in 2013, Britain's oldest wine merchant, Berry Bros. & Rudd, announced that they were stocking four wines from ChangYu.

Recent history illustrates China's astounding ability to out-compete business rivals around the world. China has rapidly gained the upper hand in markets, leaving the previous global business competitors to fight over a smaller remnant of market share. China's advantages imply a nation involved in global markets and using its accumulate trade surpluses to purchase controlling interests in other countries' natural resources industry (e.g., the less developed South American wine producing areas). It is already expanding agricultural production in other nations. In the past, international trade worked to the advantage of all trading parties, because the fixed boundaries between countries limited the extent of economic advantages in any one nation. In the past, the economic theory of Comparative Advantage applied, but much less so today, because of the fluidity of factors of production to cross borders.

According to the Factor endowment theory, some nations that are endowed in one or more of the factors of production are relatively better off than other nations, and therefore have a competitive advantage.

These factors of production are categorized as land, labor, capital and technology. The outcome with globalization, and the awakening of a previously sleeping giant, China, we find that it has advantages in all factors of production, and the giant has the potential in the near future of becoming the world's most important seller of wine; this is modern China.

Over time, in an open globalized economic system that fosters mobile capital and technology, market strategies alone are unlikely to win against China's combination of economic advantages in all the major factors of production. Time will tell if this happens in the wine industry as well. Nonetheless, peering into the future, we see people drinking glasses of wine supplied from a multitude of vineyards that will increasingly be in the hands of Chinese control and ownership.

Summary of Major Findings and Global Future Expectations

As we have noted, wine consumption is related to several factors, including economic conditions, government laws affecting production and consumption, rates of taxation, and lifestyle choices, such as those based on an increasing awareness of healthy alternative choices available to consumers.

Examining the vast array of data and the seeming appearance of trends reveals that the consumers are continuing to switch from the local traditional drinks to those that better fit modern consumer lifestyle changes. From a global standpoint, this benefits the worldwide wine market, because wine is generally perceived as upscale and fashionable, as well as more healthful. This trend can also be reinforced by changes in tax regulations. In the past, governments tended to impose higher taxes for imported alcohol products, while taxing alcohol beverages traditional to their region rather lightly. However, this practice has been changing somewhat. For example, under pressure from the EU, with the increased membership and a desire to bring about increased opportunity for market access throughout member countries, the recent changes have eliminated such practices, and this has significantly narrowed the price differences between European home grown products and imported products from EU member countries. Similarly, any lowering of taxes on non-EU wine producing countries would cause greater imports from these producers.

Europe is still the largest alcohol-consuming region of the world, per-capita. Nevertheless, the overall average per capita consumption has been decreasing since the mid-1970s. This is largely due to the substitution of wine, which has lower alcohol content, for high-alcohol spirits. Indeed, there has been increasing consumption of wine in the northern countries, as wine has been substituted for hard-spirits. This amounts to less alcohol being consumed. In fact, 11 liters of pure alcohol consumed per adult each year versus 15 liters during the middle of the past century. Over the past half century, we also see a harmonization in average consumption levels across countries, rising in central and northern Europe and falling in southern Europe. Wine has made significant advances in beverage preference and now accounts for a third of alcohol consumed in the EU member countries. The overall trend in consumption represents aspects of significant cultural convergence. In fact, these forces are likely to continue this pattern into the future, and we can also see the likelihood of equilibrium, because the rates of change are moving in that direction.

Another factor in wine's popularity is the increased connectivity of communication and ease of trade brought about by the modern methods in transportation. In addition, the Internet and the worldwide-web, along with the rapid adoption of the "smart phone" as a single platform for all types of communications and purchasing transactions are the latest technologies helping to inform and assist consumers as they chose wines. There is the relaxation of tax differentials and the increasing ease of international trade that helps leverage global marketing and standardized advertising strategies.

Furthermore, these processes are ongoing, and can be expected to promote further uniformity in attitudes and beliefs. Global economic activity is expected to increase, despite lower rates of economic growth in the previously developed Western nations. This will result in even greater convergence in terms of standards of living and lifestyles between countries. Such factors will conspire to surpass national boundaries and will lead to even more uniform consumer product preferences. We also find that the growth in popularity of wine has been and can be expected to continue in other areas of the world that previously were not significant wine producers or wine consumers. Therefore, our forecast is that consumer preferences for wine will continue to trend toward similar consumptive patterns over time and across cultural regions. All the data and related forecasts support this view of the future.

The wine industry is expected to see some downward pressure on pricing due to cyclical oversupplies and occasional record grape harvests, from increased production capacity in China and Eastern Europe, and from a probable overall slower growing western economy. Nevertheless, despite lower than previous economic growth rates for the developed Western nations, the overall demand for wine seems likely to increase, due to continued growth in Asia-Pacific region. This should prove to be the case over the next ten years.

The perceived health benefits of red wine is expected to continue to play a part in advancing wine's share of the overall alcoholic drinks market. Organic wine brands may also be expected to benefit from the urban consumers' demand for organic food in general. Increasing consumer preference for particular brands can be expected to advance development of the quality segments. These consumer preferences are driven by marketing and also by rising levels of disposable income in previously lower income countries.

Some of the New World producers can be expected to gain advantage over Old World producers, as successful marketing and branding strategies reach across the globe. The development of global brands involves targeted marketing to specific consumer groups in diverse geographical locations. Products will be designed, packaged and marketed to appeal to specific target market segments, such as the increasing population of older consumers in many national economies. Products are also being aimed at the financially independent women whose numbers are expected to continue to advance.

The wine market will see further consolidation, as more competitors seek to position themselves as global wine producers. New World producers and Asian producers will be seeking acquisitions in both New and Old World countries. The goal of consolidation will be acquiring control over more valuable acreage and building global brand portfolios. Once again, the data and related forecasts support this view of the future. Many new wine labels will be increasingly displayed with the pride of their national origin as an indication of brand quality. Increasingly better quality wines will become ubiquitous and available at lower price points. Wine connoisseurs and consumers in general will benefit from all these factors affecting the international wine industry.

24085309R00117

Printed in Great Britain
by Amazon